Chambers

LOST LORE

A CELEBRATION
OF TRADITIONAL WISDOM
FROM FORAGING AND FESTIVALS
TO SEAFARING AND SMOKE SIGNALS
BY
UNA McGOVERN
AND
PAUL JENNER

Chambers

CHAMBERS
An imprint of Chambers Harrap Publishers Ltd
7 Hopetoun Crescent, Edinburgh, EH7 4AY

Chambers Harrap is an Hachette UK company

First published by Chambers Harrap Publishers Ltd 2009

Database right Chambers Harrap Publishers Ltd (makers)

A CIP catalogue record for this book is available from the British Library.

ISBN 978 0550 10521 9

10 9 8 7 6 5 4 3 2 1

www.chambers.co.uk

Designed by Mark Blackadder
Typeset in Golden Cockerel and Lamar Pen by Chambers Harrap Publishers Ltd, Edinburgh
Printed and bound in Italy by Printer Trento srl

Contents

Contents

HOUSEHOLD

OUTDOOR LIFE

Introduction

lore n *learning, esp of a special, traditional, or out-of-the-way miscellaneous kind.*

The Chambers Dictionary

lost adj *parted with; no longer possessed; missing; not able to be found; thrown away; squandered, wasted*

The Chambers Dictionary

The idea for this book came from the realization that the miniature abacus on my mantelpiece was a purely ornamental object as I had no idea how to use it. Not so long ago (in the great scheme of things), this knowledge was common to many. This book collects together other such areas of "learning of a special, traditional, or out-of-the-way miscellaneous kind" and describes how that learning was practised in the past.

On their journey through cleaning shoes, cranking cars and forecasting the weather, the authors outline the historical background to these skills and use quotations from original sources and literature to bring the subject to life.

Knowledge can all too easily be lost from the collective consciousness as advances in new technology supplant traditional manual methods. This process of change brings many positives but it can also leave us diminished. At the very least, we would be seriously inconvenienced should we find ourselves lost in the wilderness, needing to perform calculations without a calculator, or lacking toothpaste. This book aims to keep such knowledge alive and make it entertaining, even if you never actually have to make a posset, charm a wart or predict the sex of a baby yourself.

Patrick White, Publisher

About the Authors

Una McGovern worked in reference publishing for a number of years before becoming a freelance editor and writer, with books on a wide range of subjects to her name, including the forerunner to this book, *Lost Crafts*. She lives in a small Dartmoor town with her partner and young son.

Paul Jenner is a writer and journalist specializing in lifestyle subjects. He lives with his partner, three horses, two dogs and two sheep, in the foothills of the Spanish Pyrenees, where, when he's not working, he enjoys hiking, riding, cycling, sailing, swimming, diving and snowboarding. His other books include *Teach Yourself Living Longer, Living Well* and *Teach Yourself Happiness*.

Other Contributors

Copy Editor: Janice Mcneillie
Picture Research: Sharon McTeir
Additional Picture Research: Kate Sleight, Patrick White
Proofreader: Graham Frankland
Prepress: Becky Pickard
Project Managers: Hazel Norris, Patrick White

Health and Wellbeing

Using Natural First Aid

FIRST AID FROM NATURE

Today, many of us never stray far from medical aid, or at least from a well-stocked first-aid kit (including antiseptic wipes, sterile bandages and the like). In the past, a little more ingenuity was required when it came to treating cuts and wounds – although inclusion doesn't necessarily mean recommendation when it comes to some of the traditional remedies listed below.

CUTS

One of the most widespread traditional remedies for a cut, said to stop it bleeding, is the cobweb. Pliny recommended cobwebs in his *Natural History* (AD 77), and Shakespeare certainly knew about the spider's web treatment:

I shall desire you of more acquaintance, good Master Cobweb; if I cut my finger I shall make bold with you.
> William Shakespeare, *A Midsummer Night's Dream* (c.1594)

Cobwebs were thought to bind and seal the wound and staunch the flow of blood, and their use as natural first aid seems to have lasted until at least the 19th century, if not much later:

Apply a mixture of flour and salt and wrap with cloth or common paper; or press cobwebs and brown sugar over the cut.
> Jerry Mack Johnson, *Country Wisdom* (1974)

When bleeding is not a concern but cleaning a small wound is, sliced onions or cloves of garlic are sometimes recommended for their cleansing properties, freshly cut and rubbed over the scratch or cut.

BURNS

There are many age-old treatments for burns, both herbal and magical. Samuel Pepys noted a charm for remedying burns in his diary, different versions of which remained in popular circulation for many years. While the words vary, the theme is essentially the same – angels, frost and fire combine to soothe the burn:

> *There came three angels out of the east;*
> *The one brought fire, the other brought frost –*
> *Out fire; in frost.*
> *In the name of the Father and Son and Holy Ghost. Amen.*

For a herbal treatment of burns, a poultice made from the crushed leaves of the house leek was favoured (at one time this plant was also thought to be capable of protecting your house from fire or lightning). A rather smelly remedy, certainly not to be endorsed, comes from 19th-century Ireland:

> *For a burn.*
> *There is a pretty secret to cure a burn without a scar: 'Take sheep's suet and the rind of the elder-tree, boil both together, and the ointment will cure a burn without leaving a mark.'*
>
> Lady Francesca Speranza Wilde, *Ancient Legends, Mystic Charms, and Superstitions of Ireland* (1888)

STINGS FROM INSECTS AND PLANTS

Nettle stings

Nettles are one of the most common stinging plants in Britain, so it is particularly useful to have some natural first-aid remedies in mind to treat the painful rash brought about by brushing against these plants. Possibly the earliest and definitely the most widely known remedy is the dock leaf, which has been used for hundreds of years to relieve the sting of nettle rash. However, while many people will still look for a dock leaf as soon as they have been stung (and they always seem to grow somewhere nearby), few know that in the past this was only half the cure:

'In dock, out nettle,' a formula of words used by children in curing the sting of a nettle, which is done by laying the leaf of the butter dock upon the part stung, and repeating by way of charm, 'in dock, out nettle,' till the pain is abated.

William Toone, *A Glossary and Etymological Dictionary* (1834)

The words of the charm which accompanied the application of a dock leaf varied greatly – one rhyme ran 'Out nettle,/ In dock./ Dock shall have;/ A new smock' – but whichever version was favoured, it was considered an essential part of the cure. A much less well-known remedy involves the use of parsley:

162. NETTLE RASH.
Rub the parts strongly with parsley. Internals profit nothing.

John Wesley, *Primitive Physic* (1747)

Bee stings

Many remedies have been suggested for the sting of the Bee, but the best remedy may be found in extracting the sting immediately, and apply a little laudanum. To prevent the swelling arising from the sting of the Bee, I know of no remedy more efficacious than Venice Treacle, or olive-oil … The juice of the onion, mixed with common salt is also a good remedy.

Frederick Butler, *The Farmer's Manual* (1819)

The Greek physician Dioscorides (c.40–c.90 AD) recommended the herb marsh-mallow for the treatment of wasp and bee stings, going so far as to say that by crushing the leaves in oil an insect repellent could be made, which may prevent the victim from being stung in the first place. The English herbalist Nicholas Culpeper (1616–54) recommended basil, saying that basil leaves applied to a sting would draw the poison to them. An apparently ancient remedy for bee stings is to rub mud (mixed from earth and water) on the area, leaving it in place until the mud dries and falls off. For a more modern alternative, the mud can be replaced by a paste of baking soda and water if preferred.

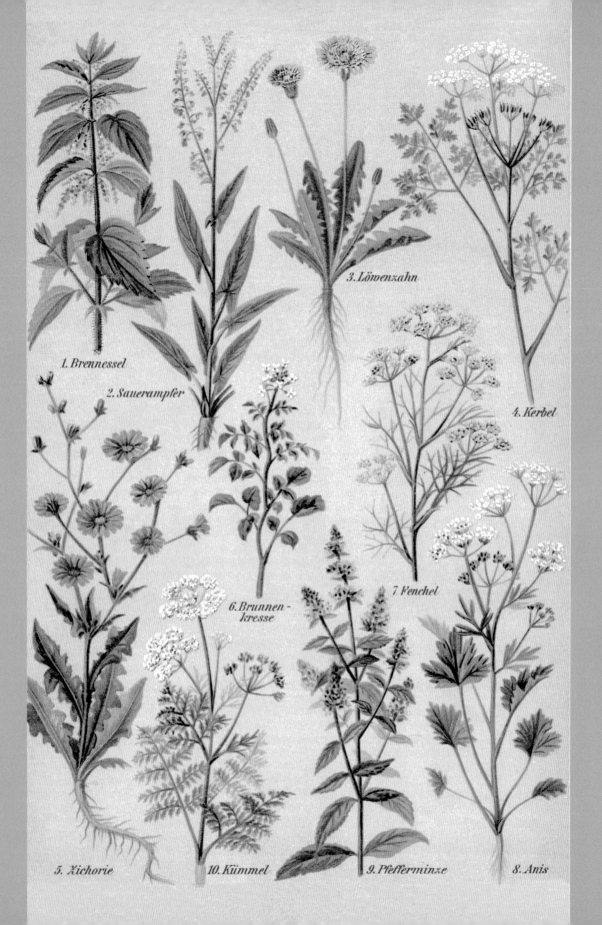

1. Brennessel

2. Sauerampfer

3. Löwenzahn

4. Kerbel

5. Zichorie

6. Brunnen-kresse

7. Fenchel

8. Anis

9. Pfefferminze

10. Kümmel

Using Natural Remedies

NATURAL REMEDIES

We can only assume that wild plants and herbs have always been collected and used medicinally. A number of Anglo-Saxon manuscripts describe the medicinal use of herbs, and in medieval times herb gardens were a feature of monasteries and country houses. Some herblore was collected in books such as *The Herball* (1597) by John Gerard, and *The Physical Directory* (1649) and *The English Physitian* (1652) by Nicholas Culpeper, but much traditional knowledge of natural or herbal remedies has been lost, as it existed in oral tradition alone, in recipes passed on between family members. However, while much knowledge was lost, interest in herbal remedies has never disappeared. Modern medical herbalists continue an ancient tradition, but what was once a rural craft, known by many, is now a specialist profession. Herbal medicine has its own professional body in the UK, the National Institute of Medical Herbalists, and to be a qualified practitioner, a herbalist must complete an approved degree in herbal medicine, or phytotherapy.

'AN EASY AND NATURAL METHOD OF CURING MOST DISEASES'

John Wesley, best known as the founder of Methodism, published widely on a number of subjects, and his *Primitive Physic, or an Easy and Natural Method of Curing Most Diseases* (1747) was reprinted throughout the 19th century. A couple of his remedies are included here, for interest rather than as recommendations.

Coughs

In an edition of Wesley's book published in 1843, remedies are included for eight different types of cough.

56. A Cough

Every cough is a dry cough at first. As long as it continues so, it may be cured by chewing immediately after you cough, the quantity of a pepper corn of Peruvian bark. Swallow your spittle as long as it is bitter, and spit out the wood. If you cough again, do this again. It very seldom fails to cure any dry cough. I earnestly desire every one, who has any regard for his health, to try this within twenty-four hours after he perceives a cough.

Or, drink a pint of cold water lying down in bed.—Tried.

Or, make a hole through a lemon and fill it with honey. Roast it and catch the juice. Take a tea-spoonful of this frequently.—Tried.

'Costiveness' (or constipation)

55. Costiveness

Rise early every morning.

Or boil in a pint and a half of broth, half a handful of mallow leaves chopt, strain this and drink it before you eat anything else. Do this frequently, if needful.

Or, breakfast twice a week or oftener, on water-gruel with currants.—Tried.

Or, take daily, two hours before dinner, a small tea-cupful of stewed prunes.

Hiccups

134. The Hiccup *(to cure.)*

Swallow a mouthful of water, stopping the mouth and ears.—Tried.

Or, take anything that makes you sneeze.

Or, two or three preserved damsons.

Or, three drops of oil of cinnamon on a lump of sugar. —Tried.

Or, ten drops of chemical oil of amber dropt on sugar, and then mixed with a little water.

HOME REMEDIES

In the past, the knowledge of many treatments was passed on within families and around communities – some have survived simply as 'old wives' tales' or superstitions, while others have some element of medical truth. A selection of traditional home remedies is given below, although, again, caution is advised before you actually try any of them:

Headaches

There have been many suggested cures for headaches over the centuries. As early as AD 77, Pliny suggested that a piece of hangman's rope would do the trick – a belief that was still current in Britain in the 16th century, when it was mentioned by Reginald Scot in his *Discoverie of Witchcraft* (1584). One simply had to 'tie a halter about your head, wherewith one had been hanged'. Equally (if not more) grisly is the cure suggested by Francis Grose in 1787:

Moss growing on a human skull, if dried, powdered, and taken as snuff, will cure the headache.

Francis Grose, *A Provincial Glossary* (1787)

A snakeskin is also said to cure a headache, worn around the head or about your hat. Remedies that are more readily available in the average domestic setting include inhaling the fumes from a saucepan of boiling vinegar, or drinking a cup of relaxing camomile tea, while early herbalists recommended feverfew. Among the recommendations in the *Primitive Physic* (1747) are rubbing the head for 15 minutes, and placing brandy and lemon zest on the palm of the hand, then holding the palm to the forehead.

Sore throats

The bark of slippery elm, ground and made into a sort of thin gruel with water or milk, was once a popular choice as a cure for a sore throat, while meatier suggestions have also been made:

Apply fat bacon or pork to outside of throat and hold in place by tying a rag around it. Keep in place until soreness is gone ... Gargle with warm salt water or apple cider vinegar, repeat often. Hold small piece of garlic in mouth for several minutes, several times during the day.

Jerry Mack Johnson, *Country Wisdom* (1974)

Alternatively, a once widespread cure for a sore throat was to tie a stocking round your neck (often the left stocking was favoured, and it was generally recommended that it be a stocking that had been worn that day).

Common cold

While there is no cure for the common cold, there have long been remedies aimed at relieving its symptoms. In *Primitive Physic* (1747) you are recommended to drink a pint of cold water while lying down in bed, or, for a head cold:

Pare very thin the yellow rind of an orange, roll it up inside out, and thrust a roll into each nostril.

John Wesley, *Primitive Physic* (1747)

The juice of oranges, and other citrus fruit, is certainly useful in warding off a cold, and has been recognized as such for some time. Other natural remedies include drinking warming ginger tea (made by steeping grated fresh ginger root in boiling water); or taking either a teaspoon of honey each morning, or honey mixed with chopped garlic (the more local the honey the better – some claim that honey from bees whose hives are within five miles of where you live will relieve hay-fever symptoms too); or taking a drink of lemon juice, honey and hot water (with whisky added if preferred).

Colds and flu: Mix and drink a mixture of cinnamon, sage, and bay leaves, and add a little lemon juice. Drink warm. Drink hot ginger tea freely ... Drink juice of citrus fruits often.

Jerry Mack Johnson, *Country Wisdom* (1974)

HERBAL TEA

The most widely used natural remedies today are herbal teas. While these are available to buy in dried form, either in tea bags or as loose leaves, many prefer to prepare their own from freshly picked leaves and flowers. Always ensure that you know which plants you are picking and take care where you pick them from (see some of the recommendations in the 'wild food' section of this book). Wash your collected leaves or flowers in cold water before making your tea. This is done by placing the herbs in a teapot, pouring on water that has just boiled, and popping on the lid (covering is said to stop the beneficial essential oils from disappearing in the steam). After five to ten minutes, strain into a cup. Don't add milk, but if you prefer, you can sweeten herb tea with honey. Herbs can have quite strong effects, and it is sometimes recommended that no more than three cups of herb tea should be drunk in a day. Also, if you want to treat a specific medical condition, or if you are pregnant, it is always best to consult a doctor, and see a qualified medical herbalist.

Dandelion tea

Dandelion tea is a diuretic, and is said to be good for cleansing the liver and expelling toxins from the body. Use a small bunch of leaves to make a pot of tea.

Nettle tea

Nettle tea is thought to be a good general tonic and system cleanser. Again, a small bunch of fresh leaves will make a pot of tea.

Nettle tea
© Arco Images GmbH /
Alamy

Peppermint tea

Peppermint has long been used to aid digestion and ease nausea. Buy a small mint plant, and simply pinch out a few fresh leaves each time you want some tea.

Elderflower tea

Tea made from elderflowers is most commonly used to ease the symptoms of colds and flu, and some believe it is also good for hay fever.

Lemon balm tea

Tea made from lemon balm leaves is a mood lifter, said to help with mild depression. It is also believed to relieve stomach upsets.

Camomile tea

Camomile flowers make a tea that has long been held to be relaxing, and to help with sleeplessness.

Preparing Antidotes to Poison

POISON

Just as early herbals contained recommendations on the herbs and plants that could be used to treat many different diseases (some of which advice had some basis in science, some of which has since proved entirely erroneous), they also contained suggestions of which plants could prevent a poison from working. Such plants could be taken after poison as an antidote, and, when carried, might preserve the body against the action of poison. Often, emetics were suggested as effective, but today, of course, medical advice should be sought in a case of suspected poisoning, as inducing the victim to vomit can actually make things worse.

MITHRIDATE

But you of learning and religion
And vertue, and such ingredients, have made
A mithridate, whose operation
Keepes off, or cures what can be done or said.

John Donne, 'To the Countesse of Bedford' (c.1608)

Historically, a mithridate was any of various medical preparations (generally distinguished by the huge number of different ingredients they contained) that were believed to be the most potent of antidotes – universal panaceas, no less. The name preserves that of Mithridates VI Eupator (120–63 BC), a ruler of Pontus who, legend has it, acquired immunity to poisons by taking gradually increased doses of them.

Mithridate was formerly, before medicine was simplified, one of the capital medicines of the shops ... The following is the recipe: Cinnamon 24 drachms; Indian spikenard, ginger, saffron, shepherd's-purse seed, frankincense, Chian turpentine, of each ten drachms; Zedoary mace, long pepper, juice of hypocistus, storax, opoponax, galbanum, opobalsam and castor, of each one ounce; scorbium, cubebs, white pepper, carrot seed, bdellium, of each seven drachms; celtic nard, gentian, dittany of Crete, red roses, wild parsley seed, cardamons, sweet fennel seeds, gum Arabic, strained opium, dissolved in wine, of each five drachms; aromatic reed, valerian root, sagapenum, aniseed, of each three drachms, catechu, St. John's wort, skinks, of each two ounces and a half, &c., &c. Another of these absurd preparations is composed of seventy-two articles.

William Hamilton Maxwell, *The Field Book* (1833)

Viper's bugloss
© STOCKFOLIO® / Alamy

HERBAL ANTIDOTES

Among the plants recommended by the renowned English physician Nicholas Culpeper (1616–54) as effective against poison if taken *before* the poison is administered (whether through paranoia or prescience he does not explain) is viper's bugloss:

It is an especial remedy against the biting of the viper, and other venomous beasts, or serpents; as also against poison, or poisonable herbs. Dioscorides and others say, that whosoever shall take of this herb or roots before they be bitten, shall not be hurt by the poison of any serpent.

Nicholas Culpeper and Peter Cole, *The English Physician: Enlarged with 369 Medicines made from English Herbs* (1826)

After poisoning, and as one of the many emetics that were previously considered a sensible course in such cases, English herbalist John Gerard (1545–1612) suggested that the 'juice' extracted from wall pepper, and taken in vinegar, 'procureth vomit, and bringeth uppe grosse and flegmatike humours', and was thus a remedy against ingested poisons. While for an example of a herb that was thought to prevent you from being poisoned simply by carrying it we turn to Culpeper again, and the herb he referred to as 'dragons':

It is excellent good against pestilence and poison. Pliny and Dioscorides affirm, that no serpent will meddle with him that carries this herb about him.

Nicholas Culpeper and Peter Cole, *The English Physician: Enlarged with 369 Medicines made from English Herbs* (1826)

Curing Warts

A WARTY PROBLEM

Warts seem to be the most popular ailment tackled by folk medicine, with more suggested cures for these unpleasant excrescences than for any other complaint. Over the centuries, warts have been charmed from the sufferer, transferred to another person or disposed of by sympathetic magic. Various vegetables have been rubbed upon them, as have slugs and pieces of stolen meat. Whether any of these traditional cures actually work is not for discussion here, but some of the better-known (and a few of the less common) remedies are described below.

MOONSHINE

In the 1st century AD Pliny the Elder (AD 23–79) is said to have recommended the removal of warts by touching them with chickpeas at the time of a new moon. Once the chickpeas were disposed of, the warts would disappear. Should you miss the new moon, Pliny had a further suggestion:

To get rid of warts, some lie in a footpath with the face upwards, when the moon is twenty days old at least, and after fixing their gaze upon it ... rub themselves with anything within their reach.

Pliny, *Natural History* (Book XXVIII, AD 77)

The moon still played a part in some wart cures in the 17th century. The natural philosopher Sir Kenelm Digby (1603–65) reported his moonshine cure to be infallible:

Amongst the marvels of Sir Kenelm's discoveries in metaphysics and alchemy, we may notice the following as far more amusing than instructive. To remove warts he recommends the hands to be washed in an empty basin into which the moon shines; and declares that the 'moonshine will have humidity enough to cleanse the hands because of the star from which it is derived'.

Robert Chambers, *Book of Days* (1869)

WARTS AND ALL

Plant cures for warts are numerous. The English physician Nicholas Culpeper (1616–54) suggests several natural remedies in *The English Physitian* (1652), including spurge, house leek and greater celandine:

[The juice of the great celandine] is good in old, filthy, corroding, creeping ulcers wheresoever, to stay their malignity of fretting and running, and to cause them to heal more speedily: the juice often applied to tetters, ring-worms, or other such like spreading cankers, will quickly heal them; and, rubbed often upon warts, will take them away.

Nicholas Culpeper and Peter Cole,
The English Physician: Enlarged with 369 Medicines made from English Herbs (1826)

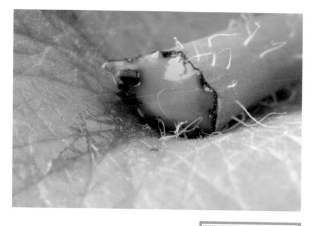

Applying greater celandine juice to skin
© Arco Images GmbH / Alamy

Some claim that dandelion juice is most efficacious, while others prefer vegetables to wild flowers and herbs, rubbing the offending wart with a slice of raw potato, for example, or the inside of a broad bean pod. Perhaps less pleasant to modern tastes are some of the animal-based cures, for example this eel remedy from the 13th-century Welsh manuscript, the *Physicians of Myddvai*:

Take an eel and cut its head off, anoint the parts, where the warts are situated, with the blood, and bury the head deep in the earth; as the head rottens, so will the warts disappear.

Physicians of Myddvai (c.1250, translated by John Pughe, 1861)

This use of sympathetic magic, where what happens to the object associated with the wart (in this instance through the action of rubbing) also happens to the wart itself, is common in wartlore. A fresh slug or snail, still living, might be rubbed on the wart, then impaled on a thorn – as the slug or snail withers and dies, so does the wart:

*Slug impaled on a
thorn
1898.71.1 © Pitt Rivers
Museum, University of Oxford*

*How to cure Warts.
Go into the field and take a black snail, and rub
with the same nine times one way, and then nine
times another, and then stick that said snail upon
a black-thorn, and the warts will waste. I have also
known a black snail cure corns, being laid thereon
as a plaister.*
Nicholas Culpeper and Peter Cole, *The
English Physician: Enlarged with 369 Medicines
made from English Herbs* (1826)

Stolen meat was used in a similar way – rubbed on the wart then buried and left to rot – but apparently the magic would not work if the meat were acquired by legitimate means:

*A gentleman well known to me, states that, when
he was a boy, the landlady of an inn where he
happened to be took compassion on his warty
hands, and undertook to cure them by rubbing
them with bacon. It was necessary, however, that
the bacon should be stolen; so the good lady took it
secretly from her own larder, which was supposed
to answer the condition sufficiently. If I recollect
rightly, the warts remained as bad as ever, which
was perhaps due to the bacon not having been
bona fide stolen.*
Robert Chambers, *Book of Days* (1869)

Similarly, a notch might be cut into a stick (often from an elder) for each wart a person was afflicted with (counting seeming to replace rubbing in this cure), and the stick would then be buried and left to rot. Alternatively, in some traditions, the stick would be left in the road and the warts would be transferred to whoever happened to pick it up next. Warts could also be transferred by wrapping a parcel of dry beans or peas, with one pulse for each wart, and leaving the parcel in the road for someone else to pick up (throwing the package over the head at a crossroads was considered the most effective way of ensuring that you 'lost' the warts).

CHARMING

But there are gifted old women who have only to slip a thread over these excrescences, or touch them with saliva, and they dry away.

Robert Southey, *Letters from England* (1807)

Wart charmers were individuals who claimed the ability to cure warts, often simply by looking at them. The charmer might recite a charm, touch the wart, or offer to buy it (although once purchased, the wart was not transferred to the charmer, but simply disappeared). Wart charming often ran in a family, with a new charmer in each generation, and while such healers often refused payment, a subsequent 'gift' was generally acceptable.

BEWARE OF BOILED EGGS

If you wish to avoid either rubbing your warts with the inside of a broad bean pod or killing innocent slugs and snails, it might be worth remembering that it was once popularly believed that warts on the hands were caused by inadvertently washing them in water that had been used for the boiling of eggs.

Degradation of Drunkenness

—

There is no sin which doth more deface God's image than drunkenness it disguiseth a person and doth even unman him. Drunkenness makes him have the throat of a fish, the belly of a swine and the head of an ass. Drunkenness is the shame of nature, the extinguisher of reason, the shipwreck of chastity, and the murderer of conscience. Drunkenness is hurtful to the body; the cup kills more than the cannon. it causes dropsies, catarrhs, apoplexies, it fills the eye with fire, and the legs with water, and turns the body into an hospital.

Curing Drunkenness

DRUNKENNESS

For as long as there has been alcohol (and it is generally agreed that beer was being brewed in Mesopotamia by 6000 BC) there have, presumably, been the consequences of alcohol – drunkenness and hangovers. While moderation or abstemiousness are the only true methods of avoiding or curing these, a number of strategies have been employed over the centuries, some of which are recorded, although not necessarily recommended, below.

SOBERING UP

In his *Medical Inquiries and Observations* (1805) Benjamin Rush described a number of methods for sobering up when drunk, including 'plunging the whole body into cold water', 'terror', 'a severe whipping' and the 'excitement of a fit of anger':

The late Dr. Witherspoon used to tell a story of a man in Scotland, who was always cured of a fit of drunkenness, by being made angry. The means chosen for that purpose, was a singular one. It was talking against religion.
> Benjamin Rush, *Medical Inquiries and Observations* (Volume 1, 1805)

In the early 19th century, it was believed that a tendency towards drunkenness could be cured by moral means, by the drunk being shown the error of his ways, as shown in this once-popular tale of the drunken goat:

Remarkable Cure of Drunkenness.—It is related of the Rev. Rees Prichard, vicar of Llandingrad, but better known, (says Rees in his History of South Wales,*) by the name of 'the vicar of Llandovery,' who died in the year 1644, that while a young man he was much addicted to drinking; and he is said to have been cured of his habit by an accidental circumstance ... In his visits to the public house, he was usually followed by a goat. On one occasion, he prevailed on his companion to participate in his enjoyments, and to drink ale until it became inebriated. This one fit of intoxication more than satisfied the goat. It could never afterwards be prevailed upon to repeat the experiment. This incident, though trifling, led the master to reflect on his own condition, and induced a resolution to abstain thenceforth from his old practice.*

The Mirror of Literature, Amusement, and Instruction (Volume XXII, 1833)

While in the New World it seems that it was once considered possible to cure drunkenness with the deterrent of hard physical labour:

Novel Cure for Drunkenness in the New World.—An American paper states, that drunkenness, in one of the newly-settled countries, has been, in a great measure, prevented, by a wholesome regulation which obliges every offender to dig up a stump of a tree, for each time he is found intoxicated; and a contemporary remarks, that this is a rather novel way of rooting out intemperance.

Robert Owen and Robert Dale Owen (Editors), *Crisis, and National Co-operative Trades' Union Gazette* (Volumes 1–2, 1832–33)

THE HAIR OF THE DOG THAT BIT YOU

The idea of curing like with like – ie that more of the thing that caused your problem will also lead to its relief – is an old one, and for many centuries 'the hair of the dog that bit you' (essentially another dose of whatever alcoholic drink caused your hangover) has been used to alleviate the symptoms encountered the day after drinking too much. As early as 1546, the saying was included in John Heywood's *Proverbs*, as 'I pray the leat me and my felow haue, a heare of the dog that bote us last night', and has proved so enduring that today the short form 'hair of the dog' is widely understood to refer to an alcoholic drink. Pepys tried this method, and mentioned it in his diary:

Up among my workmen, my head akeing all day from last night's debauch. To the office all the morning, and at noon dined with Sir W. Batten and Pen, who would needs have me drink two drafts of sack to-day to cure me of last night's disease, which I thought strange but I think find it true.

Samuel Pepys, diary entry, Wednesday 3 April 1661

Unfortunately for Pepys, and anyone else who tries the hair of the dog method, having another drink only delays your hangover, and the dog will bite you again at some point.

Another 16th-century option was to take something before drinking which it was believed would preserve you from drunkenness (and therefore from the subsequent hangover). The English herbalist John Gerard (1545–1612) recommended a number of different options, including 'colewoort' (cabbage, because there is 'a naturall enmitie between it and the vine'), lettuce (which stops 'the vapors from rising up into the head') and almonds:

And it is reported that five or sixe [almonds] being taken do keepe a man from being drunke.

John Gerard, *The Herball, or generall historie of plantes* (1597)

It is often said that in ancient Rome and Greece, such remedies as raw owl eggs and fried canaries were eaten to counter a hangover. Raw eggs still feature in the 'prairie oyster' – a raw egg (with the yolk unbroken) seasoned with salt, pepper and Worcestershire sauce, and sometimes with spirits added – a 'morning after' cure to be downed in one.

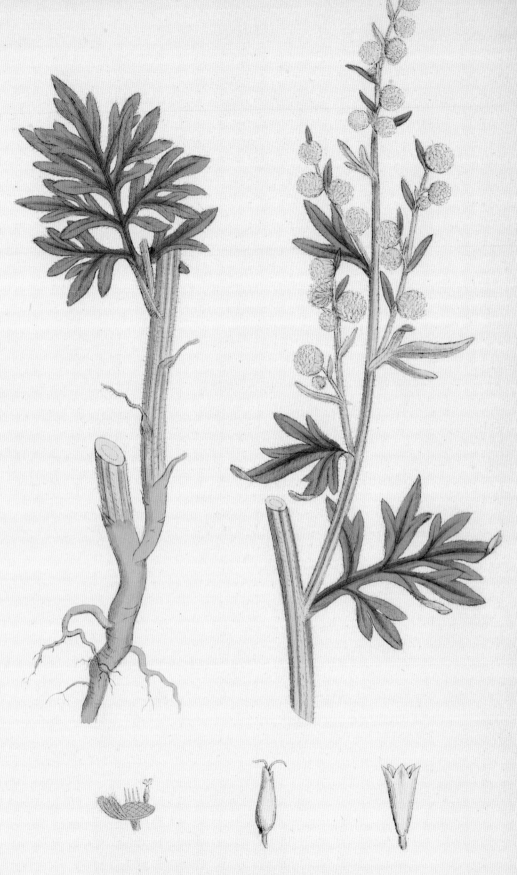

E.B. 1230.   Artemisia Absinthium.   Common Wormwood.

Improving Digestion

DIGESTION AND INDIGESTION

When our bodies fail to digest food properly, we suffer from indigestion – an age-old problem, perhaps made worse in modern times by sedentary lifestyles and processed foods. Our ancestors developed numerous methods for 'improving digestion' – some suggestions, such as taking ginger, are still practised today, whereas others, such as infusions of wormwood (which is poisonous in quantity), are mostly forgotten.

HERBAL REMEDIES

Ginger, as Dioscorides reporteth, is right good with meate in sauces, or otherwise in conditures: for it is of an heating and digesting qualitie, it gently looseth the bellie, and is profitable for the stomacke.
> John Gerard, *The Herball, or generall historie of plantes* (1597)

In addition to ginger, Gerard recommends angelica; coriander seeds; saxifrage; mint; perry (an alcoholic drink made from pears); cloves; and cinnamon:

The oyle drawne chemically prevaileth against the paines of the breast, comforteth the stomack, breaketh windinesse, causeth good digestion, and being mixed with some honie, taketh away spots from the face, being anointed therewith.
> John Gerard, *The Herball, or generall historie of plantes* (1597)

Gentian was also once a popular herbal remedy for improving digestion:

Take of gentian root, cut into pieces, half an ounce;
dried peel of Seville oranges, bruised, one drachm;
coriander seeds, bruised, half a drachm;
diluted alcohol, four ounces;
water, one pound:
First pour on the alcohol, and three hours thereafter add the water; then macerate
without heat for twelve hours, and strain. The dose is two or three drachms, at twelve
o'clock, seven in the evening, and bed-time, every day, to improve digestion.

Robert John Thornton, *A New Family Herbal* (1810)

While among the many herbal remedies suggested by the English physician Nicholas Culpeper (1616–54) is an infusion of wormwood:

The flowery tops [of Roman wormwood] are the right part. These made into a light
infusion, strengthen digestion, correct acidities, and supply the place of gall, where,
as in many constitutions, that is deficient. One ounce of the flowers and buds should
be put in a vessel, and a pint and a half of boiling water poured on them, and thus to
stand all night. In the morning, the clear liquor, with two spoonfuls of wine, should
be taken at three draughts, an hour and a half distance from one another. This,
regularly observed for a week, will cure all the complaints arising from indigestion
and wind; and a fourth part of the dose repeated afterwards, will make the cure more
lasting.

Nicholas Culpeper and Peter Cole, *The English Physician: Enlarged with*
369 Medicines made from English Herbs (1826)

TOO FREE A USE OF TEA

Heartburn is one of the most common ailments that might lead us to look for remedies to improve our digestion, although the dietary recommendations given below would probably not be endorsed by a modern nutritionist:

For heartburn.
This complaint is an uneasy sensation in the stomach, with anxiety, a heat more or
less violent, and sometimes attended with oppression, faintness, an inclination to
vomit, or a plentiful discharge of clear lymph, like saliva. This pain may arise from
various causes; such as wind, sharp humours, and worms gnawing the ... stomach;
also from acrid and pungent food; likewise from rheumatic and gouty humours, or

*surfeits, and from too free a use of tea. The diet should be of a light animal kind;
the drink brandy and water, toast and water, Bristol water; no vegetables should be
allowed; very little bread, and that well toasted.*

Mackenzie's Five Thousand Receipts in all the Useful and Domestic Arts (1831)

LAUGHTER IS THE BEST MEDICINE

Those who prefer not to take any remedies, whether synthetic or herbal,
might like to take note of the following suggestion for a method of
improving digestion:

*Laughter is favourable to digestion, for by it the organs concerned in digestion get
exercise, the exercise necessary for the process. And, accordingly, we usually find an
ample meal more easily disposed of where merriment is going on, than a light one
taken in solitude, and under a sombre state of feeling.*

Robert Chambers, *Book of Days* (1869)

Making Possets and Caudles

POSSETS AND CAUDLES

A posset is a drink made from hot milk curdled with ale or wine, once popular as a remedy for a cold. A caudle is another warm drink once administered to those in need of nourishment – and at one time especially to women who were soon to give birth – that was made from a thin gruel or eggs mixed with wine or ale. Both were popular in the later Middle Ages, and were in relatively common use until the making and taking of possets and caudles declined in the 19th century.

A MULTITUDE OF POSSETS

*A sparing diet did her health assure
Or sick, a pepper posset was her cure.*

John Dryden, 'The Cock and the Fox' (1699)

A classic, simple posset might include milk, ale, sugar, ginger and nutmeg, but many variations existed – for example, the 'pepper posset' mentioned by Dryden would have included allspice berries, or whole peppercorns, providing extra heat which was thought to help you sweat out your cold. The method for making a posset, whether with wine or ale or sherry, generally remained the same. First, the milk was brought to the boil in a saucepan, then the alcohol added. The mixture was then removed from the heat and left to curdle, before it was strained and the sugar and spices added. Possets were often served in specially designed posset pots, made from china and shaped like a covered cup with a spout. Temperance versions of the posset also existed, such as a very simple one made by warming milk and black treacle together (without curdling), or boiling milk, black treacle and lemon together (which will curdle):

And now for the posset—sweet delicious, schoolboy-beloved posset!—how often have we feigned a cold at school, in order to have a basin full of thy rich, brown bubbling mixture! Whenever you see a person—lady or gentleman, gentle or simple— whining and whimpering under the affliction of a cold, let your invariable receipt be posset—nothing but posset. It is to a cold what action is to eloquence ... Let the patient stretch himself between some warm sheets, and then swallow a basin-full of hot, curdly, shining and steaming treacle-posset ... and by the morning, his cold will have evaporated in the gentle dews of undisturbed repose.

The Idler; and Breakfast-Table Companion (Volume 1, 1837)

CAUDLES

In addition to the loan of the monthly boxes ... the society dispense occasional grants of beef-tea, and a composition of warm beer, spice, eggs, and sugar, commonly known by the name of 'caudle,' to its patients. And here again the services of the honorary members are called into requisition, and most carefully conceded. Deputations of twos and threes are sent out to visit the patients, and on these occasions there is such a tasting of caudle and beef-tea, such a stirring about of little messes in tiny saucepans on the hob, such a dressing and undressing of infants, such a tying, and folding, and pinning; such a nursing and warming of little legs and feet before the fire, such a delightful confusion of talking and cooking, bustle, importance, and officiousness, as never can be enjoyed in its full extent but on similar occasions.

Charles Dickens, *Sketches by Boz*, 'The Ladies' Societies' (1836)

While by Dickens's time, caudles were most commonly administered to women in 'childbed', and served to those who visited the mother and baby after the birth, at one time they were a fashionable choice for breakfast or suppertime. A 15th-century recipe for a caudle gives egg yolks, ale (or wine), saffron, salt and sugar as its ingredients. To make this early caudle, the egg yolks and ale are beaten together, then heated in a saucepan, while stirring continually. As soon as the mixture comes to the boil (by which time it should be thick and frothy), the sugar, saffron and salt are added, and the caudle is ready to be served. A gruel-based caudle is made first by creating the gruel: two tablespoons of oatmeal are boiled in around

600 millilitres (1 pint) of water for a few minutes. The mixture is then strained, and sugar and spices (such as ginger and nutmeg) are added, and a beaten egg if one is being used. After some gentle heating, the drink can be finished with the addition of ale, wine or brandy.

Living Longer

LONGEVITY

Throughout human history man has always sought to live longer. Stories of longevity (of individuals living for much longer than they should) have abounded, often serving to reinforce an elder's credentials of wisdom and authority – in the Old Testament, the Hebrew patriarch Methuselah is said to have attained 969 years of age. Today, because of better living conditions and medical and social care, generally people do live longer – but more often by following a healthy lifestyle, and due to genetic factors, than by chasing the myths that some of our ancestors hoped for.

FOUNTAINS OF YOUTH AND ELIXIRS OF LIFE

The legend of a spring that can restore health and youth, and even bestow immortality on the drinker, appears in various mythologies. It can be found in Hindu fable, as well as in ancient Hebrew, Greek and Roman writings. As late as the 16th century, the Spanish explorer, Juan Ponce de León (1460–1521) is said to have gone in search of a fountain of perpetual youth after having heard tales of it from the natives of Puerto Rico, but as Washington Irving (1783–1859) concluded in *Spanish Voyages of Discovery* (1817), 'he may have drank of every fountain and river, and lake of the archipelago, even to the salt pools of Turk's island, without being a whit the younger'. The elixir of life, on the other hand, is made rather than looked for. Alchemists believed that it could be used to create life, as well as preserve and prolong it. The 2nd-century AD Chinese alchemical work 'The Convergence of the Three' is largely devoted to a description of the materials and procedures required to produce elixirs of long life and immortality, while among those who claimed to have successfully made it was Elizabethan alchemist Edward Kelley.

HE THAT WOULD LIVE FOR AYE

He that would live for aye
Must eat sage in May.

This old English saying reveals that at one time the humble herb sage was thought to prolong life, a belief that might have arisen after the Crusades, when the saying 'why should a man die who grows sage in his garden' became popular throughout Europe. In more recent centuries, it has been generally accepted that clean, healthy living and a pleasant temperament are key, no matter which month you eat your sage in:

Temperance in diet and regimen is necessary to preserve long life ... an easy, mild, and quiet temper [also] prolongs life; but a peevish, fretful, and irritable disposition destroys it. Many who have exceeded the usual term of human life, were remarkable for the mildness of their temper ... The neglect of exercise is, perhaps, the greatest error which sedentary persons commit ... [while] those who convert their bodies into medicine chests, seldom enjoy health or live to old age.
                    Collections, Historical and Miscellaneous (Volume II, 1823)

EXTREME LONGEVITY

Folklore offers us a number of examples of alleged extreme longevity. Katherine Fitzgerald, the Countess of Desmond, died in the early 17th century, reputedly having reached the age of around 140 years. Francis Bacon (1561–1626) refers to her in his *Natural History*:

They tell a tale of the old Countess of Desmond who lived till she was seven score years old, that she did dentire [grow teeth] twice or thrice; casting her old teeth and others coming in their place.

                    Francis Bacon, *Natural History* (1627)

Among the myths associated with the Countess is the story that she would have lived even longer had she not climbed into a tree to gather nuts (or in some versions cherries) and fallen from it, suffering injuries that led to her much-deferred demise. Another legendary case of extreme longevity from the 17th century is Thomas Parr, who, when he died in London in 1635, was reputed to have been 152 years old:

[Thomas Parr] was born at Winnington, in the parish of Alberbury, Shropshire, in 1483. His father, John Parr, was an agricultural labourer, and Thomas throughout his long life followed the same occupation. Till the age of eighty, he continued a bachelor, and then married his first wife, with whom he lived for thirty-two years. About eight years after her death, when he himself was a hundred and twenty years old, he married for a second time. Having, in 1635, attained the wonderful age of a hundred and fifty-two years and upwards, he was visited in that year by the Earl of Arundel ... who thereupon induced [him] to pay a visit to London. It would have been better, however, had Lord Arundel left the old man undisturbed in his native parish [as] ere many months were over, [he] fell ill and died.

Robert Chambers, *Book of Days* (1869)

The officially recognized world record is 122 years of age, as achieved by the Frenchwoman Jeanne Calment (1877–1993). She enjoyed a daily cigarette until she was 117, and attributed her long life to olive oil and the consumption of two pounds of chocolate a week.

Caring for Hair

HAIR

Before the advent of commercially produced shampoos, conditioners and the myriad of hair treatments that are available today, numerous traditional methods of caring for the hair were employed, generally using such natural substances as were readily available.

HAIR CARE

Tonics and rinses

Many people claim that a tonic made from nettles is excellent for the hair. To make such a tonic, simply pick some young nettle tops (it might be a good idea to wear gloves for this bit), wash them and add them to a saucepan of water. Heat slowly, then simmer gently for a few minutes, with the lid on. Allow to cool to a suitable temperature, strain, then rinse the hair several times before a final rinse with cold, clean water. It has been claimed that this tonic will help clear dandruff and leave your hair shiny and soft. Nettles (which are not only abundant but also free) have been recommended in hair care since at least the 18th century:

> *To quicken the Growth of Hair.*
> *Dip the teeth of your comb every morning in the expressed Juice of Nettles, and comb the hair the wrong way. It will surprisingly quicken the growth of the hair.*
> Pierre-Joseph Buc'hoz, *The Toilet of Flora* (1772)

Other herbal hair rinses include one made with camomile (said to help retain the lightness of naturally blond hair) and one made with rosemary (either dried or fresh). To make the camomile rinse, simmer camomile flowers in water for a few minutes, cool to a suitable temperature, strain and use as a rinse after shampooing the hair (an even simpler version, when camomile flowers are not available, uses watered-down camomile tea). Rosemary hair rinse, which is said to condition the hair, can be made by infusing rosemary leaves in boiling water, straining and adding to your rinsing water.

Washes

A good Wash for the Hair.
INGREDIENTS.—1 pennyworth of borax, ¹/₂ pint olive-oil, 1 pint of boiling water.
Mode.—Pour the boiling water over the borax and oil; let it cool; then put the mixture in a bottle. Shake it before using, and apply it with a flannel.
Mrs Isabella Beeton, Beeton's Book of Household Management (1861)

Relatively simple herbal hair washes (which, like modern shampoos, need to be rinsed from the hair rather than left in) can be made by combining herbal infusions with liquid Castile soap (a gentle soap made with olive oil). Again, a camomile wash is recommended for blond hair.

ANTHEMIS NOBILIS *Linn.*

Camomile, illustration from Medicinal Plants *by Bentley Trimen, 1880*
© *The Natural History Museum / Alamy*

BALDNESS

For centuries man has sought a cure for baldness, or at the very least a method by which the process of going bald might be slowed down. Needless to say, these remedies are included for interest, rather than as practical suggestions for what you put on your scalp.

In the 17th century, the physician William Salmon conceded that remedying baldness was tricky, but still had a number of ideas for what might be done:

[Baldness] is a hard thing to cure, yet the following things are very good. Rub the head or bald places every morning very hard with a coarse cloth, till it be red, anointing immediately after with Bear's grease: when ten or fifteen days are passed, rub every morning and evening with a bruised Onion, till the bald places be red, then anoint with honey well mixed with Mustard seed, applying over all a plaster of Labdanum mixed with mice dung, and powder of Bees: do this for thirty days.

William Salmon, *Polygraphice* (1673)

In the 18th century, John Wesley was still recommending rubbing the head with an onion, but the mice dung had been dispensed with:

11. To CURE BALDNESS

Rub the part morning and evening, with onions, till it is red, and rub it afterwards with honey.
Or, wash it with a decoction of boxwood.—Tried.
Or, electrify it daily.

John Wesley, *Primitive Physic, or an Easy and Natural Method of Curing Most Diseases* (1747)

Even Mrs Beeton included a recipe 'to promote the growth of hair' in her famous book of household management, and whether it works or not, at least it doesn't sound too dangerous or malodorous:

INGREDIENTS.—*Equal quantities of olive-oil and spirit of rosemary; a few drops of oil of nutmeg.*
Mode.—*Mix the ingredients together, rub the roots of the hair every night with a little of the liniment, and the growth of it will very soon sensibly increase.*

Mrs Isabella Beeton, *Beeton's Book of Household Management* (1861)

HAIRY SUPERSTITIONS

Friday cut and Sunday shorn,
Better never have been born.

This traditional rhyme reveals the once-widespread belief that it was unlucky to cut the hair on a Friday (Good Friday was considered a particularly terrible choice), or shave a beard on a Sunday. Nor was the day of the week the only consideration when choosing an auspicious day on which to cut your hair – the time of the month was also considered important:

Similarly the emperor Tiberius kept to the period between two moons even in having his hair cut. Marcus Varro advises the plan of having one's hair cut just after full moon, as a precaution against going bald.

Pliny the Elder, Natural History (AD 77)

That hair should be cut when the moon is waxing, to ensure its luxurious regrowth, is a belief that was apparently held from ancient to relatively modern times. Conversely, those things which you don't want to regrow well (such as corns) are suitable for trimming when the moon is waning.

Other hairy superstitions include the care that should be taken of the trimmings (in the past it was commonly thought that a witch could make use of your discarded hair to cause you ill) and the belief that if you swallowed a long hair it would twine around your heart and kill you. Hair was once also used to divine whether or not its owner was destined to have a long life – it was thrown into the fire (having previously been detached from the scalp) and if it burnt very brightly and very well a long life could be expected, whereas if it smouldered and didn't burn well, death was not very far away.

One final piece of hairlore relates to the 'widow's peak', and dates from at least the 17th century. If a person's hair suddenly grows over the forehead in such a way as to form a low point, it was thought a sure sign that they would soon be widowed.

Caring for Skin

SKINCARE

As with many areas of health and wellbeing, our ancestors often had to rely on such ingredients as were readily available to them, and recipes that were handed from generation to generation, to create their own skincare treatments (and even then, these were perhaps restricted to those who had the leisure for such frivolities).

FACE WASH

An excellent Water to clear the Skin, and take away Pimples.
Take two quarts of Water, in which a quantity of Horse-beans have been boiled till quite soft, put into an alembic, and add two handfuls of Pimpernel, the same quantity of White Tansy, a pound of Veal minced small, six new laid Eggs, and a pint of White-Wine Vinegar; distill this mixture in a water bath, and it will afford an excellent lotion to remove all eruptions on the face, if washed therewith every night and morning.
Pierre-Joseph Buc'hoz, *The Toilet of Flora* (1772)

For a less complicated, and relatively inexpensive, facial treatment than that suggested above, our predecessors might have turned to herbal infusions (made by steeping herbs in warm water) which could be used as refreshing and cleansing skin tonics – dandelion, parsley, fennel and elderflowers all have mildly astringent properties for example, which can be exploited in this way. Rosemary too has long been used in skincare, and was one of the many ingredients found in an early commercial skin lotion, marketed in the 17th century.

COLD CREAM

If you suffer from a greasy skin, at least once a day (either immediately after the
bath, or at night time) apply a generous layer of soft, emollient cold cream ...
Leave it on for three to five minutes, then remove with a little tissue or a soft towel.
Give a second dressing of cold cream; this time use a small piece of not too rough
loofah and work the cream well into the pores by circular, outward movements,
working from the centre of the chin to the middle of the forehead ... Cold cream
and friction combined will make the pores active and enable them to throw off
superfluous oils.

The Book of Hints and Wrinkles (c.1939)

At one time such cosmetic treatments as cold cream were often made at
home – although today we would find such ingredients as spermaceti (a
waxy substance obtained from oil from the head of whales, especially the
sperm whale) unacceptable:

Melt together a pint of oil of sweet almonds, one ounce of white wax, half an ounce
of spermaceti and half a pint of rose-water. Beat to a paste.
Put into a jar one pint of sweet-oil, half an ounce of spermaceti and two ounces of
white wax. Melt in a jar by the fire. Add scent.

John A Ruth, *Decorum, a Practical Treatise on Etiquette and Dress* (1880)

However, the history of cold cream is somewhat longer, and its invention
is attributed to the Greek physician Galen (c.130–c.201 AD). His recipe
for cold cream included beeswax, oil of roses and water. People still use
adapted versions of his recipe today, mixing cold cream from, for example,
beeswax, water, olive oil and and an essential oil such as lavender.

MAGICAL COMPLEXION

The fair maid who, the first of May,
Goes to the fields at break of day,
And washes in dew from the hawthorn tree,
Will ever after handsome be.

The Nursery Rhymes of Mother Goose (1913)

In the past, both in Britain and elsewhere, there was a widespread belief that May dew was beneficial to the complexion. Samuel Pepys's wife, Elizabeth, certainly joined in the tradition, on at least two occasions:

After dinner my wife away down with Jane and W. Hewer to Woolwich, in order to a little ayre and to lie there to-night, and so to gather May-dew to-morrow morning, which Mrs. Turner hath taught her as the only thing in the world to wash her face with; and I am contented with it.

                                          Samuel Pepys, diary entry, Tuesday 28 May 1667

While Elizabeth Pepys believed any May dew to be good for her skin, the dew collected on May Day morning was generally held to give you the fairest complexion. Many young women would go out early and collect the dew from the grass on 1 May, using it to bathe their faces and necks.

In Scotland there are few relics of the old May-day observances—we might rather say none, beyond a lingering propensity in the young of the female sex to go out at an early hour, and wash their faces with dew. At Edinburgh this custom is kept up with considerable vigour, the favourite scene of the lavation being Arthur's Seat. On a fine May morning, the appearance of so many gay groups perambulating the hill sides and the intermediate valleys, searching for dew, and rousing the echoes with their harmless mirth, has an indescribably cheerful effect.

                                          Robert Chambers, *Book of Days* (1869)

CALOX The Oxygen Tooth Powder

with its wonderful property of giving up oxygen, destroys the germs which give rise to decay of the teeth. It leaves a most exquisite sense of cleanliness in the mouth.

Sold everywhere in dainty metal bottles, 1/1½.

Sample and Booklet post free from G. B. Kent & Sons, Ltd., 75, Farringdon Rd., London, E.C.

Caring for Teeth

THE CARE OF TEETH

Numerous methods (some more effective than others) were traditionally used to care for the teeth before the advent of the modern toothbrush (William Addis made the first mass-produced toothbrushes in 1780) and toothpaste (produced commercially in the 19th century). Much early tooth care relied on the 'chew stick', a thin twig with a frayed end that helped to remove food particles from between the teeth. The ancient Egyptians used a powder to help keep the teeth clean, which included such ingredients as salt and mint – not too dissimilar to tooth powders used until relatively recently (the salt acts as an abrasive, an important part of the cleaning process, while mint freshens the breath). No matter how fastidious you are when it comes to tooth hygiene, in order to care for your teeth properly it is still important to remember what they should and shouldn't be used for:

Healthy teeth depend mainly on healthy digestion, and on cleanly habits as regards the teeth. They must, of course, be confined to the purposes for which they are designed. If they are employed for the purpose of cracking nuts, biting thread, unscrewing needle-cases, or turning the stopper of a smelling-bottle; if the mouth is used as a kind of portable tool-chest, in which a pair of scissors, a knife, a vice, a corkscrew, or any other instrument may be found at the time of need, then serious and irretrievable injury will eventually be done to the enamel of the teeth, which no healthiness of digestion nor cleanliness of habit will avail to remedy.

The Cottager's Monthly Visitor (Volume VI, 1826)

CLEANING YOUR TEETH

If you will keep your teeth from rotting, or aching, wash your mouth continually every morning with juice of lemons, and afterwards rub your teeth either with a sage-leaf, or else with a little nutmeg in powder; also wash your mouth with a little fair water after meats; for the only way to keep teeth sound, and free from pain is to keep them clean.

Nicholas Culpeper and Peter Cole, *The English Physician: Enlarged with 369 Medicines made from English Herbs* (1826)

Some people still recommend using fresh sage leaves to whiten the teeth (simply rub the leaves over the teeth), and lemon can help freshen and clean the teeth (by chewing on the rind of an unwaxed lemon). Lemon and salt could also be used to make a liquid tooth cleaner:

A Liquid Dentrifice.
Take Lemon Juice, two ounces, Burnt-Alum and Salt, of each six grains; boil them together about a minute in a glazed pipkin, and then strain through a linen cloth. The method of using it is to wrap a bit of clean rag round the end of a stick, dip it in the Liquid and rub it gently against the teeth. You must be careful not to have too much of the Liquid on the rag, for fear it should excoriate the gums or inside of the mouth. This Dentrifice ought not to be used above once every two or three months.

Pierre-Joseph Buc'hoz, *The Toilet of Flora* (1772)

Charcoal was another traditional tooth cleaner, used in various parts of the world:

Tooth powder.
Pound charcoal, as fine as possible, in a mortar, or grind it in a mill, then well sift it, and apply a little of it to the teeth about twice a week, and it will not only render them beautifully white, but will also make the breath sweet, and the gums firm and comfortable.

Maria Eliza Ketelby Rundell, *The Family Receipt Book* (1819)

Ashes could be used in place of charcoal, particularly the ashes of burnt hazelnuts (a double hazelnut, ie a hazelnut in which two kernels have formed, was also thought to prevent toothache when carried about the person). Other established tooth cleaning methods include rubbing the teeth with bicarbonate of soda, or, in Asia, chewing betel nuts.

TOOTHACHE – WHEN THE WORST HAPPENS

When fevers burn, or ague freezes,
Rheumatics gnaw, or colic squeezes,
Our neibor's sympathy can ease us,
Wi' pitying moan;
But thee [toothache]!—thou hell o' a' diseases—
Aye mocks our groan.

Robert Burns, 'Address to the Toothache' (c.1789)

Some time-honoured cures for toothache are herbal, whereas others are magical (where a charm is used to stop the pain). One of the cures that comes under the heading of charm takes the form of a verse, repeated to counter the pain of a toothache:

As Peter sat on a marble stone
The Lord came to him alone
Peter, what makes thee sit there
My Lord, I am troubled with the toothache
Peter arise, and go home
And you, and whosoever for my sake
Shall keep these words in memory
Shall never be troubled with the toothache.

Traditional herbal remedies include chewing yarrow leaves, wild parsley or purslane:

The leaves [of purslane] eaten rawe, taketh away the paine of the teeth, and
fasteneth them; and is good for teeth that are set on edge with eating of sharpe things.

John Gerard, *The Herball, or generall historie of plantes* (1597)

The affected tooth could be rubbed with onion juice or oil of cloves, or an elder twig could be chewed to relieve the pain, or pepper could be added to the inner rind of an elder tree and held in the mouth against the affected area:

For the Tooth-ache.
Take the inner rind of an elder-tree, and bruise it, and put thereto a little pepper, and

make it into balls, and hold them between the teeth that ache.
Nicholas Culpeper and Peter Cole, *The English Physician: Enlarged with 369 Medicines made from English Herbs* (1826)

If both herbal and magical methods failed, additional pain was sometimes recommended as a way of distracting the patient from the original source of their discomfort:

Pain in any other part of the body eases toothache, chiefly as it would seem, by affecting the mind and distracting or withdrawing attention. A box on the ear, a blow on the shin, or on the elbow, has in this way often given immediate relief. It is in this way, that any thing which smarts the mouth relieves the pain, such as hot water, tobacco smoke, or brandy, held in the mouth.
A F Crell, *The Family Oracle of Health, Economy, Medicine and Good Living* (1824)

THE BODY BEAUTIFUL

Beautifying is a centuries-old tradition – each generation tries to beat time and nature to look its best for longer. Whereas today we would, at the least extreme, look to the vast array of mass-produced moisturizers and cosmetics that are available, and at the most extreme to the surgeon's knife, in the past numerous herbal remedies and strange concoctions were said to help achieve beauty. But for all the potions that have been tried over the years, remember also the simple rule: 'try to look cheerful':

Your outlook on life is closely interwoven with your personal appearance, so watch yourself and try to cultivate the habit of looking happy, contented and cheerful. Smile and don't frown or scowl nor worry over trifles. A smiling countenance is always attractive and a far better safeguard against the onslaught of age than all the physical jerks and cosmetics in the world.

The Book of Hints and Wrinkles (c.1939)

WRINKLES

A Secret to take away Wrinkles.
Heat an Iron Shovel red hot, throw thereon some Powder of Myrrh, receive the smoke on your face, covering the head with a napkin to collect the smoke, and prevent its being dissipated. Repeat this operation three times, then heat the Shovel again, and

when fiery hot spit on it a mouthful of White Wine. Receive the vapour of the Wine also on your face, and repeat it three times. Continue this proceeding every night and morning as long as you find occasion.

Pierre-Joseph Buc'hoz, *The Toilet of Flora* (1772)

If you prefer not to expose yourself to the potential dangers of red-hot shovels, smoke and wine vapour many other anti-wrinkle remedies have been suggested over the centuries. Meat has been promoted as an anti-wrinkle treatment:

The application of slices of veal cutlet to the face, is ... said to be an excellent preservative. It is asserted that nothing is such an effectual preventive of wrinkles as this simple topic, which, in particular, keeps the skin more fresh and supple than any other cosmetic.

La Belle Assemblée, or Bell's Court and Fashionable Magazine, Addressed Particularly to the Ladies (Volume V, 1808)

Watercress
© Nic Murray / Alamy

Meat-free treatments have also been promoted:

Pomade for removing wrinkles. Take two ounces of the juice of onions, the same quantity of the white lily, the same of Narbonne honey, and an ounce of white wax; put the whole into a new earthen pipkin till the wax is melted; take the pipkin off the fire, and, in order to mix the whole well together, keep stirring it with a wooden spatula till it grows quite cold. You will then have an excellent ointment for removing wrinkles.

The Art of Beauty (1825)

FRECKLES

Freckles have, rather unjustly, been considered unfashionable at various points in history, and the discussion of their removal has been a frequent subject for inclusion in works on the body beautiful. The English physician Nicholas Culpeper (1616–54) suggested applying bruised watercress leaves, or the extracted juice of watercress, to the face at night as a way of removing freckles. Victorian ladies applied various concoctions involving lemon juice to their skin in an attempt to keep it pale and freckle-free. Marie Antoinette is said to have used buttermilk. Some suggest that a mixture of milk and freshly grated horseradish will make freckles fade, or that rubbing the face with either a fresh-cut strawberry or the dew-covered leaves from an elm tree will do the trick, but rather more drastic measures have also been suggested at various times:

Take one pound of bullock's gall, one dram of rock alum, half an ounce of sugar-candy, two drams of borax, and one dram of camphor; mix them together, stir the whole for a quarter of an hour, and let it stand. Repeat this three or four times a day for a fortnight ... till the gall appears as clear as water; then strain it through blotting-paper, and put it away for use ... Another process.—Take a bunch of green grapes; dip it in water, and then sprinkle it with alum and salt; wrap it in paper, and bake it under hot ashes. Express the juice, and wash the face with it ... Wash for removing freckles.—Take equal parts of roots of wild cucumber and narcissus, dry them in the shade, reduce them to a very fine powder, and put it into some good brandy. Wash the face with it till you begin to feel an itching, on which wash with cold water; repeat this every day till the freckles are removed, which they cannot fail to be in a short time, because this liquid is somewhat caustic.

La Belle Assemblée (Volume V, 1808)

It should be noted that, obviously, the use of potions that are 'somewhat caustic' is not to be recommended:

The receipts for removing freckles are as ignorant and absurd as all the rest. Bullock's gall and alum would require a good nose to endure. Strawberries, grapes baked in salt, milk and lemon juice, chervil water, and such like stuff, will serve, perhaps, to amuse young ladies, and cannot, at least, do them any harm. As to acrid matters, such as the juice of wild cucumber, they will certainly take off the freckles, since they will take off the skin. The ladies are at liberty to try; but we can assure them, in the mean time, that the freckles will come back again with the new skin, more brilliant than ever. It would be much better to persuade themselves that freckles were a beauty and an ornament, as is our opinion; because that will save a deal of trouble.

The London Magazine (Volume IV, 1826)

Education and Knowledge

Using an Abacus

DIGITAL ARITHMETIC

The literal translation of the Latin word 'abacus' is 'sand tray', betraying the humble counting-board roots of this remarkable piece of calculating equipment. As with much of the language and symbolism of mathematics, the origin of the word is thought to lie in Arabic – the word 'abq' meaning 'sand' or 'dust'. The framed abacus, consisting of counting beads strung on to bars (which usually represent the decimal place-value columns), can take a number of forms – those most commonly in use are the Chinese 'suan pan' and the Japanese 'soroban'.

In both abacuses, each rod or string represents a decimal place-value column (units, tens, hundreds and so on; even decimal places can be represented) – the main difference being that the soroban has four beads below and one bead above the beam (or reckoning bar) in each column, whereas the suan pan has five below and two above. Both can be used as 'memory' to remember numbers, as a counting device and to carry out calculations using all four operations (addition, subtraction, multiplication and division).

THE VENERABLE BEAD

Recording the results of counting, and mechanically 'remembering' numbers for the purposes of calculation, can be achieved through such simple means as using pebbles or scratches in the sand to represent a one-to-one correspondence between objects (such as animals) and numbers. Thousands of years ago, these methods were developed into a variety of portable counting boards in places all around the world. Counting boards using pebbles sliding in grooves were certainly in use in the Middle East, and later by the Greeks and Romans, over 2,000 years ago. By this time, number systems involving place value, or other ways to allow one symbol, pebble or bead to stand for 10, 100, 1,000 etc, were in widespread use. The use of beads on strings or wires allowed abacuses to be portable – the world's first laptop (or even palmtop) computers.

It is possible that the Roman abacus, which already used four lower beads and a bar with one above, was then introduced to the Far East in the early Middle Ages; although abacuses and counting boards were certainly in widespread use there thousands of years before. The Chinese abacus in its current form, with beads on rods within a wooden frame, appeared approximately 1,000 years ago. Since then, a number of variant framed abacuses have appeared (including some with ten beads on each wire and no bar – such as the Russian or Danish abacuses), although the Chinese and Japanese versions are those most popularly used today.

Japanese abacus in use
© Japan Art Collection (JAC)
/ Alamy

READY RECKONING

The use of abacuses for calculation could form the subject of an entire textbook or maths course. However, some of the basics of calculation using the two main types of abacus are given here. If you don't have an abacus, the principles and methods can be applied to any form of makeshift abacus using counters, pebbles or other objects. All that matters is that the different columns are clear and that there is some representation of the reckoning bar.

The abacus is used in a flat position, laying on a table, the floor or in your lap. Before any calculation, all of the beads must be moved away from the bar; in this position the abacus is displaying zero. Those who are adept in its use push the beads above the bar with their forefinger, and those below it with their thumb. As a general rule, work from left to right with an abacus (the direction we read numbers), rather than from lowest place value to highest place value (as with pen and paper methods).

To display a value in a particular column, push one lower bead to the bar for 1, two to the bar for 2, etc. When 5 is reached, one of the beads above the bar is pushed to the bar, and the lower beads are returned to the bottom. Then one lower bead is pushed to the bar for 6, two for 7, three for 8, etc. When all five lower beads reach the bar, the column is full – all the beads in the column are pushed away from the bar, and one lower bead in the adjacent column to the left (where each bead has a value ten times bigger) is pushed to the bar. Thus the Chinese abacus would appear to have redundant beads, those that are absent on the soroban. However, as you will see, these 'redundant' beads come in handy for certain methods of calculation.

The following are basic methods. These can be adapted and 'mechanized' with practice, so that they require very little active thought and can be applied with great speed.

Simple addition and subtraction

The method for simple addition (which doesn't involve 'filling' any columns) is similar on either abacus. For example, to add 23 to 614, first set the abacus to 614 by pushing one upper and one lower bead in the hundreds column to the bar, one lower bead in the tens column to the bar, and four lower beads in the units column to the bar. Then simply increase the value in the tens column by two (two lower beads to the bar) and the units column by three (clear the lower beads and move one upper bead to the bar, then move two lower beads to the bar). Simple subtraction can be completed in much the same way – for 637–23, reverse the process.

More complex calculations

An addition such as 637+48, or a subtraction such as 614–126, would (for a beginner) require a little more thought. This is where the different attributes of each abacus lead to a preference for different approaches.

For both, it is useful to know pairs of complementary numbers to five (1+4 and 2+3) and to ten (1+9, 2+8, 3+7, 4+6 and 5+5) – these are often taught in schools as 'number bonds'.

For the first calculation, set the abacus to 637. Increasing the value of the tens column by 4 (to add the 40 of 48) is straightforward, leaving the abacus set at 677. To add the 8, you could then simply count on 8 on either abacus. Otherwise, you could recognize that the 7 only requires 3 more (from the 8) to fill the column, pushing one more lower bead to the bar in the tens column, leaving 5 (from the 8) to be represented in the units column. However, there is an even quicker method. By recognizing that the complement to 10 for 8 is 2, the process of adding 8 can be changed to adding 10 and subtracting 2, so with just two flicks, one lower bead can be moved to the bar in the tens column and the two lower beads can be moved away from the bar in the units column. The abacus now shows 685.

For the second calculation, 614–126, the usefulness of the 'redundant' beads on the Chinese abacus becomes evident. The extra beads above the bar in each column allow the decomposition of the number (commonly known as 'borrowing'). Thus, once the first step of reducing the 6 (actually 600) in the hundreds column by 1 (actually 100) has been completed, a further 100 can be 'borrowed' for the tens column by moving beads in the hundreds column to show 4, and moving both upper beads to the bar in the tens column so that it effectively contains 11 (actually 110). Now the 2 (actually 20) can be subtracted. A similar process can then be used in the units column – beads moved so that 10 is 'borrowed' to make 14 from which the 6 can be subtracted. This is very similar to the decomposition ('borrowing') pen and paper method, but you work in the opposite direction. The additional upper bead can be thought of as a 'borrowing bead' – just don't say so in front of a maths teacher.

Of course, the soroban doesn't have a 'borrowing bead' in each column. This is where a beautifully simple method can be employed as an alternative to decomposition. Using the simpler subtraction 14–6, we can see how complements to 10 can help. Set the abacus to 14 (one lower bead in the tens column to the bar, and four lower beads in the units column to the bar). Now, because 6+4=10, subtracting 6 is the same as subtracting 10 and adding 4. So move the bead in the tens column away from the bar, and increase the value in the units column by 4, so it displays the answer, 8. Through practice, the use of complements to 5 and 10 becomes almost automatic, and speed increases dramatically.

Methods for multiplication and division are more complex. The most common methods rely on some basic knowledge of 'number facts' – in this instance, times tables up to 9×9=81 and an understanding of place value – and the fact that multiplication can be treated as repeated addition, and division as the repeated subtraction of groups (in much the same way as formal pen and paper methods work).

THE AGE OF THE BEAD

Abacuses are still in widespread use, particularly in the Far East. They provide a quick, portable means of carrying out complex business calculations without the need for an electricity supply. They are also extremely useful devices for teaching calculation within schools.

Using Logarithm Tables

A logarithm is a mathematical operation that was used widely in the days before electronic computing to simplify multiplication and division. Logarithms made it relatively easy to carry out calculations that had previously been extremely time-consuming.

THE DISCOVERY OF LOGARITHMS

The first person to publish a description of logarithms was the Scottish mathematician John Napier (1550–1617). An early enthusiast was Johannes Kepler (1571–1630), the German astronomer, who championed Napier's discovery and later published his own explanation of how they worked.

HOW LOGARITHMS WORK

Logarithms may sound complicated, but the principle is actually quite simple. It's most easily grasped by giving an example first:

10 × 10 × 10 = 1,000

In this equation, 10 is multiplied by itself and then multiplied by 10 again in order to reach the total of 1,000. The logarithm is quite simply the numbers of 10s; there are 3 of them in this example, so here the logarithm is 3. The number 10 itself is called the 'base', so mathematicians would phrase the example above as 'the logarithm of 1,000 to the base 10 is 3'.

Of course, a calculation might involve any number. For example, the base-3 logarithm of 81 is 4 because that's how many 3s would have to be multiplied together to get 81:

$$3 \times 3 \times 3 \times 3 = 81$$

The base is 3 and the logarithm is 4. Similarly, the base-5 logarithm of 15,625 is 6 because that's how many 5s would have to be multiplied together to get 15,625.

$$5 \times 5 \times 5 \times 5 \times 5 \times 5 = 15,625$$

The base is 5 and the logarithm is 6.

THE BENEFIT OF LOGARITHMS

Logarithms have a number of useful properties. Perhaps the most significant is that they can be used to turn multiplication problems into problems of addition. In today's era of the calculator and the computer that might not sound very significant, but in earlier times it was a huge advance. In the simple examples above it's fairly easy to work out the logarithm but imagine, for example, having to multiply 68,129.32 × 248,497.01. And then imagine you had to do hundreds of such calculations. Anything that shortened the procedure was – and still is – immensely valuable.

In mathematical terms the concept is expressed like this:

$$log\ (xy) = log\ x + log\ y$$

But the principle only helps to speed up calculations if you already know the logarithm. In other words, somebody first had to work out the logarithms and publish them in the form of tables.

THE HISTORY OF LOGARITHM TABLES

Soon after John Napier had published his description of logarithms, the mathematician Henry Briggs (1551–1630) published a table containing the logarithms of all whole numbers up to 1,000 to 8 decimal places. In 1624 he added the numbers to 20,000 as well as from 90,000 to 100,000. The missing numbers from 20,000 to 90,000 were added four years later by the

Dutch mathematician Adriaan Vlacq (1600–67). Other mathematicians expanded the tables in the decades that followed.

PRACTICAL APPLICATIONS

Although logarithms may not sound very interesting, they have various fascinating applications. For example, the human eye responds logarithmically to changing levels of brightness and a logarithmic scale is therefore used to measure the apparent brightness of stars. The Richter scale, which gives the intensity of earthquakes, is on a base-10 logarithmic scale. Even music depends on logarithms because a semitone is related to the base-2 logarithm. In fact, logarithms are used just about everywhere, from acoustics to geometry to computer science.

HOW TO USE LOG TABLES

Nowadays, log tables have been replaced by calculators, but anyone who went to school in earlier ages would have been familiar with them. They were usually four-figure tables, which were simpler than the 17th-century versions, and in order to keep the books to a convenient size they only supplied the more difficult part of the calculation.

Consider, for example, the numbers 15, 150 and 1,500 to base-10. The logarithm of 15 must lie between 1 and 2. You know this because 1×10 is 10 (which is less than 15), while 2 10s (10×10) is 100 (which is more than 15). So the answer clearly lies somewhere in between. In other words it must be 1.something. Similarly, the logarithm of 150 must be between 2 and 3, in other words 2.something. And the logarithm of 1,500 must be between 3 and 4, which is to say 3.something.

The 'something' – the number that goes after the decimal point – is known as the 'mantissa' and is the part that's printed in the tables. The number that goes before the decimal point is known as the 'characteristic' and is the part you have to work out for yourself.

If you were to look in a table of logarithms to base-10, you would see that the logarithm of 15 is shown as 1761. So the logarithm of 15 would actually be 1.1761 – that's to say, the characteristic followed by the mantissa. The logarithm of 150 would be 2.1761 and the logarithm of 1,500 would be 3.1761. And so on.

If looking up a logarithm in a table, say 14.35, you would already know that the characteristic must be 1. You would find 14 in the left-hand column, then move your finger across until you are under column 3, and see the number 1553. Moving horizontally across to the 'difference' in column 5 of the 'Mean Differences' table, you would see the number 15. Add that to the first number and you get 1568. So the logarithm, including the characteristic, is 1.1568.

Once familiar with using the table you can move on to multiplying. To tackle 14.35 × 50.98, we already know that the log of 14.35 is 1.1568. Now, using the same procedure, we would need to look up the log of 50.98 and, if done correctly, would arrive at 1.7074. Now we add the two logarithms together:

$$1.1568 + 1.7074 = 2.8642$$

We now have the sum of the logarithms. To get our final answer we have to look up that number in a table of 'antilogarithms', ie numbers of which a particular number is the logarithm.

As before, the characteristic can be ignored for the moment, as we're only concerned with the 8642. Running a finger down the left-hand column until 86 is reached and then across to column 4 results in the number 7311. Moving across to column 2 in the 'Mean Differences' table, you would see the number 3. Add that on and you should have 7314. It only remains to insert the decimal point. Since the characteristic was 2 the answer must lie between 100 and 1000. So the answer is 731.4.

You can check this on a calculator and, in fact, will find you get 731.563. This is due to rounding errors in the log tables, and was the price paid for speed before the era of the calculator.

Gr.	30		+|			
30 min	Sinus	Logarithmi	Differentia	logarithmi	Sinus	
0	5000000	6931469	5493059	1438410	8660254	60
1	5002519	6926432	5486342	1440090	8658799	59
2	5005038	6921399	5479628	1441771	8657344	58
3	5007556	6916369	5472916	1443453	8655888	57
4	5010074	6911342	5466206	1445136	8654431	56
5	5012591	6906319	5459498	1446821	8652973	55
6	5015108	6901299	5452792	1448507	8651514	54
7	5017624	6896282	5446088	1450194	8650055	53
8	5020140	6891269	5439387	1451882	8648595	52
9	5022656	6886259	5432688	1453571	8647134	51
10	5025171	6881253	5425992	1455261	8645673	50
11	5027686	6876250	5419298	1456952	8644211	49
12	5030200	6871250	5412605	1458645	8642748	48
13	5032714	6866254	5405915	1460339	3641284	47
14	5035227	6861261	5399227	1462034	8639820	46
15	5037740	6856271	5392541	1463730	8638355	45
16	5040253	6851285	5385858	1465427	8636889	44
17	5042765	6846302	5379177	1467125	8635423	43
18	5045277	6841323	5372499	1468824	8633956	42
19	5047788	6836347	5365822	1470525	8632488	41
20	5050299	6831374	5359147	1472227	8631019	40
21	5052809	6826405	5352475	1473930	8629549	39
22	5055319	6821439	5345805	1475634	8628079	38
23	5057829	6816476	5339137	1477339	8626608	37
24	5060338	6811516	5332471	1479045	8625137	36
25	5062847	6806560	5325808	1480752	8623665	35
26	5065355	6801607	5319147	1482460	8622192	34
27	5067863	6796657	5312488	1484169	8620718	33
28	5070370	6791710	5305831	1485879	8619243	32
29	5072877	6786767	5299177	1487590	8617768	31
30	5075384	6781827	5292525	1489302	8616292	30

59

Page from a book of logarithmic tables by John Napier, 1614
© *Science Museum Library*

Using a Slide Rule

INVENTION

A slide rule, so called because it resembles a ruler with a central sliding part, is a calculating device. Before the era of cheap electronic calculators, it was in common use in schools and by mathematicians, scientists and engineers. Soon after John Napier published his description of logarithms (see the section on using logarithm tables, p.60), the mathematician Edmund Gunter (1581–1626) developed a primitive device based on the logarithmic scale. Most slide rules since work on the same principle but a few have used linear scales instead. Various improvements were made culminating in a version created in 1859 by the French artillery officer Amédée Mannheim (1831–1906). The standard slide rule is no longer made, but a circular version which originated in the 1630s is still available.

PARTS OF THE SLIDE RULE

There are three basic parts to a slide rule. The main part is known as the 'stock' or 'stator' or, simply, 'body', while the movable part, in the middle, is known as the 'slide'. Answers are read off along a hairline in the third basic part known as the 'cursor' or 'indicator' which is also movable.

Along the stock and slide various scales are marked. On a simple slide rule there might be just two of each, while on a more complicated version there might be over 20. If scales are printed on just one face the slide rule is known as a 'simplex' and if there are scales on both sides it's a 'duplex'.

By aligning the scales on the stock and the slide various calculations can be made.

LINEAR VERSUS LOGARITHMIC SLIDE RULES

An ordinary ruler uses a linear scale. That's to say, the distance between the 1cm mark and the 2cm mark is exactly the same as between, say, the 21cm mark and the 22cm mark. This design was also used for some simple slide rules and made it possible to carry out addition and subtraction, not possible on the logarithmic version.

In contrast to the linear scale, a logarithmic scale is arranged so that a given *ratio* between numbers is always represented by the same distance. In other words, the distance between numbers 1 and 2, and between numbers 2 and 4, and between numbers 4 and 8 will always be exactly the same, because the second of the pair of numbers is double the first – the ratio is 2:1. When you look at a linear scale, then, the numbers are evenly spaced but when you look at a logarithmic scale, the numbers get closer and closer together as they get larger.

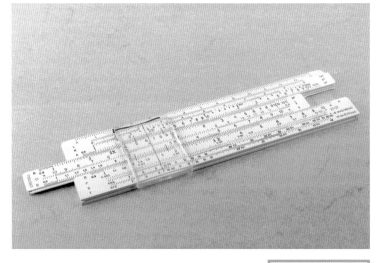

Slide rule
© Friedrich Saurer / Alamy

HOW TO USE A SLIDE RULE

The scales on a slide rule have to be identified in some way, usually with the letters of the alphabet. On most slide rules the C scale, which is on the slide, and the D scale, which is on the stock, are the ones to use for simple multiplication and division.

Let's imagine setting up a slide rule to multiply by 2. The first step is to position the '1' on the C scale of the slide against the '2' on the D scale of the stock. Every number on the D scale will then be twice the number that's opposite to it on the C scale. For example, to work out 2 × 3 you only have to move the cursor to '3' on the C scale to be able to read off the answer '6' on the D scale. Similarly, by moving the cursor to, say, 3.85 on the C scale you will immediately see that 2 × 3.85 is equal to 7.70.

For division, try dividing 9.90 by 3. Position the '3' on the C scale against the '9.90' on the D scale. Move the cursor to '1' on the C scale and read off the answer on the D scale. It should be 3.30.

Slide rules can carry out many more kinds of calculations, and advanced models even had special functions for electrical and hydraulic problems. But one of the drawbacks with slide rules, as even the simple example calculations given above demonstrate, is that accuracy depends on having sufficiently good eyesight to see exactly where the cursor is positioned.

THE DOWNWARD SLIDE

The development of electronic computers was the beginning of the end for slide rules. Nevertheless, they continued in widespread use well into the 1970s because computers were still very expensive then and even the first pocket-sized scientific calculator cost something like 20 times more than a plastic slide rule. By the end of the 1970s, however, scientific calculators were cheaper than slide rules and the market for Edmund Gunter's invention had collapsed.

WHERE SLIDE RULES RULE

Slide rules still have some advantages over electronic calculators. The biggest, perhaps, is that they don't need batteries and can work in harsh environments where electronics might be too delicate. Enthusiasts also claim that, because they require users to think about what they're doing, there's less chance of making careless mistakes. Slide rules also avoid the problem of 'false precision'. That's to say, most physical measurements can't be accurate to more than three decimal places, whereas electronic calculators can give answers to seven or more decimal places, luring users into the false belief that the answer is more precise than the input data.

Imperial Measurements

WEIGHTS AND MEASURES

Imperial measurements have their roots in the less-than-standard forms of measurement that were used throughout Britain, before finally being standardized for consistent application during the heyday of the British Empire. Despite the adoption of the decimal system, imperial measurements are still in common use, especially for the purpose of estimation, and in conversation.

RULE OF THUMB

In the early days of measuring, people formed units out of whatever came to hand – such as a foot or, indeed, a hand. Early length measurements included the Egyptian cubit (the distance from the elbow to the tip of the outstretched middle finger), the digit (roughly a finger width), the span (the distance from thumb-tip to little fingertip on an outstretched hand), and possibly the hypothetical 'megalithic yard' (approximately one pace in length, slightly shorter than the modern yard, and postulated by some modern interpreters of ancient monuments). Such measurements were, by their nature, flexible – although most were standardized at some point in history, albeit often only within an individual country or region. There were similarly vague and open-to-interpretation definitions of measures of weight, area and capacity.

In Britain, various monarchs and governments attempted to standardize certain units of measurement – notably Henry I who standardized the yard as the distance from his nose to the tip of his upwardly-pointed thumb at the end of his outstretched arm, and Edward II who set the inch at the length of three barleycorns placed end to end. However, it was not until the early 19th century that the imperial standard yard, pound and gallon (from which all other measures could be derived) were established by the British government – by which time there had already been rumblings in parliament to the effect that Britain should follow the example of France and adopt the metric system. There have since been further standardizations – the UK and US inch have been the same since 1954, ironically because they are now both standardized at 2.54cm.

Likewise, the standard for all other imperial measurements has been established by reference to exact measurements within the metric SI (Système International) system. So the yard is now exactly 0.9144 metres, the pound is now exactly 0.45359237 kilograms and the gallon (UK) is now exactly 4.54609 litres.

Despite a number of acts of parliament designed to move Britain towards the metric system, imperial measurements remain remarkably tenacious. Road signs still use miles and yards, beer and doorstep-delivered milk are still sold in pints, land is still registered in acres and precious metals are still measured in troy ounces.

Imperial measurement gauge at the Royal Observatory in Greenwich, London
© Alex Segre / Alamy

HOW THE EMPIRE WAS WEIGHED AND MEASURED

Length

Imperial measurements of length contain an obvious reference to body measurements in the word 'foot'. Similarly, a yard was originally based on a stride-length and the word 'mile' is derived from the Latin *mille* – referring to 1,000 Roman double paces. A chain was once the length of an actual surveyor's chain; originally that of Edmund Gunter (1581–1626), the same

Edmund Gunter who was influential in the development of the slide rule (see p.64).

12 inches	=	1 foot
3 feet	=	1 yard
5½ yards	=	1 rod (or 1 pole or 1 perch)
4 rods	=	1 chain (22 yards)
10 chains	=	1 furlong (40 rods)
8 furlongs	=	1 mile (1,760 yards)

Area

Land measurements were derived from the processes of ploughing, farming and living off the land. A 'rod' needed to be long enough to reach from the plough to the front of an ox, and was then used for measuring fields. A furlong was the length of a furrow (varying depending on how hard the soil was to plough and how tired your horse or ox was). A hide was once the area of land that could support a household (again, variable), and an acre was the area that could be ploughed with oxen in a day. The rod (pole or perch) was used as both a linear and a square measurement.

144 square inches	=	1 square foot
9 square feet	=	1 square yard
1 (square) pole	=	30¼ square yards
1 furlong x 1 pole	=	1 rood (40 square poles or 1,210 square yards)
1 furlong x 1 chain	=	1 acre (4,840 square yards, 4 roods, 160 poles)
640 acres	=	1 square mile

Volume

Imperial measurements of volume are often separated into measurements of capacity (for containers and quantities of fluids), and what are often referred to as 'cubic measures' for larger volumes such as quantities of timber or the internal sizes of buildings. Measures of volume in the USA are different because the standard US gallon, from which they are derived, is approximately 0.83 of a UK gallon. In addition, in the USA, slightly different measures are adopted for wet and dry goods.

The basic units of capacity are as follows. The particular units selected usually depended on the nature of the product to be measured, stored or transported.

60 minims	=	1 fluid drachm
8 fluid drachms	=	1 fluid ounce
5 fluid ounces	=	1 gill
2 gills	=	1 cup
4 gills	=	1 pint (20 fluid ounces)
2 pints	=	1 quart
4 quarts	=	1 gallon (8 pints)

For dry goods, these were extended to:

2 gallons	=	1 peck
4 pecks	=	1 bushel (8 gallons)
3 bushels	=	1 sack
8 bushels	=	1 quarter
4$\frac{1}{2}$ quarters	=	1 chaldron (36 bushels, 12 sacks)
5 quarters	=	1 load

For ales and other wet goods:

4$\frac{1}{2}$ gallons	=	1 pin
9 gallons	=	1 firkin (2 pins)
2 firkins	=	1 kilderkin (18 gallons)
2 kilderkins	=	1 barrel (36 gallons)
3 kilderkins	=	1 hogshead (6 firkins, 54 gallons)
2 barrels	=	1 puncheon
2 hogsheads	=	1 butt
2 butts	=	1 tun (4 hogsheads, 3 puncheons)

When dealing with wines, the number of gallons in a hogshead was somewhat more variable.

Cubic measures:

1,728 cubic inches	=	1 cubic foot
27 cubic feet	=	1 cubic yard

Weight

There are two systems of imperial weights – 'avoirdupois' (from the French 'to have weight') for everyday use, and 'troy' (after the French town Troyes) for precious metals. Avoirdupois weights are as follows:

16 drams (dr)	=	1 ounce
4 ounces (oz)	=	1 quarter
4 quarters (qtr)	=	1 pound (16oz)
14 pounds (lb)	=	1 stone
2 stone (st)	=	1 quarter (28 lb)
4 quarters (qtr)	=	1 hundredweight (112 lb)
20 hundredweight (cwt)	=	1 ton (2240 lb)

The troy pound is equal to 5,760 grains, as distinct from the avoirdupois pound, which is 7,000 grains. Although the system is now rarely used, gold is still sold in troy ounces.

4 grains	=	1 carat
6 carats	=	1 pennyweight (24 grains)
20 pennyweights	=	1 ounce
12 ounces	=	1 pound
25 pounds	=	1 quarter
4 quarters	=	1 hundredweight (100 pounds)

Apothecaries once used the following variations on troy weights for weighing medicines. Under their system 20 grains made one scruple, three scruples made a drachm and eight drachms made an ounce.

Converting Decimal to Pounds, Shillings and Pence

POUNDS, SHILLINGS AND PENCE

Britain finally adopted a decimal system of currency on 15 February 1971 (a date often referred to as D-day, short for 'decimal day'). The familiar lsd (pounds, shillings and pence, from the Latin *librae*, *solidi* and *denarii*), a system that had been in existence since Anglo-Saxon times, were gone, and the pound became decimal (now divided into 100 pennies, rather than the 240 of pre-decimal sterling).

THE SLOW DAWN OF DECIMALIZATION

In 1608, the English writer and army officer Robert Norton (d.1635) published *Disme, the Art of Tenths, or, Decimal Arithmetike*, a translation of a Dutch work by Simon Stevin, which promoted decimal arithmetic. At the end of the 17th century, the English natural philosopher Sir William Petty (1623–87) suggested that there should be five farthings to the penny, instead of four:

Let me add that if your old defective farthings were cryed down to five a penny you might keep all accompts in a way of decimal arithmetic which hath long been desired for the ease and certainty of accompts.

Sir William Petty, *Quantulumcunque* (1682)

In 1824, Sir John Wrottesley (1771–1841) introduced a motion in the House of Commons to 'inquire how far the coin of the realm could be adapted to a decimal scale'. He was not the first MP to propose decimalization, but his system (that '100 farthings would make a double shilling, and ten double shillings, or 1,000 farthings, would amount to a pound') was not adopted. But while full decimalization would have to wait until the 20th century, sterling had its first 'decimal' coin in 1849, when the florin (equalling one-tenth of a pound) was first minted (followed, in 1887, by the double florin). Even the final changeover was gradual – between 1967 and 1971 Britain lost the half-crown, but had already gained the new 5p (replacing the shilling) and 10p (replacing the florin) coins, as well as the 50p, claimed to be the world's first seven-sided coin.

PRE-DECIMAL COINS AND NOTES

Coins	Nickname	Value
Farthing	Jenny	$1/4$ penny
Halfpenny	Ha'penny	$1/2$ penny
Penny	Copper	$1/240$ pound, $1/12$ shilling
Threepence	Thruppence, Joey	3 pence, $1/4$ shilling, $1/80$ pound
Sixpence	Tanner, Half a bob	6 pence, $1/2$ shilling, $1/40$ pound
Shilling	Bob	12 pence, $1/20$ pound
Florin	Two bob	24 pence, 2 shillings, $1/10$ pound
Half-crown	Two and six	30 pence, 2 shillings and 6 pence, $1/2$ pound
Crown	Five bob	60 pence, 5 shillings, $1/4$ pound

Note	Nickname	Value
Ten shilling	Half a quid	120 pence, 10 shillings, $1/2$ pound
Pound	Quid	240 pence, 20 shillings

When working with pre-decimal currency, some of the key numbers to remember are that there were 20 shillings in a pound; twelve pennies (12d) in a shilling; and that the penny consisted of two halfpennies or four farthings. When converting old money to new money, sixpence equals $2^1/_2$p ('p' referring to decimal pennies, or 'new pence', rather than 'd' referring to 'old pence'), a shilling equals 5p, and half a crown equals $12^1/_2$p.

The guinea is an obvious omission from this list of pre-decimal notes and coins, but while the notion of guineas was still used until decimalization (for example, when quoting the price of a racehorse, or when discussing professional fees) the gold coin known as the guinea was only current in England from 1663 to 1817, its value being fixed in 1717 at 21 shillings (which is one pound and one shilling).

SING A SONG OF SIXPENCE

The sixpence was first minted in 1551. Later known as a 'tanner', its nickname is said to have come from the surname of an 18th-century engraver at the Mint, John Sigismund Tanner. For a time it survived decimalization, remaining in circulation with a value of $2^1/_2$p until it was officially withdrawn from use on 30 June 1980. A very popular coin, the sixpence has had numerous mentions in songs and rhymes (the crooked man who walked a crooked mile found a crooked sixpence upon a crooked stile; we 'sing a song of sixpence, a pocketful of rye'; while in another song we find 'I've got sixpence, jolly jolly sixpence'). It has also made regular appearances on the Christmas dining table, traditionally added to the plum pudding when it is made on stir-up Sunday (the Sunday before Advent). To find the sixpence in your portion of pudding was said to ensure your future wealth. Perhaps it was for all these reasons that a 'Save Our Sixpence' campaign was launched, and that the sixpence survived for so long after decimalization.

Using Mnemonics

MNEMONICS

Mnemonics are mental techniques designed to help us learn and remember specific facts and items of information. Their use can be traced back to ancient Greece where, in around 500 BC, the poet Simonides of Ceos invented the 'method of loci', in which a list of items was memorized by visualizing each item in a specific part of a familiar house or building, the list being reassembled in the mind when needed by imagining a systematic tour of the house. In the Middle Ages a method was devised of using the human hand to help with memorizing the names of musical notes. This was known as the 'Guidonian Hand' after Italian music teacher Guido d'Arezzo. Today, mnemonics often take the form of a verse or phrase, tailored as an aide-mémoire to help us recall something that might otherwise be tricky to remember.

THIRTY DAYS HATH SEPTEMBER

Thirty days hath September,
April, June and November;
All the rest have thirty-one,
Excepting February alone,
Which has twenty-eight days clear
And twenty-nine in each leap year.

This poem, of obscure origin but thought to be of considerable age, is a famous mnemonic for remembering the number of days in each month of the year. Such rhymes are often employed to aid the memory, as many people find them far easier to remember than the bald facts they allude to. Another classic example is the schoolchildren's rhyme for remembering the fate of each of Henry VIII's six wives: *Divorced, beheaded, died, divorced, beheaded, survived* – Henry divorced Catherine of Aragon; had Anne Boleyn beheaded; Jane Seymour died; he divorced Anne of Cleves; had Catherine Howard beheaded; while Catherine Parr survived, dying one year after the death of the King.

GIVING BATTLE IN VAIN

One of the traditional methods for remembering the colours of the rainbow is in the mnemonic *Richard of York gave battle in vain*. This is also a classic example of a mnemonic where the initial letters of each word in the phrase give you the key to remembering your facts – the 'r' of 'Richard' is for red, the 'o' of 'of' is for orange, the 'y' of 'York' is for yellow, and so on, until you can recall all seven hues (red, orange, yellow, green, blue, indigo and violet). This style of mnemonic has also been used to help students of music to remember the notes on the lines of the treble clef (E, G, B, D, F remembered with the saying *Every good boy deserves favour*) and to overcome tricky spellings ('because' is phonetically difficult, but becomes easier to spell when you remember that *Big elephants can always understand small elephants* – or, alternatively, *Big elephants can't always use small exits*).

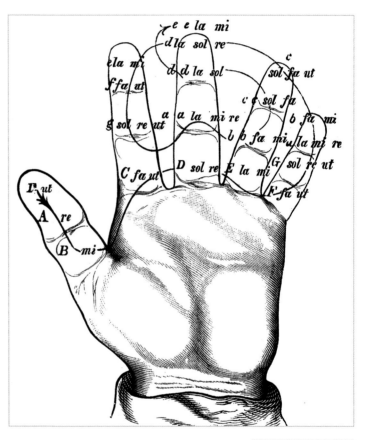

A 'Guidonian Hand'
© INTERFOTO
Pressebildagentur / Alamy

HOW I WANT A DRINK ...

The British mathematician and astronomer Sir James Hopwood Jeans (1877–1946) helped his students to remember the value of pi with the following mnemonic: *How I want a drink, alcoholic of course, after the heavy chapters involving quantum mechanics.* The number of letters in each word represents one digit of pi, hence pi equals 3.14159265358979. If pi to fourteen decimal places seems a little too much for your needs, a popular way to remember it to six places is in the phrase *How I wish I could calculate pi* (3.141592). As long as the phrase you create is memorable for you, this technique can be adopted to help to memorize any number.

FURTHER OLD CHESTNUTS

Many mnemonics have been created to help the school child recall facts of a historical or geographical nature. These are just a few of them.

Lord Nelson (1758–1805), the famous English admiral, sustained several injuries in the course of his duties – in 1794, he lost the sight in his right eye while commanding the naval brigade at the reduction of Bastia and Calvi, and following an action at Santa Cruz in 1797 he had his right arm amputated. The mnemonic for remembering the afflicted parts of Nelson's anatomy is *EARs*, standing for Eye, Arm and Right (×2).

The major royal houses of England (and later Britain) since 1066 are Norman (1066–1135); Plantagenet (1154–1399); Lancaster (1399–1461; 1470–71); York (1471–85); Tudor (1485–1603); Stuart (1603–49; 1660–1714); Hanover (1714–1901); and Windsor (1901/1917–   ). The initial letters of these (NPLYTSHW) have been learnt with the aid of a number of phrases, including *No plan like yours to study history wisely.*

The phrase *Can Queen Victoria eat cold apple pie?* has been used as an aide-mémoire for the seven hills of Rome (Capitoline; Quirinal; Viminal; Esquiline; Caelian; Aventine; and Palatine).

The five Great Lakes of North America can be remembered with the mnemonic acronym *HOMES*, for Huron, Ontario, Michigan, Erie and Superior, or, if you prefer to know them in geographical order (in this case from west to east) you can learn the phrase *Sally Mitchell hates eating oranges* (Superior is furthest west and Ontario furthest east) . If you want to recall them by size (by surface area, with the largest of the Great Lakes first), you can use the saying *Sam's horse must eat oats.*

DEVELOPING YOUR OWN MNEMONICS

Generally speaking, mnemonics ought to be individual; each individual ought to find out that method of assisting his memory which is most convenient to himself; and this will vary, of course, with his habitual associations.

Encylopædia Americana (1835)

Many of us still use a few favourite mnemonics learnt in childhood, but it is possible to develop your own – although not everyone thinks they are a good idea:

I have been troubled from childhood with a short memory, which is the more unfortunate, as I am blessed with a long name—George Alexander Edward Ezekiel Benyowski. I was yesterday lamenting to a friend, who has made great improvements in the fashionable art of Mnemonics ... that I could not always recollect the precise order in which my baptismal names were arranged. Courage! says he, nothing is easier than to fix it forever. Come with me into the yard. I accordingly attended him, with eager impatience, to learn the art of remembering my name. You see this pump, continued he ... the first thing that strikes your eye, is the shaft; I name that George; you next perceive the handle; I call that Alexander; the spear I connect with Edward; when you look at the nose you will think of Ezekiel; and the water will remind you of Benyowski. Think of them always in this order—the shaft, handle, spear, nose and water, and you will never forget your name ... This far, all went well, but this morning came my troubles. I rose at early dawn, and hastened down stairs ... opening the back-door, the first thing I saw was the handle of the pump! ALEXANDER! *said I, and began pumping with all my might. Presently the spear shewed itself at the top of the pump—Huzza! for* EDWARD! *... The servant had wrapped a piece of old carpet round the pump, last evening, to prevent the water from freezing; and I did not perceive that the nose was stopped up, until the water came over the top of the pump and drenched me sadly. I consoled myself with remembering that water meant* BENYOWSKI; *and proceeded to uncover the shaft that reminded me of my first name,* GEORGE. *I then stepped round and unstopped the nose, exclaiming, in a melancholy tone,* EZEKIEL! *The association is fixed forever! and I must subscribe myself, in all tribulation,*

Alexander Edward Benyowski George Ezekiel!
Miscellanies selected from the Public Journals (Volume II, 1824)

APRIL.

Day of Yr.	Day of Mo.	Day of Week.	Latitude of Boston. Rises.	Sets.	Latitude of New York. Rises.	Sets.	Latitude of Washington. Rises.	Sets.	East of Rocky Mts. Souths.	Boston. Sets.	New York. Sets.	Washington. Sets.	San Fran. Sets.	PHENOMENA, &c. Washington.	Tides. High Water, 1st and 15th, morn.
			h. m.	h. m.	h. m.	h. m.	h. m.	h. m.	h. m.	h. m.	h. m.	h. m.	h. m.		
92	1	Wd.	5 42	6 26	5 43	6 26	5 45	6 24	7 34	1 46	1 43	1 38	1 57	Venus sets, 10 : 2 P.M.	
93	2	Th.	40	27	40	27	42	25	8 31	2 52	2 50	2 46	2 48		
94	3	Fri.	39	28	39	27	40	26	9 26	3 35	3 34	3 30	3 34	Jupiter rises, 5 : 1 A.M.	**1st.**
95	4	Sat.	37	29	38	28	39	27	10 20	4 16	4 14	4 12	4 36	Saturn rises, 10 : 19 P.M.	Portland, 5 : 50.
96	5	S.	35	30	36	29	37	28	11 12	4 50	4 51	4 51	5 41	*Sixth Sunday in Lent.*	Boston, 5 : 37.
97	6	Mo.	34	31	34	31	36	29	morn.	rises	rises	rises	rises	Mercury rises, 4 : 40 A.M.	New York, 2 : 32.
98	7	Tu.	32	32	32	32	34	30	12 3	7 7	7 6	7 4	7 11	○ FULL MOON, 2 : 9 A.M.	Old Pt. Com. 3 : 17.
99	8	Wd.	30	34	31	33	33	31	12 54	8 13	8 11	8 9	8 15	☌♂♃	San Francis. 5 : 47.
100	9	Th.	28	35	29	34	31	32	1 44	9 16	9 15	9 11	9 17		
101	10	Fri.	27	36	28	34	30	32	2 34	10 17	10 15	10 11	10 15	☌♄☾	
102	11	Sat.	25	37	27	36	28	34	3 24	11 14	11 11	11 6	11 11		
103	12	S.	23	38	24	37	27	34	4 14	morn.	morn.	morn.	morn.	*EASTER.*	
104	13	Mo.	22	39	23	38	25	36	5 3	12 7	12 3	11 57	2		
105	14	Tu.	20	40	21	39	24	36	5 51	12 52	59	12 54	49	☾ LAST QUARTER, 5 : 26 P.M.	
106	15	Wd.	18	41	20	40	22	38	6 38	1 34	1 32	1 27	1 24		
107	16	Th.	17	42	18	41	21	38	7 24	2 13	2 10	2 6	2 9		**15th.**
108	17	Fri.	15	44	17	43	20	39	8 9	2 46	2 45	2 42	2 46		Portland, 5 : 23.
109	18	Sat.	13	45	15	43	18	40	8 54	3 19	3 23	3 15	3 16		Boston, 5 : 33.
110	19	S.	12	46	14	44	17	41	9 38	3 50	3 49	3 47	3 50	*First Sunday after Easter.*	New York, 2 : 7.
111	20	Mo.	11	47	13	45	16	42	10 24	4 19	4 19	4 29	4 22	☌♃☾ ☌♂☾	Old Pt. Com. 2 : 48.
112	21	Tu.	9	47	11	46	14	43	11 10	4 48	4 49	4 50	4 54	Venus sets, 10 : 37 P.M.	San Francis. 0 : 48.
113	22	Wd.	7	48	9	47	13	44	11 58	sets	sets	sets	sets	● NEW MOON, 3 : 12 P.M.	
114	23	Th.	6	49	8	48	11	45	ev. 48	7 49	7 47	7 44	7 53	25th, Occult. α Tauri, 4 : 26 A.M.	
115	24	Fri.	4	51	6	50	10	46	1 41	8 57	8 55	8 51	8 57	Mars rises, 4 : 12 A.M.	
116	25	Sat.	3	52	5	50	9	47	2 35	10 2	9 59	9 54	10 1	*St. Mark.* ☌♀☾	
117	26	S.	1	53	4	51	7	47	3 34	11 4	10 61	10 56	11 1	*Second Sunday after Easter.*	
118	27	Mo.	0	54	2	53	6	49	4 32	12 0	11 57	11 52	12 0		
119	28	Tu.	4 59	55	1	54	5	50	5 30	morn.	morn.	morn.	morn.	Jupiter rises, 3 : 42 A.M.	
120	29	Wd.	57	56	4 59	55	3	51	6 26	52	50	45	47	☽ FIRST QUARTER, 1 : 10 P.M.	
121	30	Th.	4 56	6 57	4 58	6 56	5 2	6 52	7 21	1 36	1 31	1 31	1 34		

Using an Almanac

ALMANAC

An almanac (or almanack) is an annual publication giving statistical information about events and phenomena, such as the phases of the moon, the times of sunrise and sunset, tides, weather and anniversaries. The word may come from the Arabic 'al-manakh'.

EARLIEST VERSIONS

It was probably the ancient Babylonians who first realized that astronomical phenomena, such as the movements of the stars, happened in a regular and therefore predictable way. As a result, they made the earliest-known almanacs around the 6th century BC, cutting their wedge-shaped 'cuneiform' letters into stone tablets. These tablets are known as the *Enûma Anu Enlil* after the first three words on the first tablet:

If on the first day of Nisannu [March/April] the sunrise looks sprinkled with blood: grain will vanish in the country, there will be hardship and human flesh will be eaten.
Anonymous scribes, *Enûma Anu Enlil* (c.6th century BC)

The predictions, however, were more concerned with the fortunes of the rulers than with the climate, making them more akin to astrology than science:

If a normal disc [of Venus] is present and one disc stands to the right: one from among the king's relief troops will take the throne.
Anonymous scribes, *Enûma Anu Enlil* (c.6th century BC)

The ancient Greeks went on to develop more sophisticated versions known as *parapegma*. Originally these were also stone tablets but with the innovation of a hole for every day. The *parapegma* were annotated with notes about the movements of the heavens and the corresponding weather forecasts. Pegs would then be inserted into the holes, to represent actual days, and in this way the almanac could be synchronized.

In the 2nd century AD, the Alexandrian astronomer Ptolemy took the idea to an even higher level with a far more comprehensive almanac that he called the *Phaseis*. His first recorded observation was in March of AD 127 and his last in February of AD 141. It was Ptolemy who put the earth at the centre of the universe with the sun, moon and stars revolving around it, a view that prevailed until Copernicus, more than a millennium later.

MEDIEVAL ALMANACS

The concept of the *parapegma* continued in use for centuries and, indeed, a version was discovered in the north of England that was known as the 'clog almanac':

It is a square stick of box, or any other hard wood, about eight inches long, fitted to be hung up in the family parlor for common reference, but sometimes carried as part of a walking-cane. Properly it was a perpetual almanac, designed mainly to shew the Sundays and other fixed holidays.

Dr Robert Plot, *Natural History of Staffordshire* (1686)

Meanwhile, the first almanac known to have been printed in England had this to say:

Saturne is hyest and coldest, being full old,
And Mars with his Muddy swerde ever ready to kyll,
Sol and Luna is half good and half ill.

Richard Pynson, *Sheapeards Kalendar* (1497)

POOR RICHARD'S ALMANACK

No less a person than Benjamin Franklin (1706–90), scientist, statesman and one of America's 'Founding Fathers', was the author and publisher of a popular annual known as *Poor Richard's Almanack*. Between 1732 and 1758 he sold tens of thousands of copies in what were then Britain's American colonies, writing under the pseudonym of Richard Saunders.

Astrology was still considered as important as astronomy, and various editions included 'The Anatomy of Man's Body as govern'd by the Twelve Constellations'. Franklin had a great sense of humour and explained his motive for publishing the almanac as having to do with far more than providing useful information:

The plain Truth of the Matter is, I am excessive poor, and my Wife, good Woman is, I tell her, excessive proud; she cannot bear, she says, to sit spinning in her Shift of Tow, while I do nothing but gaze at the stars.

Benjamin Franklin, *Poor Richard's Almanack* (1733)

Franklin was also very fond of writing proverbs and aphorisms, some original, some adapted from earlier writers, which proved a highly popular feature of his almanacs over the years:

With the old Almanack and the old Year, Leave thy old Vices, tho' ever so dear.
Who has deceiv'd thee so oft as thyself?
He that can compose himself, is wiser than he that composes books.

Benjamin Franklin, *Poor Richard's Almanack* (various editions 1732–58)

THE OLD FARMER'S ALMANAC

The Old Farmer's Almanac is the oldest continuously published periodical in North America, having first appeared in 1792 during George Washington's first term as president. Much of its early success was due to the long-term weather forecasts made by Robert B Thomas, the first editor, who used a still-secret formula involving various natural cycles. It's said his predictions were 80 per cent accurate. Apparently his formula is still in use and kept safely tucked away in a black tin box at the *Almanac* offices in Dublin, New Hampshire.

It's believed that in 1858, Abraham Lincoln, later to become president of the USA, used *The Old Farmer's Almanac* in a trial to discredit the testimony of an eyewitness by arguing the night was too dark for an accurate identification to have been made.

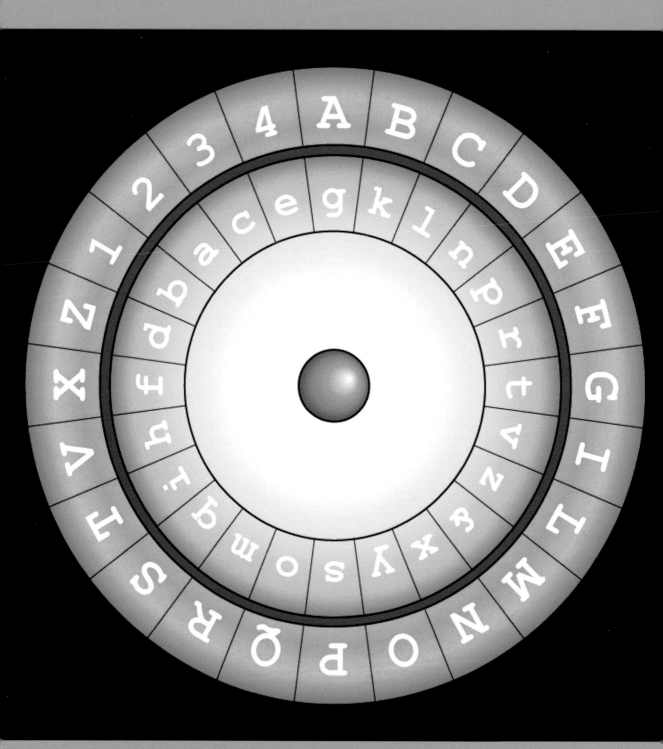

Using Codes and Ciphers

THE DIFFERENCE BETWEEN CODES AND CIPHERS

In everyday language the words 'cipher' and 'code' mean the same thing. But in technical usage they are different. Ciphers alter individual letters or, in the world of computers, individual bits. For example, changing 'cat' to 'dbu' is a cipher, achieved by substituting the next letter of the alphabet. Codes, on the other hand, use symbols or groups of letters to represent words or phrases. So semaphore signals, which use flags, are a code.

CAESAR SUBSTITUTION

Ciphers have almost certainly been in use just about as long as writing itself. One of the earliest known is Caesar Substitution which was developed by the Roman statesman and general Julius Caesar (100–44 BC). He simply replaced every letter of the alphabet with the one three places along. Using this code today, therefore, 'Julius' would become 'Mxolxv'.

Cryptologists call this 'monoalphabetic substitution' because each character is always replaced by the same cipher character. These codes are easy to crack.

Cracking monoalphabetic ciphers

In the English language the most frequently occurring letter is 'e'. Counting all the different letters in a message will therefore reveal which are the most likely candidates to represent it. One-letter words must be either an 'a' or an 'i'. And since every word must contain a vowel, concentrating on two- and three-letter words will quickly reveal which they are. Then there will be the groups of letters that appear again and again, representing 'the' 'ing' 'ly' and so on. Here's a simple example of a monoalphabetic cipher. See if you can work out what it means (solution to be found at the end of the chapter):

J cfu ju eje opu ublf zpv mpoh up efdjqifs uijt

POLYALPHABETIC SUBSTITUTION

In the 15th century, an Italian, Leon Battista Alberti, had an idea for speeding up monoalphabetic ciphers. He invented the cipher disc which consisted of two circles inscribed with the alphabet, one inside the other. One of the circles was fixed and the other, known as the 'rotor', could be moved. By moving the rotor a certain number of places a cipher could be created. For example, displacing the rotor three places would result in Caesar Substitution.

From there it was a simple step for the sender and receiver to agree that, every few letters, the rotor would be moved to a new position. For example, it might be agreed that after every six letters the rotor would be advanced two places. This made it much more difficult to decode or 'cryptanalyse' a secret message, since statistics would be of no use in searching for common letters. This 'polyalphabetic substitution' remains the basis of many ciphers today.

From then on it was simply a case of creating more and more complicated versions of Alberti's invention. In 1867, for example, Sir Charles Wheatstone (1802–75) unveiled his 'Cryptograph' which used two clock-like hands, connected by gears. The large hand was pointed to the original letter and the small hand then automatically pointed to the cipher which, because of the arrangement of gears, was different each time. He also invented the Playfair Cipher which, instead of encrypting individual letters, encrypted pairs of letters, known as digraphs. Because there are hundreds of possible digraphs compared with 26 letters in the alphabet, the Playfair Cipher is much harder to break and was still in use during World War II.

THE ZIMMERMANN INCIDENT

By the end of 1916, World War I had been raging for two and a half years, but the USA remained neutral. In January 1917, British cryptographers deciphered a telegram that was to change that. The telegram was from the German Foreign Minister Arthur Zimmermann to the German Ambassador to Mexico and began like this:

130 13042 13401 8501 115 3528 416 17214 6491 11310

When decoded the message was politically explosive and ran as follows:

We intend to begin on the first of February unrestricted submarine warfare. We shall endeavor in spite of this to keep the United States of America neutral. In the event of this not succeeding, we make Mexico a proposal of alliance on the following basis: make war together, make peace together, generous financial support and an understanding on our part that Mexico is to reconquer the lost territory in Texas, New Mexico and Arizona ...

Arthur Zimmermann, *The Zimmerman Telegram* (19 January 1917)

Once the Zimmerman telegram had been shown to the US President Woodrow Wilson and made public, the stage was set for the USA to enter the war.

ENIGMA

Breaking German ciphers also had a significant impact on the course of World War II. The German military used an updated version of a cipher machine that had been commercially available in the 1920s. Known as Enigma, it was an electro-mechanical device equipped with so many rotors that billions of combinations were possible. The German authorities were convinced that Enigma was impregnable but, with the help of Polish mathematicians who had managed to acquire a machine prior to the outbreak of war, British experts stationed at Bletchley Park cracked the Enigma, an event believed to have shortened the war by up to two years.

An even more complex German cipher machine known as Lorenz was broken by the construction of 'Colossus'. Installed at Bletchley in December 1943, Colossus had 1,500 thermionic valves and was the world's first practical electronic digital processing machine – in effect, a computer.

CODES

Codes, in the technical sense, are not necessarily designed to keep information secret so much as to improve transmission. When telegrams were in common use and the telegraph companies charged by the word, codes were used to keep the cost down. For example, using Bentley's Complete Phrase Code DIZUHRUGUB CUGYAOKGAP meant 'Contracts have been signed; commence production'. Thus, six words were reduced to two, cutting costs by two-thirds.

CREATING YOUR OWN CIPHERS

There are all kinds of ways of producing your own ciphers. You could, for example, agree to base your encryption on a favourite book. Your message would then commence with a page and a paragraph number. So 134 3 would mean 'turn to page 134 and write out the alphabet alongside the first 26 letters of paragraph 3'. The body of the message could then be deciphered but would remain secure as long as no one else knew which book was being used.

You might also like to make your own cipher disc. You only need to cut two circles of cardboard, one a little larger than the other, and fasten them together through their exact centres so they can rotate (a drawing pin pushed through them into a piece of cork will do). Next draw straight lines radiating out from the centre dividing the circles into 26 compartments. On the outer circle, fill in the letters of the alphabet. In the compartments of the inner circle you

Enigma machine
© *Ian Miles-Flashpoint Pictures / Alamy*

can also write the alphabet, or a mixture of letters and numbers, or even symbols. As long as your correspondent has an identical cipher disc you can correspond in secret.

THE FUTURE OF CIPHERS

In the age of the computer, algorithms (sets of instructions) provide the guides to encryption, whether for sending secret messages or for keeping credit card details secure. To read an encrypted message the receiving computer needs a 'key'. In the 1970s, computers used a 56-bit key known as Data Encryption Standard (DES) which provided 70 quadrillion combinations (70 followed by 15 noughts). But that is no longer considered enough, and today 128-bit keys are used, giving 300,000,000,000,000,000, 000,000,000,000,000,000 combinations.

(The coded message says: 'I bet it did not take you long to decipher this.')

Using a Camera Obscura

THE DARK CHAMBER

The camera obscura is an optical device, dating back at least 2,000 years, which is the precursor to the modern camera. The name is Latin for 'dark chamber' and that, indeed, is what the earliest examples were. A room in a building would be blacked out to allow light to enter from just one tiny hole. As a result, the image of whatever was outside would be projected onto the opposite wall inside the room.

THE INVENTION OF THE CAMERA OBSCURA

The principle was noted by ancient Chinese and Greek philosophers, but the first camera obscura known to have been built is attributed to the Arab scientist Abu Ali Al-Hasan Ibn al-Haitham (965–1039), who described it in his seven-volume *Book of Optics*, a key work in the history of physics. Using a camera obscura, he established that light moves in straight lines and that different colours and images don't blend together, like water, on passing through a small opening:

Let several lamps be positioned at various points in the same area, all being opposite a single aperture leading to a dark place; opposite the aperture let there be a wall in that dark place or let an opaque body be held facing the aperture: the lights of those lamps will appear separately on that wall or body and in the same number as the lamps, each light being opposite one of the lamps on the straight line passing through the aperture.

Abu Ali Al-Hasan Ibn al-Haitham, *Book of Optics* (1011–21)

Not long afterwards, the Chinese scientist Shen Kuo (1031–95) also experimented with the camera obscura, and in his book *Mengxi Bitan* ('Dream Pool Essays') noted that 'the image is inverted after passing through the small hole.'

USES OF THE CAMERA OBSCURA

One of the great problems facing the early astronomers was how to study solar eclipses without damaging their eyes, and the camera obscura solved it. By projecting an image of the sun, the camera obscura reduced the intensity to a safe level. Among the pioneers who used it in this way was the English Franciscan monk and scientist Roger Bacon (c. 1214–94), who described his methods in 1267.

It's not certain who was the first to attach a lens to the camera obscura but Daniello Barbaro (1513–70), a Venetian nobleman, is a strong contender. He described using not only a convex lens but also a diaphragm, and explained how to bring the image into focus:

Camera obscura, 1860s
© Mary Evans Picture Library / Alamy

Close all shutters and doors until no light enters the camera except through the lens, and opposite hold a piece of paper, which you move forward and backward until the scene appears in the sharpest detail.

Daniello Barbaro, *La Practica della Perspettiva* (1568)

Nor is it known for sure who first used the term 'camera obscura', but many scholars attribute that to Johannes Kepler (1571–1630), the German mathematician and scientist who was the first to explain planetary motion. He realized that the human eye worked on the same principle, the image being projected inverted onto the retina. As a further insight, he correctly suggested that the image was turned right way up 'in the hollows of the brain.'

The camera obscura also neatly solved the problem of true perspective, which had been missing from paintings until the Renaissance. Any artist looking at the projected image, or tracing it, would have been able to paint with far greater accuracy and realism than ever before. According to the artist David Hockney (born 1937) and the physicist Charles M Falco (born 1948) that's exactly what some Old Masters did. Their thesis is controversial only in that many critics do not believe the practice could have begun as early as Jan Van Eyck, who died in 1441.

However, only a few decades later, the great Renaissance painter and scientist Leonardo da Vinci (1452–1519) was certainly aware of the camera obscura:

When images of illuminated objects ... penetrate through a small hole into a very dark room ... you will see [on the opposite wall] these objects in their proper form and colour, reduced in size ... in a reversed position, owing to the intersection of the rays.
Leonardo da Vinci, *Codex Atlanticus* (1519)

And by the 18th century, it was common practice, as one Italian art critic made clear:

Painters should make the same use of the Camera Obscura, which Naturalists and Astronomers make of the microscope and telescope; for all these instruments equally contribute to make known and represent Nature ... the best modern painters among the Italians have availed themselves of this contrivance; nor is it possible that they should have otherwise represented things so much to the life ...
Francesco Algarotti, *Essays On Painting* (1764)

By this time, portable versions of the camera obscura were for sale all over the Western world, and by incorporating a mirror could show the image the right way up. In London they were known for a time as 'Scioptricks.' One artist who definitely experimented with the technology was Sir Joshua Reynolds (1723–92), although he warned against putting too much reliance on it. His own camera obscura is in the Science Museum in London.

The first person to put a film inside a camera obscura was the Scottish scientist Sir David Brewster (1781–1868), more famous as the man behind the kaleidoscope. By doing so he invented what we now call the pinhole camera, still occasionally used today for special effects. Extremely large-scale photographs are possible from a pinhole camera, and in 2007 the product of the world's largest pinhole camera, created from an aircraft hangar, was put on display. The photograph, printed on muslin, showed a US airbase in California and measured some 33 metres wide by 26 metres high.

In the 19th century, the camera obscura became an early form of 'cinema' with the audience grouped around a viewing table onto which the view from outside was projected. A number still survive as tourist attractions, including, in the UK, a three-lens version next to Edinburgh Castle, one overlooking the Clifton Suspension Bridge in Bristol, and one with a huge 14-inch lens that sits atop Constitution Hill in Aberystwyth.

THE CAMERA LUCIDA

In 1807, William Hyde Wollaston invented a rather different optical device to help artists. He called it the camera lucida (Latin for 'light chamber') to emphasize that it needed no closed dark box. Instead of a pinhole or lens, the artist looks through either a half-silvered mirror tilted at 45 degrees or a prism, thus seeing both the subject and the paper simultaneously. The effect is that the mind perceives the subject faintly superimposed on the paper so it can be traced.

If you'd like to draw but don't feel you have the aptitude you can still buy a camera lucida from art suppliers today.

MAKING YOUR OWN CAMERA OBSCURA

Rather than make a light-tight box, it's far easier to adapt something already in existence. A cardboard shoe box is easy to work with or, for more durability, the sort of tin that gifts of biscuits arrive in at Christmas time is ideal. But with a little ingenuity all kinds of containers can be pressed into service. The first step is to create the pinhole. Rather than make it in the box itself, a better idea is to make a larger hole in the box and then tape a piece of aluminium foil over it, in which you can make your pinhole using a sewing needle. One reason is that the thinner the material in which you make your pinhole the sharper your image will be. Another reason is that this method makes it easier to experiment with different sizes of pinholes.

The next step is to install the viewing screen. If you're using a cardboard shoe box you can simply use a craft knife to cut out a square in the end opposite the pinhole and then tape some greaseproof paper or tracing paper over it. Finish by sheathing the box, other than the pinhole and the screen, with some black plastic to make sure no extraneous light enters. Wherever you point the pinhole the image will now be thrown onto the screen although you may need to put a cover, such as a towel, over both the screen and your head in order to be able to see the image clearly.

Converting a camera obscura into a pinhole camera

In order to record an image, you'll have to devise a way of securing a sheet of film instead of the viewing screen. The most basic way is to open the box in a darkroom, tape the film into position, and close the box again. You'll also need to create a simple shutter so no light enters until you're ready – some black sticky tape will do the trick. Note that the closer the film is to the pinhole the wider the angle of view and the shorter the exposure. For a telephoto effect, on the other hand, the film needs to be further away from the pinhole, in which case the exposure will be longer.

As an alternative to making a pinhole camera from scratch, you can create one from an existing camera by replacing the lens with a pinhole – a fun idea if you happen to have an old camera with a broken lens.

Socializing and Celebration

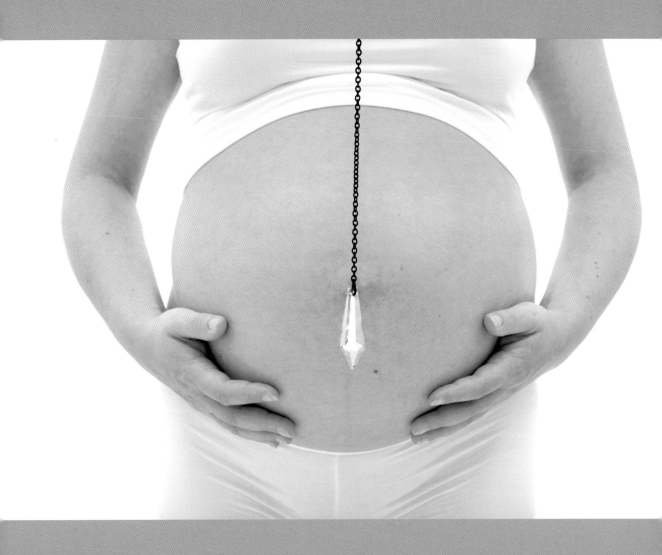

Predicting the Sex of a Baby

IT'S A BABY

Women have long sought to discover the gender of their baby before it is born, and before the advent of ultrasound scans (which themselves don't offer any guarantees), a wide variety of signs were looked for, and rituals performed, which could allegedly predict the sex of your unborn child. Today, many pregnant women follow their foremothers in these practices, but for fun, rather than in the belief that such divinatory methods provide accurate results.

Using a pendulum to predict the sex of a baby
© Cristian Baitg / Getty Images

IT'S A BOY ...

In ancient Greece, Hippocrates (c.460–377/359 BC) believed that the 'male fetus is usually seated in the right, and the female in the left side' (*Aphorisms*, Section V, number 48). That boy babies affect the right side of the mother's body was still a popular belief in the 17th century, when Jane Sharp wrote one of the earliest treatises on midwifery:

If it be a Boy she is better coloured, her right Breast will swell more, for males lye most on the right side, and her belly especially on that side lieth rounder and more tumified [swollen], and the Child will be first felt to move on that side, the woman is more cheerful and in better health, her pains are not so often nor so great, the right breast is harder and more plump, the nipple a more clear red, and the whole visage clear not swarthy.

Jane Sharp, *The Midwives Book, Or, The Whole Art of Midwifry Discovered* (1671)

Some women still believe that the size of the breasts during pregnancy indicate the sex of the baby – a larger right breast means a boy, while a larger left breast means a girl (breasts of a similar size presumably don't reveal anything). It is also said that a boy enhances his mother's beauty, improving her hair and complexion, while a girl steals some of her mother's beauty, leaving her hair dull and her skin in poor condition.

... OR MAYBE A GIRL

If the mother is said to hold the bump at the front (so that no one would know she was pregnant from behind) a boy is predicted, whereas if she carries the bump in such a way that it is obvious from behind that she is pregnant, it is a girl. If you ask a pregnant woman to show you her hands, she will present them palms up if she is carrying a girl, and palms down if she is carrying a boy. Another revealing trap to set for a pregnant woman is to ask her to pick up a key – if she picks it up by the long end a girl is on the way, by the round end and a boy is predicted, and if she picks it up in the middle then she will be blessed with twins.

THE RING TRICK

One of the most famous methods for divining the sex of a baby before it is born is that of suspending a pendulum, usually a wedding ring (or a key) on a thread (or even a hair from the mother's head), over the bump (or the palm of the mother's hand) and watching how it swings. Unfortunately, different sources disagree on which movements predict which sex – some say that if the ring moves in a circular motion, then the baby is a girl, but if it swings backwards and forwards, it is a boy. Others claim the opposite, or that the important thing to watch is whether the movement of the ring is clockwise or anticlockwise.

Celebrating Births

SURVIVING THE BIRTH

In former times, if mother and child both survived the birth it was certainly a cause for relief even if no one had any energy left for immediate celebration. The modern father, pacing up and down outside the high-tech delivery room, or more likely watching inside, has it easy. In the 18th century, the mortality rate for British women in childbirth approached 20 per cent. Fear of childbirth was enough to keep many women spinsters, including the novelist Jane Austen. As she wrote to her sister Cassandra in 1798, 'I have just received a note from James to say that Mary was brought to bed last night ... Mary does not manage matters in such a way as to make me want to lay in myself ...' In fact, four of Jane Austen's sisters-in-law died in childbirth and given the practices of the time it was hardly surprising:

> *... by the heat of the chamber, amid the breath of so many people, the whole air is rendered foul ... if she is a person in affluent circumstances, she is covered up close in the bed with additional cloaths, the curtains are drawn around the bed, and pinned together, every crevice in the windows and door are stopped closed, not excepting the key hole ... the more effectually to exclude the fresh air ...*
> Dr Charles White, *A Treatise on the Management of Pregnant and Lying-in Women* (1773)

Some relied entirely on superstition, such as sleeping with a knife under the mattress to ensure a painless and troublefree birth, or tying knots in fabrics.

Alcohol was, of course, the way of keeping the men from worrying. In

Scotland, the women of the family would hand out 'groaning malt' at the birth, together with a rich cheese known as 'ken-no'. As for the children, figures show that in 18th-century London around half died before the age of two.

PROTECTING THE INFANT

In the absence of modern science, all kinds of rituals were adopted to keep the infant safe from harm. In early times, and in many traditional societies until very recently, the placenta was considered to be a powerful magic because it accompanies the infant from the 'spirit' world of the womb. It was seen almost as a twin or, at least, a companion:

In China ... the placenta when placed under felicitous circumstances is able to ensure the child a long life and to control his mental and physical welfare.

G Elliot Smith, *Evolution of the Dragon* (1919)

For example, burying the placenta at the high-tide mark might make the baby good at digging for clams, or in the courtyard of a mosque would make the child grow up to be religious.

In some places, it was believed that prior to baptism the baby was at risk of abduction by fairies as well as the 'evil eye'. Almost anybody could be the source of the 'evil eye':

Fascination is a power derived from a pact with the devil, who, when the so-called fascinator looks at another with evil intent ... infects with evil the person.

Martino Delrio, *Disquisitionum Magicarum* (1603)

Ways of preventing these calamities included putting salt in the newborn's mouth and putting iron tongs across the cradle. Speed of baptism was essential:

The woman who carried the infant to church for baptism was also supplied with bread and cheese, to give to the first person she met on the way, in order to preserve her charge from evil influences. After returning from church, the remaining part of the day, and often a great part of the night, was spent in eating and drinking, to which 'the whole country round' was invited, and they, in return, gave presents to the child.

A W Moore, *The Folk-Lore of the Isle of Man* (1891)

PRESENTS

Coral was considered a suitable present for the newborn at one time:

Coral is good to be hanged about children's necks, as well to rub their gums as to preserve them from the falling sickness; it hath also some special sympathy with nature, for the best coral ... will turn pale and wan if the party that wears it be sick ...
Sir Hugh Plat, *Jewel-House of Art and Nature* (1653)

In Victorian times, it was common to give apostle spoons – a full set if you were rich enough, four if you were less so, one if you were poor.

Certain precious and semi-precious stones have long been held to have magical properties, but the practice of giving a birthstone seems to date only from 18th-century Poland. The stones have varied from culture to culture and era to era but many people go by the following:

Silver apostle spoons
© The Trustees of the British Museum

> *Aquarius (January 21 – February 18) Garnet*
> *Pisces (February 19 – March 20) Amethyst*
> *Aries (March 21 – April 20) Bloodstone*
> *Taurus (April 21 – May 21) Sapphire*
> *Gemini (May 22 – June 21) Agate*
> *Cancer (June 22 – July 22) Emerald*
> *Leo (July 23 – August 23) Onyx*
> *Virgo (August 24 – September 22) Carnelian*
> *Libra (September 23 – October 23) Peridot*
> *Scorpio (October 24 – November 22) Beryl*
> *Sagittarius (November 23 – December 21) Topaz*
> *Capricorn (December 22 – January 20) Ruby*

Truly
Thine

Wooing and Courting

ROMANTIC LOVE

According to some anthropologists, romantic love was only invented about 800 years ago. But if that were true, there would previously have been no wooing and courting, by love letters or anything else:

My prayer is just: let the fair one who has so lately captivated my heart love me ever, or so act that I shall love her ever ... Vouchsafe thy favours to a lover who swears that he will serve thee through the years, who knows how to love with pure and lasting fidelity.

Ovid, *Amores* (c.1 BC)

COURTLY LOVE

What some consider as the beginning of romantic love was so-called courtly love (*amour courtois*) which supposedly began in the courts of Aquitaine, Provence, Champagne and Burgundy in the 11th century. The ingredients were a noblewoman in an arranged marriage, idealized by a knight or troubadour who would woo her by reciting poems, singing, jousting and performing other heroic deeds, but without thought of anything so base as actually *making* love. By the 15th century, Thomas Malory in his *Le Morte d'Arthur* was already bemoaning the ending of the 'olde love' when 'no licoures lustis was betwyxte, and then was love triuthe and faythefulne'. But such platonic *amour courtois* probably never existed. The term only became popular after an article published in 1883 and, what's more, a manual of the time suggests sex might very well have come into it:

Love is an inborn suffering proceeding from the sight and immoderate thought upon the beauty of the other sex, for which cause above all other things one wishes to embrace the other and, by common assent, in this embrace to fulfil the commandments of love ...

Andreas Capellanus, *De Amore* (c.1186)

ST VALENTINE'S DAY

The romantic origins of St Valentine's Day are not clear. Some argue that they date back to the ancient Roman fertility rites of Lupercalia, celebrated from 13–15 February. Other scholars say that there's no mention of the romantic tradition in any books until the writings of Geoffrey Chaucer (c.1340–1400):

For this was on seynt Volantynys day
Whan euery bryd comyth there to chese his make.

Geoffrey Chaucer, *Parlement of Foules* (1382)

It's not even certain which Valentine is the 'romantic' one. Until 1969, the Catholic Church recognized eleven different Valentine's Days and those honoured on 14 February include Valentine of Rome, a priest martyred in AD 269, as well as Valentine of Terni, a bishop martyred almost a century later.

In the 17th century, the custom was not to choose a valentine but to draw lots, and a married person was just as likely to be chosen as someone single:

I find that Mrs Pierce's little girl is my Valentine, she having drawn me: which I was not sorry for, it easing me of something more that I must have given to others.

Samuel Pepys, *Diary 1667*

Pepys was referring to the custom that the person who was drawn in the lottery had to give a present and not the other way around as nowadays. A present for 'Mrs Pierce's little girl' was far cheaper than that for an adult woman.

By the middle of the 18th century, the custom seems to have changed and it was the first single person one met on St Valentine's morning who was destined to be not only the valentine but also the future spouse:

Last Friday was Valentine's Day, and the night before ... if I dreamt of my sweetheart, Betty said we should be married before the year was out. We ... wrote our lovers' names upon bits of paper, and rolled them up in clay, and put them into water: and the first that rose up was to be our valentine. Would you think it? – Mr Blossom was my man. I lay a-bed and shut my eyes all the morning, till he came to our house: for I would not have seen another man before him for all the world.

Robert Chambers, *Book of Days* (1869)

The practice of sending valentine cards must have been current well before the middle of the 19th century in Britain because it was mentioned in Elizabeth Gaskell's *Mr Harrison's Confessions*, published in 1851. From Britain the idea seems to have been exported to the USA where the first mass-produced valentine cards appeared around 1847.

BETROTHAL

Morals have changed over the centuries but there has almost always been the issue of how young people should get close enough to know one another but not close enough for sex. Chaperones were one solution but in Scotland, some other parts of Europe and, later, North America there was an altogether more practical approach known as bundling:

When a man is enamored [sic] of a young woman, and wishes to marry her, he proposes the affair to her parents ... if they have no objection they allow him to tarry with her one night ... but without pulling off their undergarments ... If the parties agree, it is all very well. The banns are published ... If not, they part, and possibly never see each other again.

Dr Andrew Burnaby, *Travels Through the Middle Settlements in North America in the Years 1759 and '60* (1775)

But in lusty Scotland, undergarments alone were not considered enough and the girl's legs would be tied together by her mother as a precaution.

In the fictionalized story of Cyrano de Bergerac, Cyrano was employed to woo the beautiful Roxane on behalf of another man. In many societies such go-betweens were a real part of the romantic culture. On the Isle of Man, the go-between was known as a *dooinney-moyllee* and it was his job not only to win over the woman but also to negotiate the 'marriage portion'. If all else failed, magic might be employed. In the 19th century, it was reported that maidens in Shropshire 'drop needles and pins into the wells at Wenlock, to arrest and fix the affections of their lovers'.

Although rolling up names in clay and bundling may strike us nowadays as charming, the lack of any meaningful wooing to explore compatibility could lead to disaster. When a woman friend suggested her sister, Mary Owens, as a wife for Abraham Lincoln, the future American president, he agreed, even though he had only seen the woman once, three years earlier:

In a few days we had an interview, and ... she did not look as my imagination pictured her. I knew she was over-size, but she now appeared a fair match for Falstaff. I knew she was called an 'old maid' and I felt no doubt of the truth of at least half of the appellation, but now, when I beheld her, I could not for my life avoid thinking of my mother ... I was not at all pleased with her. But what could I do! I had told her sister that I would take her for better or for worse ...

Abraham Lincoln,
Letter to Mrs O H Browning
(1838)

Claddagh rings
Steve Gorton © Dorling Kindersley

Fortunately for Lincoln, and probably the woman, too, she refused his proposal. The letter may not be wholly accurate (it was written on 1 April) but it certainly reflects the situation of Lincoln and many other men and women of the time. Jane Austen, the English novelist, only ever received one proposal of marriage and accepted it, but then withdrew the next morning. As she later wrote to her niece, 'Anything is to be preferred or endured rather than marrying without Affection.'

In the Middle Ages, she would have had more of a problem. A promise to marry, given in front of witnesses, was known as the 'verbum' and was considered binding.

Engagement rings

Because they form a never-ending circle, rings have long been a symbol of undying love. The modern custom of the engagement ring probably only dates from 1477 when Maximilian I, Holy Roman Emperor, gave a diamond ring to Mary of Burgundy as an engagement present.

For lovers who prefer something more unusual there's the Claddagh ring. According to one tradition, a fisherman from Claddagh, Galway, was captured by pirates and sold as a slave to a goldsmith. Upon his return home years later he was overjoyed to find that his bride had waited for him and designed, made and gave her the ring. The ring has three elements, a heart (signifying love) held between two hands (signifying friendship), topped by a crown (symbolizing loyalty). Claddagh rings continue to be worn, especially by those of Irish origin. (See also the section on celebrating marriages.)

Celebrating Marriages

MOSTLY A PRIVATE MATTER

For thousands of years 'marriage' was simply a mutual, verbal agreement, although in Roman times there was a form known as *conventio in manum* which involved a ceremony in front of witnesses. Even in early Christian times, marriage remained a private matter and it was not until the Council of Trent in 1545 that the Roman Catholic Church insisted that a ceremony be conducted by a priest. Many Protestants, however, continued to marry in an informal way, especially in the more remote areas:

This custom was termed hand-fasting, and consisted of a species of contract between two chiefs, by which it was agreed that the heir of one should live with the daughter of another as her husband for a year and a day. If, in that time, the lady became a mother, or proved to be with child, the marriage became good in law, even although no priest had performed the marriage ceremony in due form; but should there not have occurred any appearance of issue, the contract was considered at an end, and each party was at liberty to marry or hand-fast with any other.

James Browne, *History of the Highlands, and of the Highland Clans*
(c.1836)

The term 'hand-fasting' seems to have come from Old Norse, signifying to seal an agreement by shaking hands, but sometimes the couple were literally tied together by their hands, which may have been the origin of the expression 'tying the knot'. It wasn't until the Marriage Act of 1753 that a formal church ceremony was required in England and Wales. The Marriage Act of 1836 later provided for civil marriages.

BUT ALSO POLITICAL

Although marriages in early times had little to do with Church or State, they didn't necessarily have anything to do with love either. It wasn't only royal families that were more concerned with political alliances. The same applied to minor aristocracy, too:

There is preserved the agreement entered into on the 4th April 1528, between Sir William Sturton ... and Walter Hungerford ... for the disposal of Charles, the eldest son of the former, in marriage to one of the three daughters of the latter, Elinor, Mary or Anne, whichever Sir William might choose.

Robert Chambers, *Book of Days* (1869)

AROUND THE CEREMONY

They have Bride-men, and Bride-maids, who lead the young couple ... preceded by musick. When they arrive at the Churchyard, they walk three times round the Church, before they enter it.

A W Moore, *The Folk-Lore of the Isle of Man* (1891)

The white wedding dress symbolizes purity and became popular in Victorian times, because Queen Victoria wore white when she married Prince Albert. But, according to some sources, white really represents wealth, because a white dress could never be worn again.

As regards the veil, some say it was to protect the bride from evil spirits, while others argue that it was this that symbolized virginity.

The tradition that most strongly evokes the Western wedding is the tune 'Here Comes The Bride', actually the 'Bridal Chorus' from the opera *Lohengrin*, and sung for the wedding night, not the ceremony, as the original words make clear:

This sweet-smelling room, decked for love ... draw now near to where the blessing of love shall preserve you.

The Bridal Chorus from Act III of Wagner's *Lohengrin* (1848)

The wedding ring has been worn on the fourth finger of the left hand ever since the ancient Graeco-Roman belief that a nerve went directly from that finger to the heart (see also the section on wooing and courting). For the same reason it was known as the healing finger and was used to stir medicines.

The idea of the bride throwing her bouquet may stem from the belief that tearing off a piece of the bride's clothing would bring luck. Tossing the bouquet thus became a way of preserving the bride's dress.

As for tying shoes to the back of the wedding car, the origin lies in biblical times when taking off a shoe seems to have had some significance to do with property transfer. In Anglo-Saxon days, the bride's father would present her shoe to the bridegroom as a symbol of the transfer of authority over her.

THE RECEPTION

Celebrations in Britain nowadays are relatively prim affairs, to judge by earlier accounts:

Broth is served up in wooden piggins, every man having his portion allowed him. This they sup with shells called sligs, very much like ... mussel shells, but larger. I have seen a dozen capons in one platter, and six or eight fat geese in another; hogs and sheep roasted whole, and oxen divided but into quarters.

A W Moore, quoted in *The Folk-Lore of the Isle of Man* (1891)

The marriage of Queen Victoria to Prince Albert
© *Mary Evans Picture Library / Alamy*

The wedding cake goes back to at least Roman times, when it was made of wheat or barley and broken over the head of the bride by the groom to ensure fertility. The tradition spread and a 19th-century writer records how in England 'on their arrival at the door ... the bridecake was broken over the bride's head, and then thrown away to be scrambled for by the crowd ... The girls present were especially anxious to secure a piece to place under their pillows, that they might dream of their future husbands ...'

HAPPILY EVER AFTER – OR NOT

The people of Dunmow in Essex were so confident that newlyweds would soon 'have brawls or contentious strife' that a flitch of bacon was offered to any who would swear that never:

> *... since the parish-clerk said Amen,*
> *You wish'd yourselves unmarried agen,*
> *Or in a twelvemonth and a day,*
> *Repented not in thought any way ...*

The Flitch Oath

Few couples won a flitch and, indeed, it seems even as late as the final years of the 19th century some men who wished themselves 'unmarried agen' sold their wives:

> *Within the last twenty years there have been at least a dozen cases ... of men in a low station in life who have sold their wives, under the impression they could legally do so ... One husband parted with his spouse for eighteen pence and a glass of beer.*

T Sharper Knowlson, *The Origins of Popular Superstitions* (1910)

Mourning Deaths

MOURNING IN PREHISTORY

Early people have left an archaeological record of their burial practices, but as to how they mourned their dead we can only imagine. Almost certainly they would have had specific rituals by about 40,000 years ago, if not earlier, because burial sites from that time included ornaments and tools. Around 10,000 years ago ideas about death must have changed because Europeans then began to bury their dead in cemeteries, rather than in individual sites.

A BETTER PLACE?

Some religions taught that death could be a happy occasion and mourning unnecessary since the spirit was going to a better place. Indeed, in the 4th century, Bishop Ambrose of Milan instructed that Christians should look forward to death with joy as it was a necessary step on the way to Heaven. His view, however, did not prevail, partly because of the fear that a dead person might go to Hell:

I have another dream to tell you ... I soon found myself at the mouth of a frightful cave. I halted, unwilling to venture into that deep cavern ... after a long while a huge, hideous monster emerged ... Then I went back to my guide. 'Now you know who he is,' he said to me. 'I surely do! It is the devil himself!'

St John Bosco, *The Road to Hell* (1868)

According to some, one way of keeping away evil spirits was to ring a bell, and mourners sometimes paid extra to the ringers for the noise to be so loud that 'the evil spirits must go farther off':

Item, that when anye Christian bodie is in passing, that the bell be tolled, and that the curate be speciallie called for to comforte the sicke person; and after the time of his passinge, to ringe no more but one short peale; and one before the burial, and another short peale after the burial.

Anon, *Advertisements for due order* (1565)

Not everyone, however, was overly concerned about evil spirits who 'stood at the bed's foot and about the house':

Waked this morning with news ... that my Uncle Robert is dead ... So I rose – sorry in some respect; glad in my expectations in another respect ... set out about 11 or 12 a-clock ... and got well by 9 a-clock to Brampton ... My uncle's corps in a coffin, standing upon joynt-stools in the chimney in the hall; but it begun to smell, and so I caused it to be set forth in the yard all night ...

Samuel Pepys, *Diary* (1661)

THE VICTORIAN ERA

Following the death of Prince Albert in 1861, after just two decades of marriage, Queen Victoria went into deep mourning and set the style that very many others then followed. In those days, most people died at home, surrounded by family and friends, where the corpse would remain until burial. Quite often a few locks of the dead person's hair would be cut off to be made into jewellery or be kept inside a locket. Other mementos included 'death masks' and photographs of the dead person as if merely asleep – children who had died were often photographed propped up and surrounded by their toys, sometimes with their brothers and sisters.

Giving a 'decent' and therefore impressive and expensive burial was considered essential. Men weren't expected to more than nod towards mourning clothes by, for example, wearing a black hatband, but for widows almost everything had to be specially bought, from hair accessories and stationery right through to the all-enveloping black dresses in non-reflective silk, bombazine or crepe – known as 'widow's weeds' from the Old English 'waed' meaning 'clothing'. A widow was expected to remain in mourning for two years, while children whose siblings had died would have to wear mourning clothes for six months. It was a lucrative business, especially as it was considered bad luck to keep mourning clothes for future use:

MOURNING FOR FAMILIES.
JAY'S
Experienced dressmakers and milliners travel to any part of the Kingdom free of expense to purchasers ... Reasonable estimates are also given for Household Mourning at a great saving to large or small families.

Advert for Jay's of Regent Street (c. 1841)

The custom of wearing black goes back to at least Roman times, when those in mourning would have worn the *toga pulla* of dark wool. However, in the Middle Ages, white was often the favoured colour and Mary, Queen of Scots wore the *deuil blanc* following the death of her first husband Francis II of France in 1560.

Mourning dress, 1861
© Mary Evans Picture Library / Alamy

CONTACTING THE DEAD

Through the ages there has been a belief that the spirits of the dead lived on in some way. Often it was a cause for fear rather than a consolation. Australian Aborigines believed that death was the permanent separation of body and spirit but, just in case, would sometimes break the legs of the deceased to prevent them from walking around again. Many hunter-gatherer cultures would abandon the place where someone had died, for fear of the spirit, sometimes pulling their hut down over the dead body.

More usually the belief in contact with the dead was a comfort:

*The wife knows ... the skull of her husband or her child ... and there seldom passes
a day that she does not visit it, with a dish of the best cooked food that her wigwam
affords ... these women may be seen sitting or laying by the skull of their child
or husband – talking to it in the most pleasant and endearing language ... and
seemingly getting an answer back.*

> George Catlin, *The Manners, Customs and Condition of the North American
> Indian* (1841)

If anybody could make contact from 'the other side' it would surely be
someone like the English poet, artist and mystic William Blake (1757–1827)
and, indeed, his widow Catherine was sure he did. According to her
account, he used to come and sit with her for two or three hours every
day, sitting in his favourite chair, chatting, and advising her on the best way
of making money from his engravings.

Such beliefs were formalized into the spiritualist movement after
the Fox sisters in America claimed to be able to converse with the dead
through 'spirit-rapping' and, although they later confessed to deception,
the movement grew rapidly in Britain from the 1850s. Like many, the
writer Sir Arthur Conan Doyle (1859–1930) was mourning a son lost in
World War I and, destroyed by grief, fell into a lapse of judgement that
his creation, Sherlock Holmes, would have been ashamed of, becoming
a firm believer. By that time, the trickery had moved well beyond mere
tappings and table movements:

*She took up her station against the drawing-room wall ... Then three gas-burners
were turned on to their full extent ... The effect upon Katie King was marvellous. She
looked like herself for the space of a second only, then she began gradually to melt
away ... At last there was nothing but her head left above the ground – then a heap of
white drapery only, which disappeared with a whisk ...*

> Sir Arthur Conan Doyle, *The History of Spiritualism* (1926)

Observing Etiquette

AN EXCLUSIVE CLUB

Many animals have rules of etiquette (for example, as to who eats first) and it's therefore logical that early humans, too, would have had their conventions. Etiquette serves two purposes. The first is to allow members of a group to identify one another and to exclude non-members:

It is not to be disputed then, that every man, who is not determined to spend his life in solitude and the retreat of an hermitage, but in the company and assemblies of the polite, must think it of the utmost consequence, to make himself amiable and agreeable in conversation ... Whereas this elegance of manners, which depends entirely on our words and actions, even without the appendage of a good estate, gives a man influence, and the appearance of a gentleman.

Giovanni della Casa, *Galateo: Or, A Treatise on Politeness and Delicacy of Manners* (1558)

The second is simply to make it easier for people to live together without too much friction:

Put not thy hand in the presence of others to any part of thy body, not ordinarily discovered ... Spit not in the Room, but in a corner, and rub it out with thy Foot, or rather go out and do it abroad.

John Garretson, *The School of Manners* (1701)

DEALING WITH THE ARISTOCRACY

One of the earliest-known books of etiquette was written by the Egyptian Ptah-Hotep and survives in a papyrus version some 4000 years old, although he himself lived earlier (see the section on handwriting). Here he gives advice to those invited to dinner:

If you be among the guests of a man who is greater than you, accept whatever he gives you and put it to your lips ... The noble apportions a meal as his soul directs and gives unto those he favours ... If you look at him ... pierce him not with many glances ... Speak not till he addresses you ...

Ptah-Hotep, *Prisse Papyrus* (c.2000 BC)

An 18th-century British manual similarly counsels young people, 'Look not boldly or wilfully in the Face of thy Superior'. But in the 'new' country of 19th century America things were done a little differently:

Always look people in the face when you speak to them, otherwise you will be thought conscious of some guilt; besides, you lose the opportunity of reading their countenances, from which you will much better learn the impression which your discourse makes upon them ...

Emily Thornwell, *The Lady's Guide to Perfect Gentility* (1857)

Nevertheless, America was not yet the land of equality the Founding Fathers had hoped and *The Lady's Guide* noted that if 'one of lower rank' used a person's name repeatedly it should be considered an 'impertinence'.

DEALING WITH SERVANTS

'From the hour of their birth', wrote Aristotle, 'some are marked out for subjection, others for rule'. In his day and earlier, being a servant generally meant more or less the same thing as being a slave. Even so, it was considered politic to treat servants well:

Satisfy your hired servants out of such things as you have; it is the duty of one that has been favoured of the god ... Peace dwells not in that town wherein dwell servants that are wretched.

Ptah-Hotep, *Prisse Papyrus* (c.2000 BC)

Through the Middle Ages, and in some cases later, there was another class of 'servant' drawn from among the sons of gentlemen and 'waiting gentlewomen' whose duties were light and given in return for, as it were, on-the-job training. Courtiers were in a special position, unpaid and giving their services in the hope of royal favours and the opportunity to make a profit from being at the centre of power. To be successful they needed extensive skills:

To have a judgement to frame himself to the manners of the Countrey where ever he commeth.

To procure where ever he goeth that men may first conceive a good opinion of him before he commeth there.

To make his garments after the facion of the most, and those to be black, or of some darkish and sad colour, not garish.

To daunce well without over nimble footings or to busie trickes.

To be skilfull in all kind of marciall feates both on horsbacke and a foote.

Baldassare Castiglione, *Il Cortegiano* (1528)

THE END OF ETIQUETTE?

Etiquette must, by definition, always exist, but as regards the rigid and stultifying codes that had prevailed for so long, the writing was on the wall long before the end of the Victorian era:

1902 manual on etiquette
© Mary Evans Picture Library / Alamy

The first great fundamental rule of good taste is to be natural; and it is from an infringement of this that many of our worst mistakes proceed. In manner of style, affectation is the source of the most flagrant offences against taste ... Affectation is an offence against high moral feeling ... we cannot help feeling that it originates in artifice.

Emily Thornwell, *The Lady's Guide to Perfect Gentility* (1857)

Dining

WHAT WOULD YOU HAVE EATEN?

If you could get into a time machine and travel back to share a meal with early hunter-gatherers you would have no choice but to eat your food raw. Exactly when you could have got a hot meal is controversial. Some archaeologists say early humans began cooking 300,000 years ago but mainstream opinion puts it closer to 50,000 years ago. But whatever raw-food enthusiasts may think now, it was a huge advance, because cooking most foods provides many more nutrients than it destroys.

What else would have been different? Well, you would certainly have eaten insects, which, by Roman times, had become a delicacy. According to the 1st century Roman scholar Pliny the Elder in his *Historia Naturalis*, his contemporaries loved beetle larvae that had been reared on flour and wine. And as for the Greeks, Aristotle in the 4th century BC recommended cicada nymphs and females 'after copulation ... which are then full of white eggs'.

THE APPLE OF LOVE

Even some foods which we now take for granted arrived surprisingly late on the plates of British diners. Tomatoes, first cultivated in Mexico, didn't arrive in Europe until the 16th century, and it took at least a century for them to spread throughout Europe, and another century again before they became popular in Britain. The British resisted partly because the plants needed greenhouses to flourish, but also because what the French were calling the *pomme d'amour* was considered a dangerous aphrodisiac.

ONE POTATO, TWO POTATO

It was the same story with the potato. British folklore credits Sir Walter Raleigh with its introduction but, in fact, it was Spanish explorers who brought potatoes from South America, around 1570. All kinds of superstition immediately attached to the rather ugly tubers. Once again, the fear of sex had something to do with it. Known variously as 'earth's testicles' and 'Eve's apple' it was said that potatoes 'incited Venus'. It didn't help that the people of South America had rather unappetizing ways of dealing with the vegetable, the most common being *chuño*, which amounted to an early and natural form of freeze-drying high in the Andes, and *papa seca* which was dehydration. As a result, and despite championing by Queen Marie Antoinette, who wore potato flowers in her hair, it took some 250 years before the potato was widely accepted in Europe as fit for human consumption. But the Irish were early enthusiasts (planting tubers, it's said, that floated ashore from Armada wrecks) and at one point were eating up to 16 lb / 7kg a day each, in myriad forms, from boxty (potato pancakes) to this recipe for colcannon:

Chop cold boiled cabbage and potatoes quite fine; put them together, season with butter, pepper and salt, add a very little vinegar or hot water to moisten without making it wet, put it into a stew-pan over the fire, stir it well, that it may be thoroughly heated, but not burn, then take it into a dish and serve for breakfast, or with cold boiled salt meat for dinner.

Mrs Crowen, *Lady's Cookery Book* (1847)

EATING IN

Almost no aspect of etiquette arouses such passion as manners at the table. In Britain, until the 17th century, and even later, one of the worst crimes would have been to use a fork. 'God in his wisdom has provided man with natural forks – his fingers,' complained one observer of the social scene. Therefore, he concluded, using a metal fork was an insult to God.

In fact, no one in Britain insulted God with a fork until after 1600. Thomas Coryat claimed to be among the first Englishmen to be so decadent:

I observed a custome in all those Italian Cities and Townes through which I passed, that is not used in any other country that I saw ... The Italian ... doe always at their meales use a little forke ... whatsoever he be that sitteth in the company of any others at meate, should unadvisedly touch the dish of meate with his fingers ... he will give occasion of offence unto the company as having transgressed the lawes of good manners, insomuch for his error he shall be at least browbeaten, if not reprehended in words.

Thomas Coryat, *Coryat's Crudities Hastily Gobbled up in Five Months' Travels* (1611)

Dining in those days was certainly not for those of more modern sensibilities. One 16th-century observer noted how a female dining companion 'rummages the most remote cavities of her mouth and gums, with the corner of her napkin; and squirts out the soiled ablution into the water-glass, with so bold and ostentatious an air, as if she considered it as an excellence ...' As regards a knife, except in the wealthiest households, guests were expected to bring their own.

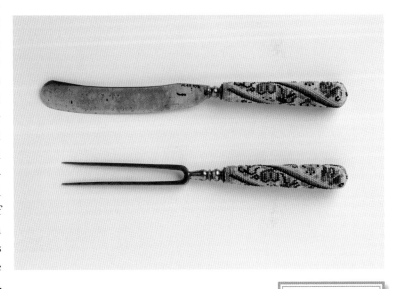

Early 18th-century steel knife and fork with beaded handles
© V&A Images, Victoria and Albert Museum

EATING OUT

Which was the world's first restaurant? According to gastronomic folklore it was, of course, in Paris and was opened by a Monsieur Boulanger in 1765 in what is now the Rue du Louvre. What's more, the sign he put outside, *Boulanger débite des restaurants divins* (Boulanger provides divine restoratives) supposedly gave the world the word 'restaurant' in the modern sense.

However, an academic, Rebecca L Spang, after an exhaustive study, has found no hard evidence. Instead, she champions a man called

Mathurin Roze de Chantoiseau in 1766. If indeed he was the first he was quickly copied because an almanac three years later lists not only him but also some 700 other caterers, innkeepers and hoteliers in Paris (and no Monsieur Boulanger).

Diners would have sat at a communal table and eaten whatever they were given, in a tradition of hospitality that goes way back (some think the word 'company' derives from *communis* meaning 'common' and *panis* meaning 'bread'). Individual tables came much later. Intriguingly, Roze saw his mission as supplying health foods, by which he meant grinding everything up into an easily-digestible soup. That only goes to show how fashions in food and everything else go round and round because four centuries earlier, in the *Canterbury Tales*, Chaucer mentioned a ground meat stew that he called *mortreux*, a recipe for which is given below:

Take hennes [chicken] and pork and seeth [simmer] hem togyder. Take the lyre [liver] of hennes and of the pork and hewe it small, and grinde it all to doust; take brede ygrated and do therto, and temper it with the self broth, and alye [thicken] it with yolkes of ayren [eggs]; and cast theron powdour fort [strong spice mix]. Boile it and do therin powdour of ginger, sugur, safroun and salt, and loke that it be stondying; and flour it with powdour ginger.

Master-Cooks of King Richard II, *The Forme of Cury* (1390)

The controversy over who was first is, however, something of an academic diversion since restaurants of various descriptions have existed for, probably, thousands of years. Back in ancient Rome you could have gone to a tavern, most likely near a bathhouse or one of the public buildings, where there would have been an L- or U-shaped stone bar with, set into it, various clay pots holding hot and cold food and drink.

Making and Taking Tea

ZEN AND THE ART OF TEA

Tea comes from the *Camellia sinensis* plant of which there are several varieties, producing over 3,000 different types of beverage. It was already drunk in China at the time of Confucius (c.551–479 BC) and probably spread to Japan in the 8th century, but didn't become popular there until a Zen Buddhist monk called Eisai introduced the famous tea ceremony in 1191. Gradually tea-drinking spread westwards becoming fashionable in Britain in the 17th century under the influence of Catherine of Braganza, wife of Charles II.

UNSTRINGING THE NERVES

Initially tea was enormously expensive in Britain but gradually it became affordable to all, such that by the 18th century there were concerns about its impact on health:

I began to observe, that abundance of the People in London, with whom I conversed, laboured under the same, and many other Paralytick Disorders, and that in a much higher Degree; insomuch that some of their Nerves were quite unstrung ... I inquired, 'Are you not an hard Drinker?' And was answered by one and another, and another, 'No, indeed. Sir, not I; I drink scarce any Thing but a little Tea, Morning and Night.'
John Wesley, *A Letter to a Friend Concerning Tea* (1748)

In 1757, Jonas Hanway published an essay attacking tea as 'pernicious to health, obstructing industry and impoverishing the nation' leading to a robust defence by one of the most famous intellectuals of his day:

... a hardened and shameless tea-drinker, who has for twenty years diluted his meals with only the infusion of this fascinating plant, whose kettle scarcely has time to cool, who with Tea amuses the evening, with Tea solaces the midnights, and with Tea welcomes the morning.

Dr Samuel Johnson, *An Essay on Tea*, published in *The Literary Magazine* (1757)

In Britain, Dr Johnson's cosy image of tea is the one that has prevailed:

... we returned into the Castle where we found Miss Skiffins preparing tea. The responsibility of making toast was delegated to the Aged ... The Aged prepared such a haystack of buttered toast, that I could scarcely see him over it ... We ate the whole of the toast, and drank tea in proportion, and it was delightful to see how warm and greasy we all got after it.

Charles Dickens, *Great Expectations* (1861)

Dr Samuel Johnson and James Boswell taking tea with Flora Macdonald
© The Print Collector / Alamy

A NICE CUPPA

In China and Japan, tea had an altogether different image. In the 8th century, the Chinese author Lu Yu wrote the *Ch'a ching* (The Classic of Tea), encapsulating a quasi-religious approach to the beverage in which every single detail had ritualistic significance. Here Lu Yu's instructions for the water are described by an early-20th-century devotee:

The mountain spring is best, the river water and the spring water come next in the order of excellence. There are three stages of boiling: the first boil is when the little bubbles like the eye of fishes swim on the surface; the second boil is when the bubbles are like crystal beads rolling in a fountain; the third boil is when the billows surge wildly in the kettle ... Salt is put in the first boil, the tea in the second. At the third boil, a dipperful of cold water is poured into the kettle to settle the tea and revive the 'youth of the water' ... O nectar!

Kakuzo Okakura, *The Book of Tea* (1904)

The result, according to one poet of the era, was an infusion that, cup by cup, induced a kind of ecstasy. 'At the fifth cup I am purified,' he wrote; 'the sixth cup calls me to the realms of the immortals. The seventh cup – ah, but I could take no more! I only feel the breath of cool wind ... Let me ride on this sweet breeze and waft away thither.'

In other parts of Asia they had a very different way of producing a 'nice cuppa':

An English traveller once journeying through Asiatic Russia was obliged to claim the hospitality of a family of Buratsky Arabs. At mealtime the mistress of the tent placed a large kettle on the fire, wiped it carefully with a horse's tail, filled it with water, threw in some coarse tea and a little salt. When this was nearly boiled she stirred the mixture with a brass ladle until the liquor became very brown, when she poured it into another vessel. Cleaning the kettle as before, the woman set it again on the fire to fry a paste of meal and fresh butter. Upon this she poured the tea and some thick cream... Half-pint mugs were handed around and the tea ladled into them...

Arthur Gray, *The Little Tea Book* (1903)

Japanese tea ceremony
© Henrik Winther Andersen
/ Alamy

Celebrating with Alcohol

FANCY SOME ETHANOL?

In all probability, people have been using alcohol for tens of thousands of years because it can be produced naturally, in the form of ethanol, when sugars in ripe fruits start to ferment. Biologists have proposed that attraction to the aroma of alcohol may even have evolved when early man roamed the forests in search of energy-rich food sources – one gram of pure alcohol contains seven calories, almost as much as in pure fat. Although some tales of wild animals getting drunk have proven apocryphal, it's known for a fact that Malaysian tree shrews and some other mammals do feed on the fermented nectar of the bertam palm flower with an alcohol content of 3.8 per cent. As to the man-made production of alcohol, archaeologists in China have found evidence dating back 9000 years and it's thought that the necessary technology developed in the Middle East at around the same time.

Ethanol is a colourless volatile liquid and can be produced from all kinds of foodstuffs, including fruit, grains, vegetables, milk, honey and sugar. Naturally, alcoholic drinks cannot reach a strength of more than around 15 per cent because beyond that level the yeasts that produce the alcohol die. Stronger drink requires distillation, a process that seems to have been known to the Babylonians at least 3000 years ago, reaching a sophisticated level in Europe by the 12th century.

THE BACCHANALIA

Perhaps as early as 6000 BC, people on the borders of Mesopotamia and

Hand-coloured woodcut of a 19th-century illustration of gentlemen toasting Queen Victoria
© North Wind Picture Archives / Alamy

129

Persia had developed an explanation for alcohol's special properties. They believed they were being possessed by a god – Dionysus, also known as Bacchus, the god of wine. The Dionysus cult was certainly a feature of life on Minoan Crete some time after 3000 BC and from there it spread to Athens and other cities, where it caused considerable consternation:

I hear that our women-folk have left their homes on pretence of Bacchic rites, and on the wooded hills rush wildly to and fro, honouring in the dance this new god Dionysus, whoe'er he is; and in the midst of each revel-rout the brimming wine-bowl stands ...

Euripides, *The Bacchae*
(410 BC)

Gin Lane, *by William Hogarth, 1751*
© Classic Image / Alamy

By 200 BC, the Dionysus cult had reached Rome in the form of the bacchanalia, probably the most infamous alcohol-fuelled festivals in history. They started in the Simila grove near the Aventine Hill on March 16th and 17th each year and initially were for women only. Fairly quickly, however, men were allowed to attend and celebrations were held as often as five times every month. It is said that the bacchanalia were a cross between an orgy and a political agitation but no reliable descriptions have survived, although there are murals depicting the female initiation process on the walls of the Villa of the Mysteries in Pompeii. Certainly the authorities were frightened enough to try to impose a ban in 186 BC, but the bacchanalia never entirely died out and, in a less extreme form, were revived under Julius Caesar around 50 BC, continuing as a kind of carnival into the time of Augustine more than four centuries later.

As Giuseppe Garibaldi, the 19th-century Italian patriot put it, 'Bacchus has drowned more men than Neptune'.

LIBATIONS AND TOASTS

In antiquity, it was a common practice, before drinking, to offer some of the wine to a god, either by pouring it onto an altar or onto the ground:

In accordance with the national custom the cupbearers gave us a cup for us to make our libations before we took our seats ... When all were sitting properly in order, a cupbearer came to offer Attila an ivy-wood bowl of wine, which he took and drank a toast ... The guests, taking their own cups, then honoured him in the same way, sipping the wine after making the toast.

Priscus, *Dinner with Attila* as quoted in *Readings in European History* (1905)

So even the 'barbarians' in the 5th century had the custom of the toast, but the actual word in English seems to derive from the 17th-century practice of putting a piece of spiced toast into the drink to improve the flavour. As to clinking glasses, one theory is that the guest would pour some wine from his own goblet into the host's goblet to be sure he was not being poisoned. Once trust was established the goblets would merely be clinked together. Others say that the custom developed because everyone once drank from a communal bowl and bringing the glasses together and clinking them serves to maintain the sense of community that otherwise would be lost.

Most probably glasses were sometimes smashed after a toast as a way of warding off evil spirits that, apparently, are frightened by noise.

BINGE DRINKING – NOT A MODERN INVENTION

After attending the coronation of King Charles II in 1661, Samuel Pepys, the diarist, got together with some friends to celebrate:

... we drank the King's health and nothing else, till one of the gentlemen fell down stark drunk and there lay spewing. And I went to my Lord's pretty well. But no sooner a-bed with Mr Shepley but my head began to hum, and I to vomit, and if ever I was foxed it was now, which I cannot say yet, because I fell asleep and slept till morning. Only, when I waked I found myself wet with my spewing. Thus did the day end, with joy every where ...

Samuel Pepys, *Diary* (1660–69)

It seems that binge drinking was as acceptable in the 17th century as in the 21st and, indeed, 'joy' became an even bigger social problem when the next monarch but one became king in 1688. Because William III was Dutch, the government encouraged gin and restricted French brandy, with the disastrous results depicted by William Hogarth's famous engraving *Gin Lane*.

Gin consumption reached 10 litres (2.2 gallons) per head of the population and the government introduced a succession of laws to try to control the 'Gin Craze'. But it took 50 years, high grain prices and properly licensed premises in place of 'dram shops' before consumption of 'mother's ruin' fell to more healthy levels. The new-style, more respectable 'Gin Palaces' would have been perfectly familiar to pub-goers today:

... the gay building with the fantastically ornamented parapet, the illuminated clock, the plate-glass windows surrounded by stucco rosettes, and its profusion of gaslights in richly-gilt burners, is perfectly dazzling when contrasted with the darkness and dirt we have just left. The interior is even gayer than the exterior. A bar of French-polished mahogany, elegantly carved, extends the whole width of the place ... Behind it, are two showily-dressed damsels with large necklaces, dispensing the spirits ...
Charles Dickens, *Sketches by Boz* (1836)

GOOD HEALTH – OR MAYBE NOT

'Good health' is a common toast all over the world but the balance between alcohol's beneficial and harmful effects remains controversial:

It sloweth age, it strengtheneth youth, it helpeth digestion, it cutteth phlegm, it abandoneth melancholy ... it healeth the strangury, it pounceth the stone, it expelleth gravel, it puffeth away all ventosity ...
Theoricus, 16th century, quoted in *The Critical Review* (1813)

That alcohol is a poison is attested by all chemists and other scientific men; taken undiluted it destroys the vitality of the tissues of the body with which it comes in contact as readily as creosote or pure carbolic acid.
Martha M Allen, *Alcohol: A Dangerous And Unnecessary Medicine* (1900)

Although various species have their courtship 'dances', and birds, whales and gibbons have songs, only humans truly seem to respond to the rhythms of music. Proof of the earliest date for human dancing is in the cave paintings at Bhimbetka in India, which are around 9000 years old. But many specialists in prehistory believe *Homo ergaster* (a common ancestor of both Neanderthals and sapiens) was already dancing. All theories remain controversial but a link between sex and the origin of dance is widely accepted.

SOCIAL DANCING

While some dances, especially those like the can-can and the belly dance, have always been associated in repressed British minds with sex, even our homegrown and often more genteel dances can't escape these long-established associations. In the British court dances of the 17th century, sexual connotations were not entirely suppressed:

By and by comes the King [Charles II] and Queen, the Duke and Duchesse, and all the great ones; and after seating themselfs, the King takes out the Duchesse of Yorke ... After that, the King led a lady a single coranto ... Very noble it was, and a great pleasure to see. Then to country dances; the King leading the first which he called for; which was, says he, 'Cuckolds all a-row' – the old dance of England.

Samuel Pepys, *Diary* (1660–69)

But at the French court, by contrast, the style had become something quite effete under the dance enthusiast Louis XIV (1638–1715), known as the Sun King. Elegance was everything and every little movement was studied:

The position is correct when the feet are in a certain symmetry, the toes turned out an equal amount ... There are five correct positions. The first is when the two heels are together. The second is when the two feet are open and separated by a distance of the length of one foot ...

Raul-Auger Feuillet, *Choréographie*
(1700)

It was Feuillet's *Choréographie*, published in 1700, that was the first to set out a system of dance notation, using charts to show people exactly how to perform various steps. He defined such movements as *ballonné, jeté, pas de bourrée* and *pas de menuet* thus helping the French style to spread across Europe.

The big 18th-century dance was the *minuet*, possibly because it was the least technically complicated of the era. Even so, it involved four figures requiring considerable precision, with each step spread over two measures of 3/4 time. First there was an S or Z figure, followed by the giving of right hands, then left hands and finally the giving of both hands. Handel, Bach, Haydn and Mozart all composed minuets.

But even if dances were no longer sexually expressive, balls were nevertheless opportunities for the better-off of both sexes to mingle:

Postcard image of couple dancing a waltz at a ball, early 20th century
© *Lebrecht Music and Arts Photo Library / Alamy*

There were only twelve dances, of which I danced nine, & was merely prevented from dancing the rest by the want of a partner ... There were but 50 people in the room; very few families indeed from our side of the Country, & not many more from the other. My partners were the two St Johns, Hooper Holder – and very prodigious – Mr

Mathew, with whom I called the last, & whom I liked the best of my little stock. There were very few Beauties ...

Jane Austen, *Letter to Cassandra Austen* (1800)

And even Jane Austen was not altogether immune to the sensual pleasures of dance. As she observed in her novel *Emma*, 'when the felicities of rapid motion have once been, though slightly, felt – it must be a very heavy set that does not ask for more'.

AT THE BALL

'A ball is not a place where one comes to find some romantic dream', advises one book on manners. 'If you see someone who has not yet had an opportunity to dance, make sure she is given that opportunity.' The elegant and precise protocol of the ballroom probably reached its height in 18th-century France, where the minuet was the dance of the moment. Because it wasn't physically difficult, every aspiring member of the bourgeoisie used it to display his or her own refinement, while revelling in the errors of others. A lady never asked a gentleman; instead she would have to wait for a man to ask her permission for a specific dance. When the dance was over he would offer her his arm, conduct her back to her seat, bow, and wait to be released. Even well into the Victorian era these rigid codes of ballroom conduct prevailed:

A lady should not attend a public ball without an escort ... Ladies should not be too hasty in filling their programme on their entrance to the ball room ... An introduction in a public ball room must be understood by the gentleman to be for that evening only ... If a gentleman, without proper introduction, should ask a lady with whom he is not acquainted to dance or promenade, the lady should positively refuse ...

Lucien Carpenter, *Universal Dancing Master* (1880)

Celebrating the Seasons

NEW YEAR

Scotland has always been the place to celebrate New Year. Exactly why 31 December is known as Hogmanay nobody knows for sure. One plausible theory is that the name comes from the old Scandinavian *hogenat* – *hogg* indicating the killing of animals in preparation for the feast. At midnight, the head of the house would have a bowl of hot, spiced wine and as the bells rang out the old year and rang in the new he would drink to the health of the family, toasting *waes hael* (see also the section on celebrating Christmas). The bowl would then be passed round. If you'd like to make your own mulled wine for Hogmanay then, according to a traditional recipe, you should spice it with cardamoms, cloves, nutmeg, mace, ginger, cinnamon and coriander, sweeten it with sugar and thicken it with beaten egg.

Getting back to work on the first Monday after New Year's celebrations wasn't easy:

> *Plough Monday, next after that Twelfth-tide is past,*
> *Bids out with the Plough; the worst husband is last:*
> *If Plowman get hatchet, or whip to the skrene,*
> *Maids loseth their cocke, if no water be seen.*
>
> Traditional verse, quoted in Thomas Tusser's *Five Hundred Points of Good Husbandry* (1573)

The explanation is as follows:

Plough Monday puts them in mind of their business. In the morning the men and the maid servants strive who shall show their diligence in rising earliest. If the ploughman can get his whip, his plough-staff, hatchet, or anything that he wants in the field, by the fire-side, before the maid hath got her kettle on, then the maid loseth her Shrove-tide cock, and it wholly belongs to the men.

Daniel Hilman, *Tusser Redivivus* (1710)

SPRING

Spring was the time of renewal, of rising energy and, of course, of love, especially the Monday and Tuesday following the second Sunday after Easter, known as Hock-tide. On the Monday, men would 'capture' women and only release them on payment of a kiss. The next day the women would have their revenge:

On this day it was the custom for the women to go out into the streets and roads with cords, and stop and bind all those of the other sex they met, holding them till they purchased their release by a small contribution of money ... The custom may be traced, by its name at least, as far back as the thirteenth century, and appears to have prevailed in all parts of England.

Robert Chambers, *Book of Days* (1869)

The big 'spring-cleaning' festival was known as Beltane, when all the old floor coverings and bedding would be dragged outside and burnt on bonfires. (Before carpets, floors were simply strewn with straw or rushes and possibly some nice-smelling herbs, too.) Beltane dates from at least Roman times because Julius Caesar described it, but it probably goes back much earlier than that. A dark side of the festival is that it may originally have involved human sacrifice. Later, the sacrifice became symbolic – a special Beltane cake would be baked and the person who received the part known as the carline would be treated as if dead for the rest of the evening.

SUMMER

Festivities to celebrate Midsummer's Day, technically 21 June, go back thousands of years. The evidence is in the alignment of numerous stone circles, the most famous of which is Stonehenge, dating from 3100 BC.

When Christianity was adopted, however, the festival became St John's eve and day, commemorating the birth of St John the Baptist, and was held instead on the 23rd and 24th. But its origins as a Celtic fire festival were not forgotten:

... this wheel was taken up to the top of a mountain and rolled down from thence; and that, as it had previously been covered with straw, twisted about it and set on fire, it appeared at a distance as if the sun had been falling from the sky.

John Brand, *Popular Antiquities* (1777)

Most people on St John's eve, however, contented themselves with the traditional bonfire, the more daring men and boys jumping through the flames. Apparently there was a belief that the highest jump would be the height of that year's harvest.

St John's eve was also thought to be a time, like Hallowe'en, when the spirit world touched the everyday world, as reflected by the strange and colourful events in Shakespeare's *A Midsummer Night's Dream*. Indeed, you could become a bard yourself if you spent the night at a sacred site – but at the risk of being taken away by the fairies.

Druids celebrating the summer solstice at Stonehenge
© *Robert Harding Picture Library Ltd / Alamy*

AUTUMN

When all produce was local, the success of harvest season (known as the 'ingathering' or the 'harvest-home' in the south of England, the 'mell-supper' in the north, and the 'kirn' in Scotland) was vital. Everyone looked forward to it but the work could be hard and monotonous and the labourers therefore invented various ways to make it more amusing:

In Buckinghamshire and other counties, 'a lady' was elected as well as 'a lord', which often added much merriment to the harvest-season. For, while the lady was to receive all honours due to the lord from the rest of the labourers, he (for the lady was one of the workmen) was required to pass it on to the lord. For instance, at drinking-time, the vassals were to give the horn first to the lady, who passed it to the lord, and when he had drunk, she drank next, and then the others indiscriminately. Every departure from this rule incurred a fine. The blunders which led to fines, of course, were frequent, and produced great merriment.

Robert Chambers, *Book of Days* (1869)

The custom of ducking for apples on Hallowe'en, the night of 31 October, when spirits 'walk abroad', is well known. In some areas it was also called Nutcrack Night:

It is a custom in Ireland, when the young women would know if their lovers are faithful, to put three nuts upon the bars of the grate, naming the nuts after the lovers. If a nut cracks or jumps, the lover will prove unfaithful; if it begins to blaze or burn, he has a regard for the person making the trial. If the nuts named after the girl and her lover burn together, they will be married.

John Brand, *Popular Antiquities* (1777)

WINTER

In the old Celtic calendar, the last day of October wasn't autumn, but the first day of winter and known as Samhain. Animals not for breeding were slaughtered and their meat salted and stored, while the others were mated. It was also a fertility festival for people – on the eve of Samhain in Irish mythology the god Dhaghda made love to Morrigan as she straddled the river Unius, symbolizing the transition from light to darkness. Later, winter was considered to begin on 11 November, known as Martinmas or St Martin's Day after a Roman soldier who was baptized as an adult and became a monk. From the late 4th century until the late Middle Ages St Martin's eve was a night of hearty eating and drinking because it was followed by 40 days of fasting.

The tradition of kissing under the mistletoe when it bears fruit around the time of the winter solstice goes back to a Scandinavian legend of Frigga, the goddess of love, marriage and destiny. Baldur, her son, was killed by a dart made with poison from mistletoe and it was Frigga's tears that formed the milky white berries. Baldur was then magically restored to life and Frigga, in gratitude, exhorted everyone to make peace and kiss beneath the 'plant of love'. The poison – diluted – was used as a medicine by the Celts and the plant was also believed to protect buildings from fire and lightning. The other 'winter plant', of course, is the holly, significant to the Romans as part of their *Saturnalia* festival, the Celts, and later Christians, for its cheery red berries:

> *So now is come our joyful feast;*
> *Let every man be jolly;*
> *Each room with ivy leaves is drest.*
> *And every post with holly.*
>
> George Wither, poet (17th century)

In the mid-19th century, winters were much colder than now. On one Sunday in January 1861, tens of thousands of people were recorded as skating on the ponds in the London parks and at night there were 'torches being used to illuminate the scene, which was one of the greatest animation and gaiety', according to a contemporary report. With global warming, we're unlikely to see such scenes again.

Celebrating a Traditional Christmas

THE FIRST CHRISTMAS

The day officially chosen by Pope Julius I in 350 to celebrate the birth of Christ was 25 December. Although Jesus was probably born in early autumn, it was thought it would be more popular to opt for a time that coincided with the Roman feast for Saturn, their god of agriculture, and the pagan Yule feast which honoured the birth of Mithras, the sun god. The first actual celebration of a church mass for Christmas – then known as Christ's Mass – was probably in Germany around the middle of the 16th century.

CHRISTMAS TRADITIONS

Happy, happy Christmas that can win us back to the delusions of our childish days.

Charles Dickens, *Pickwick Papers* (1836)

Christmas trees

The first public Christmas celebration involving a tree seems to have been in Riga, Latvia, in 1510. Not many details are known except that the event was attended by men wearing black hats and that the tree was ceremoniously burned afterwards. But, privately, evergreen trees had often been brought into homes in winter as a symbol of hope, and the Druids, whose ceremonies date from pre-Christian times, used trees as religious totems. The Christmas tree only became popular in Britain after

Prince Albert, the German-born husband of Queen Victoria, established it at Windsor Castle in 1841.

Father Christmas

Father Christmas really existed. He was Saint Nicholas, the Archbishop of Myra (near Anatolia in present-day Turkey) during the 4th century AD. But, beyond that, separating fact from fiction is difficult. According to legend, he hailed from a wealthy family, but distributed his riches to the poor. There is a story that he climbed on the roof of a house to drop a purse of money down the chimney and that it landed in a stocking hanging by the fire to dry – the source of the well-known tradition. As to the title 'Santa Claus', it comes from the Dutch *Sinterklaas*, itself a corruption of Saint Nicholas, and for many north Europeans he comes on 6 December, riding a white horse. Exactly how the British came to believe that Santa Claus lived at the north pole and drove reindeer is uncertain, because the Dutch are quite sure that *Sinterklaas* now lives in Spain.

Christmas pudding

This traditional dish can be traced back to the early 14th century when it was known as *frumenty* and had a porridge-like consistency. It seems to have been almost a meal in itself, the ingredients including beef, mutton, raisins, currants, prunes, alcohol and spices. Because it was so rich the Puritans banned it along with Christmas itself and it only again became a Christmas dish for polite society after its endorsement by King George I in 1714.

Oh! All that steam! Oh! That smell! Thirty seconds later Mrs Cratchit entered, her face crimson, but smiling proudly. With the pudding resembling a cannon ball, all speckled, very firm, sprinkled with brandy in flames and decorated with a sprig of holly stuck in the centre. Oh! The marvellous pudding!

Charles Dickens, *A Christmas Carol* (1843)

Carols

A *carole* was an Old French word for a circle dance but accompanied by singers. By the mid-12th century carols were popular dance songs and by the 14th century had become standards during processions. However, the British tradition goes back much further, possibly even to pre-Christian times, in what came to be known as *wassailing*, from the Anglo-Saxon toast *waes hael* or 'be thou hale'. Wassailing was particularly popular in the 16th and 17th centuries when peasants and employees would call on their masters, sing carols, and be given a *wassail* – a spiced alcoholic drink made of ale or cider. It was important that these rounds should not be seen as begging but rather as Christmas good cheer and the words of the Wassailer's Carol reflect this:

> *We are not daily beggars*
> *That beg from door to door;*
> *But we are neighbours' children*
> *Whom you have seen before.*

Boxing Day

Like so many other traditions, the concept of Boxing Day probably goes back to pre-Christian Rome, where gifts were given for the festival of the Saturnalia. Early Christian leaders seem to have denounced the custom for its pagan origins but eventually the Church embraced the practice so that by the 12th century, churches would open their collection or *alms* boxes and give gifts to the poor of the parish. From there the idea spread, rather feeding on itself, and certainly not to everyone's satisfaction:

Wassailers receiving a wassail bowl
© *Mary Evans Picture Library*

This custom of Christmas-boxes ... was formerly, and even yet to a certain extent continues to be, a great nuisance. The journeymen and apprentices of trades-people were wont to levy regular contributions from their masters' customers, who, in addition, were mulcted by the trades-people in the form of augmented charges in the bills, to recompense the latter for gratuities expected from them by the customers' servants.

Robert Chambers, *Book of Days* (1869)

THE LAST CHRISTMAS

For almost 20 years of the 17th century, Christmas was actually banned in Britain. By that time it had grown into a boisterous 12-day festival for which normal shops and businesses closed and only ale houses and taverns flourished. That all changed from around 1644, as the Puritans tightened their grip on the country. In some areas, especially central London, troops patrolled to enforce the new law and anybody found celebrating – by, for example, buying, making or eating anything that resembled a Christmas feast – risked a fine or imprisonment. According to one Puritan social reformer:

More mischief is that time committed than in all the year besides ...
What dicing and carding, what eating and drinking, what banqueting and feasting is
then used ...
To the great dishonour of God and the impoverishing of the reign.

> Philip Stubbes, *The Anatomy of Abuses* (1583)

For better or worse, Christmas was restored in 1661 under Charles II.

Letter Writing

TRIFLES AND NEGLIGENCES

'Letters' probably existed long before writing. Native Americans, for example, had messengers specially trained in both memory and running, as Hernan Cortez discovered soon after landing at Chianiztlan in 1519. Within 24 hours the Aztec ruler Montezuma had full details 260 miles away.

Nevertheless, the ability to convey ideas, not just to those within earshot but to many people far away, through written documents was an advance comparable to the invention of the wheel.

It has been estimated that, before the era of the email, the average person would have written around 18,000 letters in a lifetime. But some people have been hugely prolific. More than 11,000 of the letters of the novelist E M Forster survive, as do tens of thousands of those of the playwright George Bernard Shaw. Virginia Woolf's published letters run to six volumes and those of D H Lawrence to seven. The record, perhaps, goes to the novelist Horace Walpole 4th Earl of Oxford (1717–97), whose letters fill almost 50 volumes.

Walpole nevertheless felt that women were better letter-writers than men, paying them a somewhat backhanded compliment. 'Our sex is too jealous of the reputation of good sense,' he wrote, 'to condescend to hazard a thousand trifles and negligences, which give grace, ease, and familiarity to correspondence.'

ADVICE ON LETTER WRITING

No sooner than there were letters it seems there were manuals on how to write them, and high expectations of the standards required of both letters and their authors.

It is felt that the public have a right to expect a Letter Writer up to date, practical, sensible, and concise, written in a style suitable for everyday correspondence; and not in the stilted, and verbose language, common to the Letter Writer of thirty years ago.
'A Member of the Aristocracy', *The Correct Guide to Letter Writing*
(1910 edition)

Indeed, by the 20th century, the giving of advice had become a whole industry:

A 'sloppy' letter with the writing all pouring into one corner of the page, badly worded, badly spelled, and with unmatched paper and envelope – even possibly a blot – proclaims the sort of person who would have unkempt hair, unclean linen and broken shoe laces. ... if a young man wishes to choose a wife in whose daily life he is sure always to find the unfinished task, the untidy mind and the syncopated housekeeping, he may do it quite simply by selecting her from her letters.
Emily Post, *Etiquette in Society, in Business, in Politics and at Home* (1922)

But modern letter writing is nothing compared to the complication of just beginning a letter in ancient times. 'To my Lady, the most reverend and divinely favoured deaconess Olympias, I John, Bishop, send greeting in the Lord' was how St John Chrysostom wrote from 4th-century Constantinople. Nor was it enough to finish a letter with a mere signature; it was necessary to record exactly where the writer was, as in this example by a famous poet:

Written on the thirty-first day of March in the confines of Tuscany from beneath the springs of Arno, in the first year of the most auspicious passage of the Emperor Henry into Italy.
Dante Alighieri, *Letter to the Florentines* (1311)

All through the Middle Ages, even personal family letters could be surprisingly formal:

*Right worshipful and my most entirely beloved mother, in the most lowly manner
I recommend me unto your good motherhood, beseeching you daily and nightly of
your motherly blessing, ever more desiring to hear of your welfare and prosperity, the
which I pray God to continue to your heart's desire ...*

Elizabeth Poynings, *Letter to her mother Agnes Paston* (1459)

Samuel Richardson, the author of *Pamela* and *Clarissa*, also joined the
advice industry with a book 'directing the requisite style and forms to be
observed in writing familiar letters'. However, it was somewhat tongue-
in-cheek, as in this template for a gentleman who 'resents his mistress's
fondness of a monkey':

*But while I am dying beneath your frowns, how can you be profuse in your
caresses to so mean a competitor? Condescend to view us in the same light. What
valuable qualification is Mr Pug endowed with, which I am destitute of? Is it a
recommendation in him that he wears no breeches? For my part, I will most willingly
surrender mine at your feet.*

Samuel Richardson, *Letters Written to and for Particular Friends* (1741)

ROMANTIC LETTERS

That love letters may be read by others, either at the time or years later,
is a danger for which one early 20th-century book of etiquette had this
remedy: 'Of course the best advice to a young girl who is impelled to write
letters to men, can be put in one word, *don't!*' As for men writing love
letters:

*One of the fundamental rules for the behavior of any man who has the faintest
pretension to being a gentleman, is that ... he never, therefore, writes a letter that can
be construed, even by a lawyer, as damaging to any woman's good name. ... there
must be no hint of his having received especial favors from her.*

Emily Post, *Etiquette in Society, in Business, in Politics and at Home* (1922)

Careful lovers, therefore, were recommended to use a sort of code. 'We all
missed you at the picnic' was about as strong an intimation of attraction
as was prudent in the Victorian era. Other manuals of letter-writing style,
however, were not so hesitant:

From a Gentleman to a Lady he has seen but Twice.
I am afraid you will accuse me of acting upon impulse only, from my venturing to write to you on so short an acquaintance, but were I to wait for months it would make no difference in my feelings towards you. I have met you, it is true, but twice, and my declaration of affection may perhaps appear precipitate in your eyes, but will you not make allowances for this in consideration of the true and lasting feeling of regard with which you have inspired me? I am convinced I shall never love anyone but you ...

'A Member of the Aristocracy', *The Correct Guide to Letter Writing*
(1910 edition)

The Irish writer James Joyce sent his partner, Nora, very clear instructions on how love letters should be composed while he was temporarily in Dublin in 1909 and she was left behind in Trieste where the couple were living. Make the letters long and full of the smallest personal details, he begged, of things that are 'obscene and secret and filthy'. Nora evidently obliged but, unfortunately, her letters have been lost. Joyce's letters to her have, however, survived and, as Emily Post feared, they did eventually become public.

Penny Black and 2d Blue, 1840
© *Antiques & Collectables / Alamy*

They could be seen as a foretaste of his most famous novel *Ulysses* which was published in 1922 in Paris but banned in both the USA and Britain for obscenity – and, at first, even Nora wouldn't read it.

DELIVERY

If you wanted a letter delivered throughout most of history you would have had to make your own arrangements. In Britain, the postal service began when King Henry I (1068–1135) appointed special messengers to deliver government letters, but it wasn't until 1635 that the Royal Mail became available to the general public. It's worth reflecting that in the 17th century a letter 'posted' in London in the morning might be delivered to another

London address within hours, a much better service than today's. It was normally the recipient who had to pay by the page and as a result of that the sender would strive to make the letter as entertaining, informative and densely written as possible. Rowland Hill (1795–1879) convinced Parliament that adopting a flat rate of prepayment would be a good idea and thus in 1840 the Penny Black became the world's first proper postage stamp.

PERSONALIZING YOUR OWN LETTERS

From early times, letters have been sealed with wax. Wax is still on sale and you can even commission a seal to create your own design in it.

As a further refinement you might like to use scented ink. Put about 100 drops of an essential oil such as rose or lavender into a teaspoon of vodka and add slowly to around 50 millilitres of ink.

Writing by Hand

THE INVENTION OF WRITING

According to legend, the Egyptian god Thoth was the inventor of writing, claiming it would improve people's memories and make them wiser. But the Egyptian king at the time, Thamus, was not convinced:

The fact is that this invention will produce forgetfulness in the souls of those who have learned it because they will not need to exercise their memories ... And as for wisdom, you're equipping your pupils with only a semblance of it, not with truth.

Plato, *Phaedrus* (360 BC)

In reality, Egypt was, indeed, the birthplace of writing as we know it in the West. By 2700 BC the Egyptians had a set of 22 hieroglyphs for consonants and a 23rd for vowels, descended from stone-carved symbols that had been in use in the Middle East as much as 5,000 years earlier. The 'Prisse Papyrus' is the earliest surviving example of writing on papyrus, dating from around 2000 BC. It has been called 'the world's oldest book' and includes advice from a man known as Ptah-Hotep:

Let thy mind be deep and thy speech scanty.

Ptah-Hotep, *Prisse Papyrus* (c.2000 BC)

All, or nearly all, world alphabets are descendants of the Egyptian. It led to the Greek alphabet, which emerged about 400 BC, and which, in turn, led to every other European alphabet. The ancient Greeks could also be said to be the inventors of the notebook, using a stylus made of bone or metal to make marks on wax-coated tablets. As a refinement, the tablets were made as hinged pairs which, like a modern notebook, could be closed to protect the contents.

When it came to ink, however, the Chinese were probably the first in that field almost 5,000 years ago, mixing soot with oil and gelatine from animal hides, with which to black the surface of stone-carved hieroglyphs. The Chinese also invented wood-fibre paper in AD 105, but it didn't reach Europe until the 8th century and wasn't in widespread use until the 14th century.

X MARKS THE SPOT

Until the industrial revolution, writing materials were extremely expensive in Britain and it was this, as much as educational factors, that restricted literacy. Even in 1841, a third of men and almost half of women in England signed their marriage certificates with marks as a substitute for a signature, for example an X.

HANDWRITING ANALYSIS

The idea that a person's handwriting reveals a great deal about character is almost as old as handwriting itself. Some 2,500 years ago, the Chinese sage Confucius observed that: 'Handwriting can infallibly show whether it comes from a person who is noble-minded or from one who is vulgar'. And a century or so later, Aristotle wrote that: 'Just as all men do not have the same speech sounds, neither do they all have the same writing'.

The first book on the subject was written in the 17th century by an Italian doctor:

It is obvious that all persons write in their own peculiar way. Characteristic forms ... cannot be truly imitated by anybody else.
Camillo Baldi, *A Method to Recognize the Nature and Quality of a Writer from his Letters* (1622)

But it wasn't until the French priest and archaeologist Jean-Hippolyte Michon (1806–81) that anybody made a thorough and systematic study. Michon gave this new 'science' the name 'graphology':

As I write these lines quickly ... it is impossible for me to think of disguising my handwriting in any way ... I cannot but produce this tormented script ... in which my letters slope sometimes this way, sometimes the other, sometimes even in the same word.

Jean-Hippolyte Michon, *A System of Graphology/Practical Graphology*
(1875)

Some of Michon's ideas have since been discredited but many of the principles he described are still in use today.

MAKING YOUR OWN ANALYSIS

Although sceptics say there's little scientific basis to graphology, others argue that something as personal and immediate as handwriting must be revealing of character as well as state of mind at the time. Here are some of the more widely-believed principles.

Legibility

A person who makes an effort to write clearly has confidence in the subject. On the other hand, a person who writes illegibly may feel guilty, nervous, unsure, inferior or, simply, agitated.

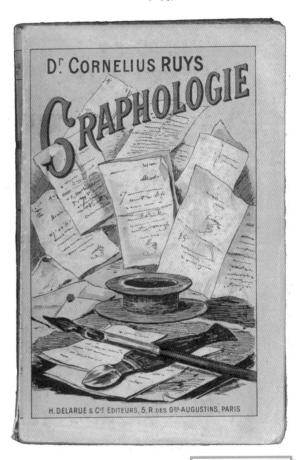

French manual on the study of handwriting
© Mary Evans Picture
Library / Alamy

Zones

Handwriting is divided into three zones. The upper zone (the tops of hs, ts and so on) is said to be related to intellect, imagination, fantasies and religious outlook. The middle zone (all of as, es and so on) is believed to be linked to emotion. The lower zone (the tails of ys, gs and so on) is the unconscious.

If projections into the upper zone are limited then the writer is considered to be materialistic, whereas very high projections suggest a vivid imagination and a dominant intellectual life.

A middle zone of approximately three millimetres suggests a well-balanced personality. A much larger size indicates egotism, whereas a smaller middle zone implies modesty.

The lower zone can be especially revealing. If it's dominant it suggests vigour, athleticism and a strong sex drive. A stunted lower zone, by contrast, is said to show sexual repression.

Slant

People who are self-absorbed, sensitive and undemonstrative are said to have writing that slants to the left. An extreme slant would suggest a fear of meeting people. Handwriting that slants to the right, by contrast, is the hallmark of the extrovert. An extreme right slant implies impulsive and even reckless behaviour. Writing that is more or less upright is associated with people who are charming but restrained and even aloof.

Slope

Lines of writing that slope up to the right suggest enthusiasm, optimism and determination. Lines that slope downwards indicate tiredness or even depression. Lines that are consistently horizontal imply persistence and reliability. Note, however, that when horizontal lines waver up and down the writer may be expressing excitability.

THE FUTURE OF HANDWRITING

Will handwriting survive? Nobody can answer that for sure. But with the range of alternatives expanding and improving all the time – keyboards, voicemail, texting and so on – it's quite possible that handwriting may become as redundant as the stone hieroglyph.

Household

Living Thriftily

MR MICAWBER

Probably the most famous piece of advice about thrifty living comes from the character Mr Micawber in Charles Dickens's novel *David Copperfield*. Mr Micawber was inspired by Dickens's own father who was sent to debtors' prison:

Annual income twenty pounds, annual expenditure nineteen six, result happiness. Annual income twenty pounds, annual expenditure twenty pounds ought and six, result misery.

Charles Dickens, *David Copperfield* (1850)

Genteel thrift was one thing in earlier times but poverty was quite another. Until the end of the Victorian era and beyond, it was generally believed that the poor were entirely responsible for their situation:

Vagabonds, idle and suspected persons shall be set in the stocks for three days and three nights and have none other sustenance but bread and water and then shall be put out of Town.

Vagabonds and Beggars Act (1494)

There were a few, however, who saw poverty as character-forming and, therefore, a good thing, provided it didn't go on too long.

If there is anything in the world that a young man should be more grateful for than another, it is the poverty which necessitates starting life under very great

disadvantages ... A young man who cannot stand this test is not good for anything.
Timothy Titcomb, *Titcomb's Letters To Young People* (1861)

LASH NOT OUT TOO LASHINGLY

In the 16th century, an English poet-farmer set out his 'Ladder To Thrift'. Altogether, there were 37 'rungs' of which the first six went like this:

1. *To take thy calling thankfully, And shun the path to beggary.*
2. *To grudge in youth no drudgery, To come by knowledge perfectly.*
3. *To count no travel slavery, That brings in penny saverly.*
4. *To follow profit, earnestly, But meddle not with pilfery.*
5. *To get by honest practisy, And keep they gettings covertly.*
6. *To lash not out, too lashingly, For fear of pinching penury.*

Thomas Tusser, *Five Hundred Points of Good Husbandry* (1557)

Here, then, is advice, both past and present, on how to avoid lashing out too lashingly.

General purchases

The first step is to follow Mr Micawber's advice and keep expenditure below income by working out a budget. Don't buy things that you don't actually need. If you need them, try to pool resources with friends and neighbours – for example, rather than each buying a lawnmower that is idle most of the time, buy one as a group and share it. Or try barter (see www.ukfreecycle.org or www.u-exchange.com). Or hire. In Victorian times, the poor even used to rent umbrellas.

Food

Prepare meals from fresh ingredients. Buy in bulk and freeze when appropriate. Buy direct from farmers. Grow your own if you have a garden (to swap seeds see www.seedysunday.org). If you don't have a garden, there are schemes under which you can 'borrow' someone else's (see www.totnes.transitionnetwork.org). Here's one solution:

... it becomes the duty of every woman who has the responsibility of providing food for a family, to avoid a variety of tempting dishes. It is a much safer rule, to have only one kind of healthy food, for each meal.

Catharine Esther Beecher and Harriet Beecher Stowe, *Principles of Domestic Science* (1869)

Clothing

In real terms, clothes are generally cheaper than ever before. In the 18th century, the better-off purchased fabrics and then took them to tailors to be made up. Later, the tailors supplied the fabrics, which aroused a certain suspicion and, as to ready-to-wear, that was beyond contemplation:

Some acquaintance with the manufacturer's qualities and prices of materials may form some check on exorbitant charges ... where fashionable dress-makers are employed, there is likewise some reason for looking into the details of their accounts ...

A still cheaper way is to purchase ready-made in the shops; but this is one of the worst modes, as there is often some kind of imposition practised, besides the great uncertainty of finding clothes that fit well.

Thomas Webster and Mrs William Parkes, *An Encyclopaedia of Domestic Economy* (1844)

Today, the inexpensive and increasingly trendy way to find clothing is to swap (see www.swishing.org.uk, www.whatsmineisyours.com or www.bigwardrobe.com).

Credit

Don't borrow money by credit card. Try to pay off your balance from income; if you can't, enquire about cheaper sources of finance.

Energy

The cost and availability of energy is not a modern concern, which makes it all the more extraordinary that it has taken so long to develop alternatives to fossil fuels:

Peat is … a vegetable substance taken in blocks from marshes … It is a slow-burning fuel which is cheap in its own locality … Economy of fuel is a world problem, for it is evident that the coal supply will be exhausted in course of time, and this is also true of coal oil or petroleum.

Anna Maria Cooley, Foods and Household Management (1914)

Modern advice includes: use energy-efficient light bulbs; turn off lights that aren't needed; don't leave appliances on stand-by; don't heat unused rooms; consider turning down the thermostat; wash clothes at a lower temperature, or even in cold water; dry clothes on a washing line, not in a drier.

Cycling to work
© Eric Nathan / Alamy

Transport

Don't drive when you don't need to – walk or cycle; don't have empty seats in your car but share lifts instead (see www.liftshare.com).

The law

Mrs Beeton was not much bothered by concerns over thrift, having married a wealthy publisher, Samuel Beeton, in 1856. But, even so, she felt the need to warn against the costly perils of the legal system:

… those learned in the law, when they do give advice without the usual fee, and in the confidence of friendship, generally say, 'Pay, pay anything rather than go to law;' while those having experience in the courts of Themis have a wholesome dread of its pitfalls.

Mrs Isabella Beeton, Beeton's Book of Household Management (1861)

She also had advice for men contemplating the expensive business of falling in love. 'A husband', she cautioned, 'is liable for his wife's debts contracted before marriage.'

Laying a Fire

FIRE LIGHTING

Before the widespread use of central heating, the ability to light a fire, quickly and efficiently, was a necessary part of daily life. Whether starting a fire in your wood-burning stove, or in a small grate designed for coal, the same first principle applies. The chimney must be free from obstruction – it should be swept at least once a year, or more depending on your choice of fuel and the frequency of your fires – otherwise you will, at best, end with a smoky room and a fire that puts itself out, or, at worst, you will set your chimney on fire.

LAYING A GOOD FIRE

Fire-lighting, however simple, is an operation requiring some skill; a fire is readily made by laying a few cinders at the bottom in open order; over this a few pieces of paper, and over that again eight or ten pieces of dry wood; over the wood, a course of moderate-sized pieces of coal, taking care to leave hollow spaces between for air at the centre; and taking care to lay the whole well back in the grate, so that the smoke may go up the chimney, and not into the room. This done, fire the paper with a match from below, and, if properly laid, it will soon burn up; the stream of flame from the wood and paper soon communicating to the coals and cinders, provided there is plenty of air at the centre.

Mrs Isabella Beeton, *Beeton's Book of Household Management* (1861)

When lighting a fire, the first task is, if necessary, to clear out the ashes

Stages in laying a fire
© Kate McLelland

from any previous fires (if your ash pan is too full, the fire will not draw – ie not enough air will circulate – and it will not be a success). Then remember to open the damper, if one is present, as this again will improve the draught, making the fire draw better and giving your fire-lighting activities a happier outcome. If you have some old newspaper to hand, place some very lightly scrunched balls of this in the bottom of the grate. On top of this, add some good kindling (small sticks either cut for the job or collected from the ground and allowed to 'season', or dry). Place the kindling in two layers, with the sticks in the second layer criss-crossing those in the first. On top of the kindling, add some coal, or fairly small logs – then light the paper. If the fire doesn't catch, you can increase its chances by increasing the amount of air that is getting to it, either using bellows, or by holding an open newspaper across the mouth of the fireplace (but beware, when it works the newspaper will catch fire too, so be ready to put it into the fire before it goes up in flames).

POKER LORE

If a fire does not burn well, and you want to 'draw it up', you should set the poker across the hearth, with the fore part leaning across the top bar of the grate, and you will have a good fire—if you wait long enough; but you must not be unreasonable, and refuse to give time for the charm to work. For a charm it is, the poker and top bar combined, forming a cross, and so defeating the malice of the gnomes, who are jealous of our possession of their subterranean treasures; or else of the witches and demons, who preside over smoky chimneys. I had seen the thing done scores of times; and understanding that it was supposed to create a draught, like a poor weak rationalist as I was, I once thought to improve the matter by setting up the shovel instead of the poker; but I might as well have left it alone—the fire wasn't to be taken in, or the witches balked, by such a shallow contrivance, and I was left in the cold.

Robert Chambers, *Book of Days* (1869)

The custom of leaving a poker across the grate, as described above, was apparently quite common from the 18th century onwards. If you happen to be in a stranger's house and you decide to place the poker so that it leans across the top bar of the grate, remember that you must not be tempted to poke the blaze first:

You mustn't poke your neighbour's fire until you have known him seven years or been drunk with him three times.

Notes & Queries (Volume 174, Number 8, 1938)

PATENT
"WELLSTOOD" RANGES.
Indispensable for High-class Cooking.

No other Cooking Range is so perfectly constructed for **Saving Labour,** for **Ensuring Cleanliness,** or for **General Utility,** and **no other** range will do so much work with as **Little Fuel** as the "Wellstood." All the flues are in iron, and are controlled by **Automatic Indicating Dampers.** With both hands holding a dish, the **Pedal** enables the oven door to be opened with a slight pressure of the foot. No heat escapes from the oven, as the doors are **Packed** and lined with **Pure White Enamel.** The **"Hot Blast" Ventilators** allow the oven to be ventilated without risk of spoiling the most delicate dishes.

All **"Wellstood"** Ranges have **Open or Close Fires** and **Improved Rising Bottom Grates.**

PATENT "WELLSTOOD" RANGES are made in sizes and styles to suit all requirements.

Cooking with a Range

FIRE CHAMBERS

Although the Chinese had closed clay stoves more than 2,000 years ago, the English cooked on open wood fires until the 16th century and beyond. The brick-built fire chamber, enclosing the wood on three sides, was the first attempt to reduce the danger and improve efficiency, but it was not until the French 'Castrol stove' in 1735 that Europe had its first fully enclosed range. But even in the middle of the 19th century the 'range' at the City of London Club House in Broad Street was still an open bank of fires in front of which meat was impaled on spits. There was then the problem of turning the meat to make sure it cooked evenly:

The common wind-up kitchen jack is ... a barrel, round which is coiled a line of considerable length, and having one end fastened to a compound pulley, containing three or four sheaves, to which is appended a weight, which, by descending slowly, moves the barrel round with the proper velocity ... When the weight has descended as far as it can, it is again wound up by a handle ...

Thomas Webster and Mrs William Parkes, *Encyclopaedia of Domestic Economy* (1844)

An alternative method was that 'poor boys did turn the spits, and licked the dripping-pan, and grew to be lusty knaves'.

The quintessential range, the Aga, was devised by Swede Gustaf Dalén in 1922 as a labour-saving device that could not only cook but simultaneously heat the house, dry washing, heat water and even press clothes. The first imports arrived in England in 1929.

167

CONSTANT HEAT

The heat produced by an old-fashioned open range could be considerable and it was usual to place a kind of screen in front of it, to reflect the heat back and to keep the rest of the kitchen at a reasonable temperature. Lined with 'tin plate' these screens often had shelves to keep plates warm.

The closed range made life in the kitchen more comfortable but many people thought it came at the expense of taste. 'Every nice palate can distinguish between meat baked in a common oven, and that which has been roasted before an open fire,' observed one 19th-century cookery writer. The solution was what was known as the 'Rumford roaster':

… a method of dressing meat … by which it could be roasted quite as well as is usually done before a large open fire … by shutting it up in an apparatus somewhat resembling an oven … no one could distinguish between a joint properly cooked in this machine, and one done before a fire.

Thomas Webster and Mrs William Parkes, *Encyclopaedia of Domestic Economy* (1844)

LIFE ON THE RANGE TODAY

The rule with the modern cooking range is that you don't so much set the heat as *find* it. That is to say, there are different temperatures in the different parts of the various ovens. Here are some tips for an Aga and similar ranges:

The temperature of the Roasting Oven is approximately 240–260°C (475–500°F). There is a significant difference in temperature between the top and the bottom of the oven.
Grill at the very top of the Roasting Oven.
Oven fry on the floor of the Roasting Oven to minimize splashes.
Start dishes in the Roasting Oven to get them hot then move them to the Simmering Oven.
You can slow cook things overnight in the Simmering Oven.
Use the Simmering Plate as a griddle.

If uncertain, cook on the grid shelf on the floor of the Roasting Oven and, if the item starts to brown too quickly, shield it using the cold plain shelf.

Choosing Produce

FOOD POISONING

Food may or may not have tasted better in earlier times, but it almost certainly caused more cases of poisoning than today. A sample of Victorian ice cream examined by the London County Council medical officer was found to contain lice, bedbugs, fleas, straw, the hair from humans, cats and dogs and various bacteria. The Privy Council in 1862 estimated that one-fifth of meat in England and Wales came from animals that were diseased. And food was often adulterated with dangerous chemicals, such as strychnine in rum and beer, sulphate of copper in various preserves, lead chromate in mustard, sulphate of iron in tea, bisulphate of mercury and Venetian lead in confectionery, and lead in wine. As for bread, the pioneering health investigator Dr Arthur Hassall found that in 1872 half contained alum, which was used in dyeing. By then, almost nobody baked bread at home – that's a romantic myth.

The average housewife in Victorian times or earlier was probably blissfully unaware of most of this, especially as the connection between acute gastric illness and a specific organism was not made until the 1880s. But in that era before commercial refrigeration, cheap domestic refrigerators, and artificial preservatives, freshness was nevertheless paramount and many housewives would go food shopping every day. Just from the point of view of taste it was essential to know what was fresh and what was old.

IN ITS PRIME

Most foods contain enzymes, natural chemicals and micro-organisms that cause them to deteriorate. Below are details of how well-informed Victorians judged what was in its prime and what was not (advice that is still sound today).

Meat

Beef. The test was to press the meat with a finger. If it quickly recovered its shape it was considered good, but if the dent lingered the meat was inferior.

Veal. The Victorians wanted a delicate white. However, Thomas Webster in his *Encyclopaedia of Domestic Economy* (1844) reported that, 'Butchers, it is said, bleed calves purposely before killing them, with a view to make the flesh white; but this also makes it dry and flavourless.'

Mutton was considered to be in its prime when the animal was about five years old. The way to tell was to pinch the meat. If the animal was too young it felt tender, but if it was too old the meat would wrinkle.

Pork. The rind should feel cool. If, however, it was flaccid and clammy, that suggested the animal had been dead too long.

Bacon. The Victorians wanted a thin rind with the fat tinged red.

Ham. The test was to plunge a knife in as far as the bone. If, on withdrawing, there was an unpleasant smell or particles of meat adhering to the blade, it was considered that the ham had not been properly cured.

Venison. The Victorians liked the fat to be thick, clear and bright.

Poultry. The eyes should be clear and the feet moist. A greenish discoloration above the vent was a sign that the bird had been dead too long. For geese, the bills and feet should be yellow.

Fish

Flat fish. The eyes should be clear and bright and the underside a rich cream colour – a bluish-white was a sign that the fish wasn't fresh.

Salmon:

The flavour and excellence of this fish depends upon its freshness and the shortness of the time since it was caught; for no method can completely preserve the delicate flavour it has when just taken out of the water. A great deal of what is brought to London has been packed in ice, and comes from the Scotch and Irish rivers, and, though quite fresh, is not quite equal to Thames salmon.

Thomas Webster and Mrs William Parkes, *An Encyclopaedia of Domestic Economy* (1844)

By the time that was written, in fact, salmon had all but disappeared from the Thames and it was only in 2007 that attempts were made to reintroduce them.

Fruit and vegetables

Avocados. Cradle the fruit in your hand and squeeze. If it yields, it is ready for eating. An avocado that is hard can be ripened more quickly by putting it in a brown paper bag with an apple.

Leafy vegetables. Avoid those that are limp or pale.

Melons. All melons, irrespective of variety, should feel heavy for their size. The best indicator that a melon is ripe is a lovely, sweet aroma.

Peaches don't ripen well off the tree so it's important to buy them at their best. The background colour should be cream to gold – green means the fruit isn't ripe.

Pears, unlike peaches, ripen best *off* the tree. Just keep them in a fruit bowl until the stem end yields slightly when you press.

Pineapples. Colour is no longer an indicator of ripeness because there are now varieties ranging from green to gold. Instead, go by smell. A sweet pineappley aroma means the pineapple is ready. If there's no perfume, the pineapple isn't ripe. If the smell is unpleasant the pineapple is past its best – and will probably feel soft in places.

Pod and root vegetables. Choose those that are slightly smaller than average.

These are the main harvesting times for vegetables grown out of doors in Britain:

Smelling a melon is the best way to check if it is ripe
© *UpperCut Images / Alamy*

Artichokes (globe): July–September
Asparagus: May
Beans (runner): August–September
Beetroot: June–September
Broccoli (purple): February–April
Broccoli (green): August–September
Brussels sprouts: October–February
Cabbage: April–October
Carrots: July–October
Cauliflower: March–November
Celery: September–February
Cucumber: August–September
Leek: October–April
Lettuce: all year
Onion: July–September
Pea: March–October
Potato: June–October
Sweetcorn: August–September
Tomato: August–September

Other items

Everyone loves the smell of fresh ground coffee, which only goes to emphasize the advantage of buying whole, unground products whenever possible, including pepper and spices. Similarly, fresh herbs have far more flavour than dried.

Making the Most of Meat

ONE DAY'S DINNER INTO TWO

Until the late 19th century, families were very much larger than they are today and, consequently, there was considerable emphasis on avoiding waste, especially where something as expensive as meat was concerned. Here are some Victorian ways for making the most of your *viande* ('lobscous' is a stew with vegetables or biscuit; 'podovies' are beef patties):

By such means as are here about to be suggested, with very little additional expense, one day's dinner may supply two or more dishes for that of the succeeding day.

Roasted beef may be warmed again as 1. Lobscous; 2. Podovies; 3. Olives; 4. Fried (as Staffordshire beef steaks); 5. Collops (with eschalot or walnut-pickle); 6. Hashed and prepared like haricot mutton (with carrots, turnips, and onions); 7. Slices put into a pie-dish with a gravy, and seasoning of eschalots and pepper, then covered over with a coating of mashed potatoes, and baked before the fire. The fat of the inside of cold sirloin will make an excellent pie or pudding crust; the bones well stewed with peas and onions, and seasoned with pepper and salt, form sufficient stock for old pea soup.

Cold boiled beef: 1. Minced and warmed up in fresh beef gravy (flavoured with eschalot or onion); 2. Potted; 3. Fried with cabbage (bubble and squeak); 4. Fried with a casserole of mashed potatoes. The water in which beef has been boiled, if not extremely salt, may serve as the stock of pea or carrot soup.

Veal may be re-cooked: 1. In thin slices with white sauce; 2. Fried as cutlets (with egg and bread-crumbs); 3. As a ragout (with green peas); 4. As currie (with rice); 5. Made into rissoles with grated ham; 6. Patties with ham or oysters.

Calf's head, boiled, makes an excellent hash; the gravy may be procured by reducing the liquor in which it was boiled. It is sometimes eaten cold with vinegar and mustard, like brawn.

Cold mutton may be hashed in several ways: 1. It may be cooked like venison (with red wine and sweet sauce); 2. It may be simply hashed and flavoured with mushroom catsup; 3. It may be made into haricot with vegetables; 4. Fried with egg and bread-crumbs, and served with a made mutton gravy; 5. Broiled, and served on a rock of mashed potatoes.

Cold lamb may be: 1. Fried, and put into a hot stew of cucumbers for a short time previous to serving; 2. Fried with egg and bread-crumbs and chopped parsley, garnished also with sprigs of crisp parsley.

Chops from cold loin may be fried and served on a dish of spinach.

Pork, of cold leg or loin, in slices or chops, will be excellent nicely fried in butter and surrounded with a thick purée of apples. Pea soup may be made of the liquor in which a leg has been boiled, if not too salt.

Cold poultry. Turkey, which has been either boiled or roasted, may be again served by pulling the fleshy parts from the bones which must be warmed in a gravy made with the bones and carcase of the turkey, and thickened with cream; the legs, pinion and gizzard should be highly deviled, broiled and laid on the top of the hot mince. Cold fowls may be made into a good currie, and served with a turban of rice.

Thomas Webster and Mrs William Parkes, *Encyclopaedia of Domestic Economy* (1844)

JOINTS.

1.—Sirloin of Beef.   2.—Boiled Beef.   3.—Leg of Mutton.   4.—Roast Ribs of Beef.

Joints of meat illustration, Beeton's Book of Household Management, 1907 edition
© Mary Evans Picture Library / Alam

A soup for a family of twelve made from beef bones and vegetables was said to cost one shilling in the middle of the 19th century, while a calf's head cost four shillings and sufficient beef for twelve cost seven shillings and sixpence.

A WORKHOUSE RECIPE

Although those living in the workhouse were supposed to be given as much as they could eat, in reality it seldom turned out that way. Here's a workhouse recipe for a meat broth:

3 ozs. Raw Meat without bones (Beef Stickings or similar quality) cut up small.
1 oz. Vegetables.
Dried Herbs and Salt and Pepper to taste.
2 ozs. Bones, cut up.
1 oz. Haricot beans.
¹/₂ oz. Flour
¹/₂ oz. Fat (Dripping)
Water, a sufficiency.

Put the meat and bones into a pot with cold water; boil, skim, add vegetables and haricot beans previously well washed, cook slowly till reduced to one pint. Put the bones in a net, and remove when the stock is finished. Brown the flour in the dripping (a chestnut brown), dilute with some hot water and pour into the prepared stock. Stir till it boils, and cook for another twenty minutes. Season to taste.

Anon, *Manual of Workhouse Cookery* (1901)

CURED, SMOKED AND SALTED FOOD

Curing is an ancient method of preserving food through salting and smoking. Originally important in ensuring a year-round supply of food, these methods are now often employed simply for the flavour they produce in meat and fish. Popular cured foodstuffs today include smoked salmon (which may be salted first, then smoked) and bacon (which can be either salted, then eaten 'green', or salted and then smoked).

LONG HISTORY

Food has been preserved through salting and smoking for thousands of years. To begin with meat or fish was smoked in order to preserve it, a process which dates back to before recorded history. Even by the Middle Ages in Europe, fish could not be transported far from the port at which it was landed unless it had been heavily salted or smoked. By the mid-19th century, perishable goods could be transported quickly, via steamships and railways, and while the need for smoking declined, an appreciation of the flavour of mildly smoked foods remained.

Two forms of smoked fish that we now regard as traditional were allegedly developed just as the need to smoke was on the wane – the kipper and the Yarmouth bloater. The modern-day kipper is said to have been accidentally invented by John Woodger, at Seahouses, Northumberland, in 1843 (the word kipper was in use before this, but was used to refer to smoked salmon, while Woodger's kipper was a herring). The story goes that Woodger left some split and salted herring in a shed where a fire was left burning overnight. At first he thought that the smoke would have ruined the fish, but once cooked it became apparent they were delicious. The Yarmouth bloater (a herring again, but traditionally left whole and ungutted, rather than split) is claimed by some to date back to the 1830s, when it is said to have been invented by a fish-curer who found that a batch of fresh herring had been overlooked – left neither gutted nor cured. He did not want to waste them, so he decided to see what happened if they were salted and hung in the smokehouse. He went on to perfect the Yarmouth bloater – although the story (and its date) could be a red herring.

Scotland also has a rich fish-smoking heritage, and the Arbroath smokie is another delicacy said to have been discovered by accident. Legend has it that a fire broke out in a cottage in Auchmithie in which haddock had been hung to dry. The house was ruined, but the haddock were delicious. Later, many people from Auchmithie moved to Arbroath, taking their smoked haddock with them, and the fish became known as the Arbroath smokie. In 2004, the designation 'Arbroath smokie' was recognized as a 'Protected Geographical Indication' by the European Union. Also conferred on such delights as champagne and Parma ham, in the case of the smokie this means that to be called an Arbroath smokie, the fish must be haddock, and it must be smoked in the traditional way within 8 kilometres (5 miles) of Arbroath.

HOT OR COLD SMOKE

While exact smoking methods vary greatly, there are a few basic principles of smoking that are generally consistent. Fish or meat is first cured, using salt – salt is either rubbed onto the surface of the food, or, commonly, it is left in brine. During the curing process, moisture is drawn from the meat or fish. This is the first stage in preserving the food. After curing it can then be either hot smoked or cold smoked. Hot-smoked foods (such as Arbroath smokies and smoked mackerel) are cooked as well as smoked, so are ready to eat. Some cold-smoked foods (such as cold-smoked salmon) are also ready to eat, but many (including smoked bacon, kippers and Yarmouth bloaters) require cooking. For hot-smoked foods, a shorter brining time and a hotter smoking temperature are used. Cold-smoked foods are kept in brine for longer, and are also smoked for longer at lower temperatures. The scientific explanation for the efficacy of smoking lies in the fact that certain extracts in the smoke inhibit the growth of bacteria which would cause the food to spoil.

SMOKING AT HOME

If you have an open fire, the simplest method of smoking at home is to place your meat or fish high up in the chimney and keep a hardwood log fire burning below – always use wood and never coal, as coal smoke is too toxic to use in food preparation. It is also possible to buy specially designed smokers (which look something like a barbecue), create your own smokehouse (self-sufficiency expert John Seymour used an outside, brick-built lavatory, converted to the purpose with a wood-burning stove), or use a barrel, as Mrs Beeton suggested:

TO SMOKE HAMS AND FISH AT HOME
Take an old hogshead, stop up all the crevices, and fix a place to put a cross-stick near the bottom, to hang the articles to be smoked on. Next, in the side, cut a hole near the top, to introduce an iron pan filled with sawdust and small pieces of green wood. Having turned the tub upside down, hang the articles upon the cross-stick, introduce the iron pan in the opening, and place a piece of red-hot iron in the pan, cover it with sawdust, and all will be complete. Let a large ham remain 40 hours, and keep up a good smoke.
Mrs Isabella Beeton, *Beeton's Book of Household Management* (1861)

Preserving by Drying

DRYING

Drying is another ancient method of preserving food. Foods such as berries, nuts, fruit and cereals have been dried in the sun and stored for later use since prehistoric times. Meat has also been sun-dried, and fish has been preserved by drying it in the air or wind in such cold dry areas as northern Scandinavia, or in the sun in warmer climes. The principle behind preserving food by drying is to remove all moisture in order to inhibit the development of the enzymes that cause food to rot. As with other forms of preserving, drying was once an essential part of ensuring a year-round supply of food and preventing waste during times of glut. At home, herbs, some fruit, and some vegetables lend themselves readily to successful drying.

Oregano, lavender and mint drying in bunches
© Clay Perry/Corbis

HERBS

To dry herbs for winter use.
On a very dry day, gather the herbs, just before they begin to flower. If this is done when the weather is damp, the herbs will not be so good a colour. (It is very necessary to particular in little matters like this, for trifles constitute perfection, and herbs nicely dried will be found very acceptable when frost and snow are on the ground ...) They should be perfectly freed from dirt and dust, and be divided into small bunches, with their roots cut off. Dry them quickly in a very hot oven, or before the fire, as by this means most of their flavour will be preserved, and be careful not to burn them.
Mrs Isabella Beeton, *Beeton's Book of Household Management* (1861)

If you find yourself with more fresh herbs than you can use, drying them for later use is a relatively simple yet satisfying process. As Mrs Beeton suggests, the herbs should be picked from plants just before they begin to flower, and on a dry day. They should be washed and shaken until dry. They must be dried in a warm, well-ventilated place, to eliminate the moisture in them as quickly as possible, whilst retaining maximum flavour. Some people also claim that drying herbs somewhere dark, for example in an airing cupboard, will help them to keep the best colour and flavour. Either hang the herbs in small bunches, loosely wrapped in muslin to keep the dust off (a method more appropriate for herbs with small leaves such as thyme, parsley and rosemary), or strip the leaves from the stems, spreading them in a single layer on a tray or rack covered with muslin (a method which is good for herbs with large leaves, such as bay, sage, basil or mint). Check the herbs regularly for a couple of days, turning them if necessary, and once they are dry either crush them or leave them as whole dried leaves, and store them in airtight jars. They are best used up during the winter after they have been dried, but beware: they have a more concentrated flavour than their fresh counterparts, so always reduce the quantity used if you are following a recipe that calls for fresh.

FRUIT

To dry pears without sugar.
Take Norwich pears, pare them with a knife, and put them in an earthen pot, and bake them not too soft; put them into a white plate pan, and put dry straw under them, and lay them in an oven after bread is drawn, and every day warm the oven to the degree of heat as when the bread is newly drawn. Within one week they must be dry.

Hannah Glasse, *The Art of Cookery Made Plain and Easy* (1784)

A number of fruits can be dried in thin slices, but it can be tricky to ensure that the air is both warm and dry enough to dry the fruit before it goes mouldy. If you have a cooking range, apples and pears can be dried fairly successfully – string thin slices of the fruit together in such a way that no two pieces are touching, and hang in the warm dry air above the range until dry.

VEGETABLES

If you grow your own vegetables, and wish to dry some of your crop of peas and beans, let them fully ripen on the plants, then either pull up whole plants and hang them from their roots somewhere dry and airy, or pick off the pods and dry them in a single layer on trays covered in newspaper. When the pods split, remove the peas and beans and leave to dry fully before storing in airtight containers (remembering that they will need plenty of soaking before use).

Pea Soup.

Soak dry peas over night, putting a quart of water to each quart of peas. Next morning boil them an hour in this water, and ten minutes before the hour expires put in a teaspoon of saleratus [bicarbonate of soda]. Change them to fresh water, put in a pound of salt pork, and boil three or four hours, till the peas are soft. Green peas need no soaking, and must boil not more than an hour. When taken up, add butter.

Catharine Beecher, *Miss Beecher's Domestic Receipt Book* (1850)

A glut of chillies can be strung together and hung anywhere there is good air circulation, and if the summer seems sunny enough, cut tomatoes in sections and dry them outdoors (or, perhaps more realistically, above a radiator).

Preserving by Pickling

PICKLES

Pickling vegetables
© Bon Appetit / Alamy

Pickles are made by preserving raw or cooked foods (most often vegetables) in either vinegar or brine. In the USA, 'pickle' refers specifically to a cucumber preserved in brine, the most popular pickled vegetable there. In Britain, small onions pickled in vinegar, which grace every pub-served ploughman's lunch, are the most common pickle.

FAMOUS FANS

The ancient Greeks and Romans held their pickles in high estimation. They consisted of flowers, herbs, roots, and vegetables, preserved in vinegar, and which were kept, for a long time, in cylindrical vases with wide mouths. Their cooks prepared pickles with the greatest care, and the various ingredients were macerated in oil, brine and vinegar, with which they were often impregnated drop by drop.

Mrs Isabella Beeton, *Beeton's Book of Household Management* (1861)

It is thought that people have been pickling vegetables for more than 4,000 years – archaeologists believe that the Mesopotamians were pickling cucumbers by around 2000 BC. It is often said that Aristotle praised the pickled cucumber as being beneficial to health, and that Cleopatra believed that eating pickles contributed to her beauty. Pliny the Elder, and the emperors Julius Caesar and Tiberius are also said to have enjoyed pickles. Amerigo Vespucci, the Italian merchant turned explorer after whom America is named, was described by the author Ralph Waldo Emerson as 'the pickle-dealer at Seville', and it does seem that in his

capacity as merchant Vespucci had pickles loaded on ships, reducing the risk of scurvy in sailors on long journeys.

Britons have long enjoyed pickles too. Elizabeth I was apparently a fan, and Samuel Pepys (who also mentions pickled oysters in his diaries) dined at least once on brawn and pickled gherkins:

We did this day cut a brave collar of brawn from Winchcombe which proves very good, and also opened the glass of girkins which Captain Cocke did give my wife the other day, which are rare things.

Samuel Pepys, diary entry, Sunday 1 December 1661

WORLDWIDE PURSUIT

Different pickles have developed in different parts of the world – pickled red cabbage is associated with Eastern Europe; fermented cabbage, or sauerkraut, with Germany; Japanese umeboshi, pickled ume fruit (related to apricots); and various Korean pickles called kimchi. Indian delights such as lime pickle or aubergine pickle are now known to many in the West. India has a rich tradition of such dishes, although these are relishes or chutneys rather than straightforward pickles, as are the British piccalilli and famous Branston Pickle.

PICKLING DECLINE

Before canning and freezing, pickling was a way of ensuring that vegetables were preserved for winter. Also, it is in the nature of vegetables to provide a glut, rather than a steady supply of produce, and pickling ensured that the surplus did not go to waste. At one time, pickling in summer would have been an annual event to ensure good food in the leaner months. As with many other things, the decline in home-pickling came with refrigeration, the industrialization of food and the importation of out-of-season foods from other parts of the world. Now the flavour of pickles is more important than the dose of vitamins they can supply in winter, although the craft is enjoying something of a revival now that more people are 'growing their own', and in the summer months often find themselves with a backlog of fresh but uneaten vegetables.

VINEGAR AND BRINE

PICKLES

These are an important class of culinary preparations, and one about which the cook and notable housewife make no little bustle, and feel no small pride ... The only general rules that can be given for the proper and safe preparation of pickles, are, to have sound vegetables, not over ripe, and gathered on a dry day ... it is miserable economy to employ bad vinegar for pickling ... [while] the spiceries used in pickling are so well bestowed that we give no rule for the quantity, except that it should not be so great as to overcome the natural flavour of the article pickled; for pickles like every thing else, should be what their name imparts,—either onion or cucumber, &c. and not a hodge-podge of conflicting flavours.

Margaret Dods, *The Cook and Housewife's Manual* (1826)

You can pickle many things, and little equipment is needed. Two key things to remember when you make pickles are: use fresh produce (and wash it carefully), and make sure that the jars you are going to store your pickles in have been sterilized and have good seals and lids that won't rust away. If you are an enthusiastic pickler, you might want to make your own vinegar, while at the other end of the effort scale, you can buy spiced vinegar, ready for pickling. A midway approach is to buy vinegar, then spice it yourself. A description of one spiced vinegar recipe is given below (although you can add any spices you like), as is the method for pickling onions. If you are going to buy vinegar to spice yourself, you will find a wide range to choose from. Wine vinegars are perhaps the best-tasting, but they are also the most expensive. Malt vinegar is the most economical, and still produces good results. The only rule is that the vinegar must have a minimum acetic acid content of five per cent.

To make spiced vinegar, you will need:

1.1 litres (2 pints) vinegar

1 cinnamon stick

15 millilitres (1 tablespoon) whole allspice berries

15 millilitres (1 tablespoon) blade mace

6 cloves

6 peppercorns

2$^1/_2$ millilitres ($^1/_2$ teaspoon) mustard seeds

To make 'quick' spiced vinegar, place all the ingredients in a saucepan, cover, and bring to the boil. Then remove the pan from the heat, and leave

for around two hours before straining – leave the lid on, it will preserve the flavours, and the smell of hot vinegar is very strong. For a better flavour, the spiced vinegar must be started at least one month before it is needed. Simply add the spices to unheated vinegar, and leave for one to two months before straining, ready for use.

Rules to be observed in Pickling.

Always use stone-jars for all sorts of pickles … for these not only last longer, but keep the pickle better: for vinegar and salt will penetrate through all earthen vessels; stone and glass are the only things to keep pickles in. Be sure never to put your hands in to take the pickles out, it will soon spoil it. The best method is, to every pot tie a wooden spoon, full of little holes, to take the pickles out with.

Hannah Glasse, *The Art of Cookery Made Plain and Easy* (1784)

Spices used in pickling (clockwise from top left): cloves, cinnamon, star anise, nutmeg, allspice
© *D. Hurst / Alamy*

To use your spiced vinegar for pickled onions you will need pickling onions, salt and water. Dissolve 225 grams (8 ounces) of salt in 2.3 litres (4 pints) of water to make a brine. Put 1.4 kilograms (3 pounds) of pickling onions (unskinned) in a bowl, and pour the brine over. Place a plate on top of the onions to keep them submerged (put a weight on the plate if needed). After twelve hours, pour the brine away and skin the onions. Make up a fresh brine, and pour this over the onions, covering them with a plate again. Leave for two to three days. Finally, drain and rinse the onions, pack them into your jars, pour over the spiced vinegar and seal. Freshly pickled onions need to be left for at least two months before they are really good to eat.

Different vegetables require different treatments, but recipes for pickles are readily available in general cookery books as well as specialist ones, and online. As a quick guide to some of the most popular pickles: beetroot are cooked, then peeled and sliced and pickled in vinegar, or baby beetroots are cooked, peeled and pickled whole; apples, especially crab-apples (often pickled in the past) also need to be cooked first; red cabbage, cauliflower and gherkins (as with the onions described above) are placed in brine rather than being cooked before they are pickled. It is generally said that pickles are best eaten within six months of making them, although some claim they can be kept much longer.

Pickled walnuts

Make a brine of Salt and Water ... put the Walnuts into this to soak for a week, or if you wish to soften them so that they may be soon ready for eating run a larding pin through them in half a dozen places—this will allow the pickle to penetrate, and they will be much softer, and of better flavour, and ready much sooner than if not perforated—put them into a stew pan with such brine, and give them a gentle simmer ... drain—then ... let them stand in the air till they turn black ... put them in Glass or unglazed stone Jars, fill these about three parts with the Walnuts, and fill them up with the following pickle. To each quart of the strongest Vinegar put an ounce of Black Pepper, same of Ginger, same of Shallots, same of Salt, and half an ounce of Allspice, and half a drachm of Cayenne. Put these into a stone jar, cover it ... and set the jar on a trivet, by the side of the fire, for three days, shaking it up three times a day, and then pour it while hot to the Walnuts.

William Kitchiner, *The Cook's Oracle; and Housekeeper's Manual* (1830)

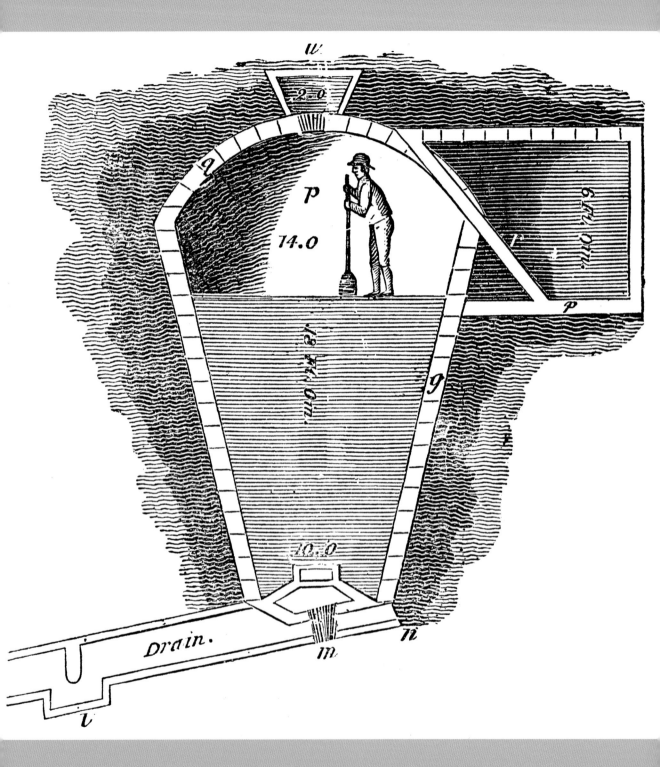

FREEZING

Freezing is certainly not a new way of preserving food. It is known that ice was used in Mesopotamia nearly 4,000 years ago, and when Spanish explorers reached South America they found the indigenous people in the Andes had developed a method for freeze-drying potato into a product known as *chuño*. In Britain in the 17th century, the winter weather also provided a natural means of freezing food:

I sat by ... some East Country merchants ... and then they told us the manner of putting their nets into the water through holes made in the thicke ice ... And then the people comes with sledges upon the ice, with snow at the bottome, and lay the fish in and cover them with snow ... And he hath seen when the said fish have been frozen in the sled, so as that he hath taken a fish and broke a-pieces, so hard it hath been; and yet the same fishes ... brought into a hot room, will be alive and leap up and down ... Fowl killed in December (Alderman Barker said) he did buy; and putting them into the box under his sled, did forget to take them out to eate till Aprill next, and they then were found there and were, through the frost, as sweet and fresh and eat as well as at first killed.

Samuel Pepys, *Diary* (1663)

Around the same time, the first ice houses were introduced into England. Basically, they were deep pits or wells which would be lined with straw or wood and filled with ice in winter, usually from the nearest lake. An experiment carried out in Cumbria in 1980 demonstrated that, once filled, the ice would easily last through the summer until the following winter.

Artificial refrigeration was first demonstrated by William Cullen at the University of Glasgow in 1748, but the man credited with the invention of the refrigerator as we know it was Carl von Linde in 1876 – his company is still in business today. Early refrigerators used gases that were toxic and there were several fatalities from the leakage of methyl chloride, which did little to boost popularity. The first refrigerator to enjoy widespread use was General Electric's 'Monitor Top' in 1927.

BOTTLING

Bottled fruits were very common at one time but have now become something of a luxury. To kill micro-organisms and inactivate enzymes it is essential to heat the fruit to the correct temperature for the right length of time. The fruit can be bottled in water but looks and tastes better in syrup:

A solution of sugar prepared by dissolving two parts of double-refined sugar (the best sugar is the most economical for preserves) in one of water, and boiling this a little, affords a syrup of the right degree of strength, and which neither ferments nor crystallizes.

Isabella Beeton, *Mrs Beeton's Book of Household Management* (1861)

The next stage is preparation of the fruit. This varies from fruit to fruit but basically involves removing stalks and any stones, and the peel and pith from citrus fruit. The old-fashioned way was then to simmer the fruit in the syrup in a pan:

Put the apricots into the pie-serving-pan with sufficient syrup to cover them; let them boil up three or four times, and then skim them; remove them from the fire, pour them into an earthen pan, and let them cool till next day. Boil them up three days successively, skimming each time, and they will then be finished and in a state fit to be put into pots for use.

Isabella Beeton, *Mrs Beeton's Book of Household Management* (1861)

Nowadays, there are faster ways, of which the quick water bath method is probably the simplest. Pack the prepared fruit into special screw-band jars and fill to the brim with hot syrup (60°C/140°F). Put on the covers but leave screw bands loose to allow steam to escape. Stand in a pan with a false bottom (the glass must not be in direct contact with the base of the pan – if nothing else is available a thick pad of newspaper will do). Pour in warm water (38°C/100°F) to cover the jars completely. Heat slowly until the water starts to simmer (88°C/190°F) and then continue simmering. Note that different fruits require to be simmered for different lengths of time. Remove the jars from the pan and place on a dry wooden surface (a cold wet surface risks cracking the jars). To make it easier to remove the jars, ladle some of the water out of the pan and then use a thick cloth to take hold of them. The screw bands should be tightened immediately and the jars left to cool.

THE EASY WAY

There is a traditional method, however, that does not require the preparation of syrup and which is extremely simple:

Many fruits, when preserved by boiling, lose much of their peculiar and delicate flavour as, for instance, pine-apples; and this inconvenience may, in some instances, be remedied by preserving them without heat. Cut the fruit in slices about one fifth of an inch thick, strew powdered loaf sugar an eighth of an inch thick on the bottom of a jar, and put the slices on it. Put more sugar on this, and then another layer of the slices, and so on till the jar is full. Place the jar with the fruit up to the neck in boiling water, and keep it there till the sugar is completely dissolved, which may take half an hour, removing the scum as it rises. Lastly, tie a wet bladder over the mouth of the jar, or cork and wax it.

Isabella Beeton, *Mrs Beeton's Book of Household Management* (1861)

Storing Vegetables, Fruit and Wine

VEGETABLES

The traditional way of storing root crops, especially potatoes, was clamping. First of all, the newly dug potatoes would be left to dry a little. Then, after a few days, a square would be dug out to a depth of about two spades and filled with dry straw. Onto that the potatoes would be piled up into a pyramid to, perhaps, waist height, depending on the quantity. Finally, the pile would be covered with a thick layer of straw, followed by tightly packed earth. If you want to copy this, be sure to leave some straw poking out at the top of the pyramid, and in one or two places around the bottom for air to get in, but make sure there are no holes through which rats or mice might enter. For a small family, it's better to make several clamps rather than one big one because, once opened, the potatoes will need to be used fairly quickly.

Beet, carrots, parsnips and turnips could also be stored in clamps but were better in dry sand inside barrels.

In southern areas of England, the tops of root vegetables were sometimes cut off and the vegetables left in the ground until needed. Leeks were 'heeled in' which meant they were dug up and the tops cut off. Then they were arranged together in bundles, replaced in the ground and the soil lightly pressed down with the heel.

Garlic and onions were simply hung up, initially out of doors to 'cure' for a few weeks and then inside in a cool, dry place.

Before refrigeration, many households had another alternative – the root cellar.

Clamping potatoes for the winter, 1935
© Topham Picturepoint

195

Your own root cellar

A root cellar could simply be a deep hole dug in the ground and lined with rocks. A shed would then be built over it with a trapdoor in the floor for access, via a ladder. An easier way, landscape permitting, was to excavate into the side of a hill. Nowadays, a root cellar is still a good idea because it uses no electricity and can provide far more storage space than a freezer. If you have a cellar below ground level you already have the basis for a root cellar. All you have to do is create a separate room down there. Don't worry if the cellar is a touch damp because a little humidity is beneficial. On the other hand, air must be able to circulate freely, so you will need an air vent at floor level and another at ceiling height, and the shelving should be slatted and two or three inches away from the walls.

In a well-designed root cellar produce should last as follows:

Aubergines: 1–2 weeks
Beetroot: 4–5 months
Broccoli: 1–2 weeks
Brussels sprouts: 3–5 weeks
Cabbage: 3–4 months
Carrots: 4–6 months
Cauliflower: 2–4 weeks
Parsnips: 1–2 months
Potatoes: 4–6 months
Pumpkins: 5–6 months
Radishes: 2–3 months
Tomatoes: 1–2 months
Turnips: 4–6 months

FRUIT

In addition to a root cellar, large houses would also have a fruit room – a cool, dark place with constant humidity. Only ripe but unspoiled and undamaged fruit could be stored in this way. Each fruit was individually cleaned and placed on slatted shelves without touching its neighbour. Fruits such as cherries, currants, gooseberries and grapes were kept on the branch and then put into special bottles filled with water, which would have to be topped up from time to time. Like this the fruit could last all year.

WINE

Having carefully counted the bottles, they are stored away in their respective binns, a layer of sand or sawdust being placed under the first tier, and another over it; a second tier is laid over this, protected by a lath, the head of the second being laid to the bottom of the first; over this another bed of sawdust is laid, not too thick, another lath; and so on till the binn is filled ... but the cellar must be kept at a perfectly steady temperature, neither too hot nor too cold, but about 55 or 60, and absolutely free from draughts of cold air.

Isabella Beeton, *Mrs Beeton's Book of Household Management* (1861)

To which may be added that the ideal humidity is 65–75 per cent. The four key words are dark, cool, still and sideways.

Monastery wine cellar
© Mary Evans Picture
Library / Alamy

Storing Clothes

STORING CLOTHES

When it comes to storing clothes safely, man has always battled against the humble clothes moth. Less talked about perhaps than they were in the past – moths eat clothes made from natural fibres and disdain modern synthetic fabrics – moths can still cause serious problems in your wardrobe. They do their damage when they are in their larval stage, so many of the traditional remedies to keep clothes moths at bay are intended as repellents – the aim being to dissuade the female moth from laying her eggs in the first place.

MOTHS

Two thousand years ago, the Roman statesman, orator and writer Cato the Elder (234–149 BC) recommended 'amurca' – a bitter paste left over when olives were pressed for their oil – as a deterrent for clothes moths:

To protect clothing from moths: Boil amurca down to one-half its volume and rub it over the bottom, the outside, the feet, and the corners of the chest. After it is dry, store the clothing and the moths will not attack it.

Cato the Elder, *De agri cultura* ('On Agriculture').

Centuries later, the English herbalist John Gerard (1545–1612) recommended a number of different herbs 'to keepe garments from motheating', including wormwood and rosemary, as well as wood shavings from the cypress tree:

The shavings of the wood laid amongst garments preserveth them from mothes, the Rosin [resin] killeth mothes, little wormes and maggots.

John Gerard, *The Herball, or generall historie of plantes* (1597)

More recently, camphor and cedar chips have been employed:

Preservatives against the devastation of Moths.
Take woollen and fur garments not worn, late in the spring, and put them in a chest with some camphor gum …Tobacco and cedar chips are a good preventative. When moths get into garments, hang them in a closet, place a pan of coals in it, and make a strong smoke of tobacco.

A L Webster, *The Improved Housewife, or Book of Receipts* (1855)

Nowadays a number of traditional moth repellents are still used. One suggested preventative to losing your fine woollens to the ravages of these creatures is to fill small muslin bags with a concoction of herbs – such as rosemary, thyme, lavender, cloves and cinnamon – and hang them in the wardrobe. Pieces of cedar wood are sold for the purpose of sending the clothes moth packing, although they are most effective if you remember to sand them down once in a while to keep the scent fresh. Bog myrtle is another herbal remedy long associated with moths, while some suggest that conkers do the trick (these useful fruits of the horse chestnut tree are also said to prevent piles and rheumatism). But one of the key ways to avoid losing your clothes to moths is to ensure that the clothes are entirely clean when you put them away, as moths are particularly attracted by sweat and food stains, and to check periodically for lurking beasts.

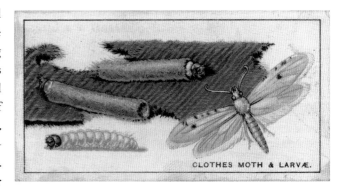

CLOTHES MOTH & LARVÆ.

The clothes moth and its larvae
© *Mary Evans Picture Library*

Furs, Feathers, and Woollens require the constant care of the waiting-maid. Furs and feathers not in constant use should be wrapped up in linen washed in lye. From May to September they are subject to being made the depository of the moth-eggs. They should be looked to, and shaken and beaten, from time to time, in case some of the eggs should have been lodged in them, in spite of every precaution; laying them up again, or rather folding them up as before, wrapping them in brown paper, which is itself a preservative. Shawls and cloaks, which would be damaged by such close folds, must be looked to, and aired and beaten, putting them away dry before the evening.

Mrs Isabella Beeton, *Beeton's Book of Household Management* (1861)

PROLONGING THE LIFE OF YOUR CLOTHES

The careful storing of clothes not only keeps them safe from moths, but can also prolong their useful life:

Clothing will last twice as long if properly looked after, and an appreciable amount of money can be saved by taking care of your clothes in the following way.
Hang them up on hangers immediately they are taken off, brush them carefully, and remove small stains immediately, airing them by hanging them in a draught before putting them away.
Keep light dresses in dustproof bags, hats on stands and shoes on trees.

The Book of Hints and Wrinkles (c.1939)

Repairing Clothes

A STITCH IN TIME SAVES NINE

Darning and patching were the norm until the 1950s. Fashions changed slowly up to the end of the Victorian era, and most better-off women and men would have had their clothes made to measure from good quality fabrics and cherished them, sending them back to the tailor from time to time for repair. For those middle-class housewives who preferred to do the job themselves, the 1890 edition of *Good Housekeeping* recommended setting aside a regular 'Mending Day' on the basis that 'Ounces of prevention ... are worth pounds of cure'. The poor, meanwhile, were very used to patching, probably buying their clothes second-hand and already quite worn. According to one enquiry into social conditions in England in the 1840s conducted by Friedrich Engels, large numbers of workers wore 'extremely ragged clothing, which is either incapable of being patched any more or has been so often patched in the past that the original colour can no longer be detected'.

ALTERATIONS AND HAND-ME-DOWNS

Because clothes were expensive they were not thrown away as fashions changed, but altered to create a new look:

A waiting-maid who wishes to make herself useful, will ... employ her spare time in repairing and making up dresses which have served one purpose, to serve another ...
Isabella Beeton, *Mrs Beeton's Book of Household Management* (1861)

Similarly, clothes would be adapted for other members of the household:

Repairing and making over cover a wide field in woman's work. Some general directions can be given for it, but each woman must study well the best way to prolong the usefulness and good appearance of the article ... Men's clothing can be cut down advantageously for boys. First rip up and clean ... After pressing, lay the patterns out thoughtfully, and cut with as little waste as possible. Large pieces can be joined together to line the waists ...

Anon, *Good Housekeeping* (1888)

DARNING

Darning, according to one old manual, 'is a method of renewing the part of the cloth destroyed or weakened by wear, and in some cases is really hand-weaving'. Here's how it's done:

To darn a hole in a stocking or in a woollen underclothing (if large), first draw the edges together as near as possible with fine cotton; then make straight lines of darning between the two opposite sides of the hole, and leave a loop of the thread at the end of each line of turning, to allow for shrinking; darn across the hole in like manner at right angles to these lines. Each line of darning should begin 1 in. or more beyond the edge of the hole, and at the left side of the worn or thin place. In one line pass the needle over the first thread and under the second, over the third and under the fourth, and so on, and in returning on the next line pass the needle over the threads taken up before, and under the threads left down.

Mending a boy's trousers, from a humorous postcard with the inscription 'His only pair'
© thislife pictures / Alamy

Catherine F Johnson, *The Art and Practice of Needlework* (1908)

Ideally, the darning was done *before* washing, not after, on the basis that the hole would then tend to close up, making the repair less visible.

PATCHING

The first step, of course, was prevention. On Mending Day, said *Good Housekeeping*, each garment should be laid out and examined for any pulled threads. 'If these are noted in time it is easy to catch up the broken thread and prevent it from spreading into a large hole which might need a patch.'

But if you weren't in time you then had to search out a patch, matching it not only to the garment but also to the direction of the threads:

A darned-on patch is used for heavy cloths, especially in mending boy's trousers. If possible, use a patch of irregular edges, as when sewed down it is less noticeable than one with straight edges, and can, with care, often be made almost invisible.
By fine overcasting of cotton or silk secure the patch to the right side of the garment, the stitch being taken through the upper surface of the edge of the patch. This brings the upper surface of the patch nearly to the level of the cloth of the garment. Then the darning stitches should be taken below the surface of the patch and the garment, never showing on the top. To hide the turning at the end of the lines of darning, take a stitch diagonally (always under the surface) from the end stitch of the line finished to the place where the next line is to begin. Pare off as little as possible of the ragged edges beneath, and catch them down securely to the under side of the patch with herringbone stitch so that the stitches do not show through.
Catherine F Johnson, *The Art and Practice of Needlework* (1908)

Nowadays, you can buy an iron-on patch or, if you think it looks good, just make the hole even bigger and fray the edges.

Dyeing

USING WHAT COMES NATURALLY

Early Britons would have used all kinds of natural things to add colour to their textiles – flowers, leaves, roots, insects, molluscs and so on. That was easy. The problem was in fixing the colours so they didn't fade away in sunlight, rain or washing. In fact, only a few natural dyes – such as those from lichens – 'fix' themselves. They are known as 'substantive' or 'direct' dyes. The vast majority, known as 'adjective' dyes, require a chemical, called a 'mordant', to fix them insolubly to the fabric.

THE SOUL WHICH ANIMATES

Because lichens were fairly readily available, and needed no mordant, they were the usual dye for Scottish tartans as well as Harris tweed, to which they imparted a distinctive scent. They included crottle lichen and sea ivory, which produced tones from gold to brown, rock tripe, which produced mauve, and cudbear, which produced pink to crimson. The last two, though, required the addition of urine to obtain the right colour.

In fact, dyeing could be a pretty unpleasant business such that in 1587 a proclamation banned mills using woad (the plant *Isatis tinctoria*) within three miles of a royal residence, market town or city because the smell was so offensive. Nevertheless, many unfortunate housewives or servants still had to cope with the processes at home:

If ye will dye yealow with weld* [dyer's rocket], take off the weld leaves, and cut off the rootes, then cut them in peeces, and lay them to soke in lye of comon ashes three *houre, then seeth it a quarter of an houre, till ye thinke it be meetely well sodde. Then put therein two quarts of water, and as much stale Urine of six dayes old at the least, so let them seeth together a little, then cleanse it thorow a siue, and then put unto the same againe, of lye and Urine as aforesaid. Then straine it thorow a faire cloth and seeth it, and to two pound of weld take two pound of Verdegreace, with the lye that ye have sod, your weld and al, putting them in your sayd colour, which must be medled and well stirred all together. Then shall ye boyle it all a little, and it shall be well.*

Anon, *A Profitable Booke* (1605)

* The original work *T Bouck va Wondre* was in Dutch and this English translation mistakenly used the word 'wood' for 'weld' or dyer's rocket. Here, the correct term has been reinstated.

As dyeing became more complicated and skilful, so standards – and the dyers themselves – were protected by a guild system. The 'Art of Dyeing', explained one early 18th century manual, was divided into two parts, 'the great or good Dye, and the lesser and slight'. As a result, only master dyers were allowed to use the best, fast dyes.

Nowadays, with the invention of synthetic dyes, we take colour for granted, but in earlier times, clean, vibrant, fast colours were difficult to achieve and became something of a status symbol. According to *The Whole Art of Dyeing* (1705), colour was 'the Soul which animates' fabrics, without which 'they would be Spiritless Bodies'.

THE INVENTION OF SYNTHETIC DYES

One day in 1856, in his apartment in London, a student chemist called William Perkin attempted to synthesize quinine for the treatment of malaria. He didn't succeed but the liquid he ended up with was a startling purple. At that time, purple dye, known as Tyrian purple, came from molluscs and was extremely expensive. Perkin realized he was on to something good, called it mauveine, and patented it. He was only 18 and mauveine was to make him wealthy. It was the first truly synthetic dye and others soon followed, including Perkin's Green. Not only were synthetic dyes generally cheaper than natural equivalents but they were also more consistent and faded less. But it wasn't quite the end for natural dyes which, today, are gaining in popularity once again, with the revived interest in old crafts.

TRY DYEING

A whole range of plant materials can be used as natural dyes. Just chop them up, add twice as much water as plant material, bring to the boil, simmer for an hour and strain. Always remember to wear rubber gloves when preparing dyes or dyeing. Here are some ideas:

Blue: red cabbage, woad, grapes, blackberries.
Red: dandelion root, beetroot, rosehips, dried hibiscus flowers.
Pink: strawberries, cherries, raspberries.
Green: artichokes, spinach leaves, nettles.
Yellow: saffron, onion skins, marigold blossoms, dandelion flowers, daffodils,
tea, turmeric.
Brown: oak bark, walnut hulls,
tea bags, coffee grounds.

Your fabric or garment will first have to be simmered for an hour in a fixative to limit the amount of colour that washes out. For dyes made from berries, use ¹/₂ cup of salt per eight cups of cold water. For dyes made from other parts of plants, use one part of vinegar per four parts of cold water. After fixing, rinse until the water runs clear. Then put the fabric or garment into the dye bath you prepared and simmer until the colour is a little darker than you want – it will lighten on drying.

Unspun wool dyed using natural plant dyes
© John Henshall / Alamy

Anyone who has ever prepared or eaten beetroot knows that it produces a vibrant crimson dye, and this is therefore one of the easiest plant dyes to begin with. On clean, scoured wool it gives a range of tones from rust through to red. Although you can fix it with vinegar, in this recipe we use alum and tartaric acid (available from dye and craft suppliers) for a more permanent result:

1. *Weigh the wool.*
2. *Weigh out the alum. You will need 10 per cent of the weight of the wool.*
3. *Weigh out the tartaric acid. You will need 5 per cent of the weight of the wool.*
4. *Fill a sufficiently large pot with water, heat and add first the alum and then the tartaric acid.*
5. *Rinse the wool so it's damp, put it into the water and simmer for about an hour.*
6. *While the wool is simmering, dice approximately 1 kg of beetroot and cook in 4.5 litres of water for one hour.*
7. *Strain the red beet liquid into your dye bath, add the wool and simmer for one hour.*
8. *Drain, rinse the wool and let dry.*

Garments that have been dyed with plant material should always be washed separately.

Laundering

LAUNDRY

It was not until the mid-20th century that doing the laundry became the relatively simple task that it is today. Prior to that, household laundering was a day-long task consisting of soaking, boiling and drying the family linen. Earlier still, clothes were often washed at the river, with linen pounded against the rocks to remove stains. (For information on early and home-made detergents, see the section on 'soap making'.)

GOOD DAYS FOR LAUNDERING

Most of the folklore relating to laundering refers to the day on which this task is carried out, rather than the manner in which it is done.

> *They that wash on Monday, have all the week to dry*
> *They that wash on Tuesday, are not so much awry*
> *They that wash on Wednesday, have half the week past*
> *They that wash on Thursday, are very near the last*
> *They that wash on Friday, wash in haste and need*
> *They that wash on Saturday, are sluts indeed.*

This is one of the versions of a 19th-century rhyme dictating which days of the week are appropriate for doing the laundry – Monday is always recommended as the best choice, with the suitability of a washday decreasing as the week progresses, until Saturday, which for laundering is the antithesis of good housewifely practice. For many years, Monday was indeed the most popular day for washing, but not merely to fall in line with the rhyme. Some claim that Monday's popularity was down to there being leftovers from the Sunday roast for dinner, thereby allowing the housewife time for the laundering to be done.

It was not only the day of the week that was important when it came to choosing your washday – there were a number of days of the year when superstition dictated that laundering was forbidden. In the West Country in particular, both New Year's Day and Holy Innocents' Day (28 December) were never given over to washing. Good Friday was also a day on which to avoid doing laundry – if you did the washing on this day it was said that you ran the risk of the soapsuds turning red, or of blood appearing on the clothes as they dried upon the line.

WASHDAY TIMETABLE

Suggested timetable for washing day

Let us assume breakfast is over by 8.30. Immediately set the boiler going, and let the clothes boil while you do the most urgent household tasks (clearing away breakfast things, tidying room, opening beds, getting clothes lines ready).

9–9.15 a.m. Start washing boiled clothes, rinse, blue and get them on the line as quickly as possible; sheets and bath towels first, smaller articles after. By eleven o'clock at the latest, if you are reasonably experienced, all whites should be on the line.

11–12 a.m. Wash, rinse, mangle and hang woollens, then coloured articles.

12–12.30 p.m. Wash silks.

From time to time check up on how the drying is progressing and remove from the lines those clothes ready for mangling or ironing.

12.30–2 p.m. Lunch interval. Make beds and tidy bedrooms.

2 p.m. Starching.

2.30 p.m. Start ironing or mangling articles which are dry.

Thus by early evening, everything connected with the home laundry should be out of the way.

The Book of Hints and Wrinkles (c.1939)

The boiler mentioned in this very busy timetable for a washing day was most likely a free-standing wash boiler, which would be filled with water which was then kept continually hot. Early boilers (or coppers) were large metal cauldrons which were built into the chimney above an open fire, either in the kitchen or in an outhouse. Laundry 'blue' was used to make whites appear whiter, and took the form of a small blue bag that was stirred into the water of the final rinse of the wash. From the mid-19th century, factory-produced blue was available, the main ingredient of which was synthetic ultramarine (famous brands included 'Reckitt's Blue' and 'Dolly Blue'). In earlier times blue was often made from a pigment derived from the indigo plant, mixed with starch and made into lumps, or from Prussian blue. The resultant mixture was often known as 'stone blue', 'fig blue' or 'blue starch'.

TUBS, DOLLIES, WASHBOARDS AND MANGLES

Domestic mangle
© East Lothian Museums Service. Licensor www.scran.ac.uk

Before the advent of washing machines, tubs, dollies, washboards and mangles were all part of the process of laundering. Tubs were made of wood, and could either be trough-shaped (easier to use with a washboard) or shaped like a barrel (easier to use with a dolly). Stubborn stains could either be rubbed against the ridged surface of a washboard, or loosened through the action of a dolly – a wooden shaft attached to a disc with projecting arms, used for beating and stirring the clothes in their tub. The earliest mangles were rather unwieldy, horizontal affairs, in which a heavy box (weighted with stones or sand) was drawn backwards and forwards over the clean linen in order to press it. It was not until the 19th century that the more familiar upright mangle was invented, suitable for squeezing the water out of the washing or flattening it – bed linen, for example, was left to dry for some time before being passed through the mangle as an alternative to ironing it.

THE IRON AGE

Simple flat irons (also known as sad irons) were made from the late Middle Ages. These were designed to be heated next to a fire or on a stove, and at least two were required for efficient ironing (so that one was always heating up while the other was being used). Various weights of flat irons were developed, with heavy irons used for thick material, and light irons for light material such as muslin. By the early 19th century, very large households (with a number of servants) often had specially designed laundry stoves, on which several flat irons could be warmed at once. The work was very hard, and it took experience to know when an iron was hot enough to be useful, but not so hot as to scorch the cloth it was being used upon.

A later ironing development was the box iron. Rather than needing to be heated on a stove, box irons were designed to have something hot placed inside them – either a heated iron slab, or hot coals or charcoal. The rather dangerous-sounding petrol irons and methylated spirit irons were further additions to ironing heritage, although all these irons were eventually superseded by the electric iron, first patented in America in 1883.

Nearly all articles that require ironing should be ironed when still damp (tussore silk is an exception) ... White and coloured cotton and linen articles need an iron that is fairly hot; it should be first tested on a cotton rag to see that it does not scorch it. For silks and other fine fabrics the iron should be tested on a piece of newspaper ... To get the best result, work quickly and with even pressure on the iron. Attend to the small parts first (straps, belts, neckbands, cuffs, yokes, sleeves, and so on), then take the larger parts ... Sleeves of blouses and dresses should be ironed on a sleeve board. If you do not possess one, iron on both sides from the inside seam to within an inch or so of the fold, then open the sleeve out with the unironed strip uppermost and iron that. If you do this with care you will avoid the ugly outside crease that so often mars newly ironed sleeves.

The Book of Hints and Wrinkles (c.1939)

STARCH

To make Starch.

INGREDIENTS.—*Allow* ¹/₂ *pint of cold water and 1 quart of boiling water to every 2 tablespoonfuls of starch.*

Mode.—Put the starch into a tolerably large basin; pour over it the cold water, and stir the mixture well with a wooden spoon until it is perfectly free from lumps, and quite smooth. Then take the basin to the fire, and whilst the water is actually boiling in the kettle or boiler, pour it over the starch, stirring it the whole time ... when sufficiently cool that the hand may be borne in it, starch the things.

Mrs Isabella Beeton, *Beeton's Book of Household Management* (1861)

Luckily, it is now socially acceptable not to wear uncomfortable starched collars, but at one time starching was an inevitable part of the wash day. Starch is a naturally occurring stiffener (it is the principal reserve food material stored in plants). Available in powdered form, starch was mixed into a paste, as described by Mrs Beeton, and those clothes which were to be stiffened were dipped into the starch pan. Starch is still available today, for those who prefer extremely crisp linen.

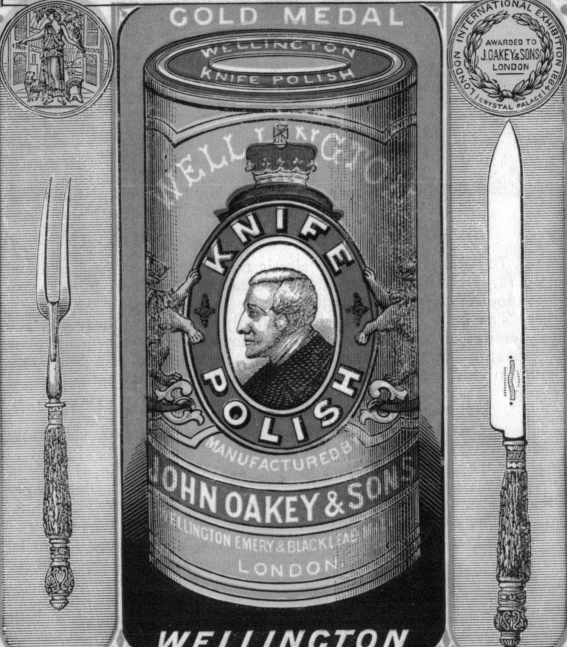

Cleaning

CLEANLINESS AND GODLINESS

How dirty were houses in earlier times? Over the centuries standards of hygiene have waxed and waned. Even cave-dwellers 4,000 years ago used twig brooms to keep things tidy and the Romans in Britain brought their knowledge of aqueducts and sewers. But, after they left, it took until 1848 for a Public Health Act to require proper plumbing in every home. Meanwhile, to judge from an account by Erasmus (c.1466–1536), the Renaissance scholar, the average English home was pretty filthy. Floors were covered in rushes which, in theory, could easily be renewed. But in practice the lowest layer might rest undisturbed for a decade or more. Fortunately, the Victorians believed that cleanliness was next to godliness and especially as well-to-do families all had servants, it's quite possible that their standards were higher than today's.

DEALING WITH FABRICS

Certainly, even in the 16th and 17th centuries, there was no shortage of advice on the best ways to clean household fabrics, albeit water had to be collected in a bucket:

Take of Unquenched lyme two ounces, of Oake ashes two ounces, of cleare water two pound. Then meddle them well all together, and so let them rest a quarter of an houre, and then clarifie that water, & therewith wash your cloth, & it will returne to his first colour and wax faire againe as before.

Anon, *A Profitable Booke* (1605)

Just as we have commercial stain removers, so earlier times had their home-made equivalents:

Take one pound of roch Allom burned and made into a fine poulder. Also take of the rootes cald flames of florance (so called in Dutch) halfe a pound: then beate it into a poulder. Then take a new layd egge, & of white sope two pounde & a halfe, then blend your poulder and your egge and sope altogether well, and thereof make pellots or bals ... then take of the said pellots, and rubbe all over the spots in the cloth: so done, then wash out the filth ...

Anon, *A Profitable Booke* (1605)

Not all of the traditional ways were quite so complicated. Here are some of the simpler ways (be warned, you should always carry out a test on a small unimportant area of fabric first, just in case it reacts badly).

Blood: fresh blood rinses out with cold water, but if it's dried on, soak the fabric in salt water for several hours.

Water-based ink: lay the stained area over an old white towel, pour on a little water and then blot from behind with another towel; afterwards, rub with soap, leave for five minutes and wash in the warmest water suitable for the fabric.

Permanent ink: this is very hard to remove. Begin by blotting with gin, using the two-towel method as above, then apply nail-polish remover. Rinse, then rub in baking soda, and rinse again.

Ballpoint ink: blot with gin, then apply nail-polish remover and rinse. Rub with soap, leave for five minutes, then wash at the warmest suitable temperature.

Grease: blot up as much as possible with paper towels. Then place the front of the stained area against a clean white cloth and apply dry-cleaning fluid from the back using another clean white cloth. (See also *Some tricks with Coca-Cola*, below.)

GLASS

Keeping glass sparkling clean has been a problem ever since it was invented. The Victorian solution to cleaning windows was to put some 'putty powder' (the pulverized oxide of tin, or of tin and lead) on a damp leather and polish away, buffing up afterwards with a dry cloth. Another traditional method was white vinegar, or a mixture of vinegar, ammonia and surgical spirit, plus water, finishing off with a wad of newspaper. However, no method will work if the dirt isn't completely washed off, and too much rubbing only creates static which attracts more dirt.

The professional way is to use a squeegee and a bucket of warm water with just a squirt of dishwashing liquid. Work over the glass from one top corner, making S-patterns. Clean off with the rubber blade, wiping it dry when necessary with a lint-free cloth. Finally, dry the edges and corners with a damp chamois. For small panes a squeegee can be cut to size with a hacksaw – after washing, pull the squeegee blade down the pane in a single action. Really stubborn stains can be removed with a powder containing oxalic acid.

If you don't like cleaning windows, you can now cut the work by half by installing 'self-cleaning' windows embedded with titanium dioxide.

A BIT OF BULLING

The traditional method of making your shoes or boots really shiny, favoured by soldiers and butlers for decades, is a good bit of spit and polish or 'bulling'. The secret to obtaining a mirror shine is to build up five or six layers of polish, so this is not a five-minute task.

RAF cadet 'bulling'
his shoes for
inspection
© Annie Griffiths Belt/Corbis

As you apply each layer with a duster, use your index finger and make small circles as you work the polish into the leather, adding saliva to the duster or directly onto the shoe. After leaving to dry, a final rub down with cotton wool and cold water will bring out the shine.

As an alternative to polish you can try olive oil, but test it first on a small, inconspicuous area of the leather.

SILVER

Silver tarnishes when exposed to the air and is damaged by, among others, rubber, table salt, vinegar, fruit juice, salad dressings and eggs. The traditional method of cleaning was to make a paste with baking soda and water. Rub it over the silver, rinse off and polish dry. Anything that had an intricate design was put into a pan of water in which a teaspoon of baking soda and another of salt were dissolved and boiled for three minutes, together with a sheet of aluminium foil. A modern trick is to take an old soft toothbrush and gently work toothpaste all over the item, using a little warm water as necessary. Rinse and buff.

THE MECHANIZATION OF CLEANING

The Victorians had a sort of dishwasher which resembled a vertical wooden drum inside which were brushes. Knives and forks (already rinsed and wiped free of grease) were put into slots and the handle turned, after which the cutlery would emerge thoroughly buffed – vital in the age before stainless steel. The late Victorians also had washing machines, invented by William Blackstone in Indiana in 1874. And they had carpet sweepers, using brushes activated by the wheels. But they didn't have electric vacuum cleaners, so rugs had to be dealt with like this:

Air, sunshine and water are the great purifiers, plus muscular energy ... If you live in a suburb or in the country, brush, shake, and beat articles to be cleaned out of doors, noticing the way of the wind that the dust may not be carried back into the house.

Helen Kinne and Anna Maria Cooley, *Foods and Household Management* (1914)

In fact, the first electric vacuum cleaner appeared in 1905, completing the range of essential labour-saving devices. On top of that, World War I brought about big social changes, fewer people worked as servants and keeping the house clean became the responsibility of the housewife, aided or not by her partner.

SOME TRICKS WITH COCA-COLA

Coca-Cola was invented at the end of the Victorian era and, owing to its acidity, was soon discovered to have useful cleaning properties.

Burnt saucepans: boil Coca-Cola in them.

Oil stains on a concrete driveway: pour on Coca-Cola, leave and hose off.

Limescale in a kettle: pour full of Coca-Cola and leave for a day.

Limescale in a toilet: pour in Coca-Cola and leave for at least an hour.

Corrosion on battery terminals: pour Coca-Cola over them.

Grease on clothing: wash in a mixture of warm soapy water and Coca-Cola.

Permanent markers on carpet: soak with Coca-Cola, wash off and vacuum when dry.

The Coca-Cola Company plays down suggestions that its product can be used as a cleaner, but will admit that basting ham with Coca-Cola produces a delicious gravy.

Polishing Furniture

OLD-FASHIONED POLISHING

Before proprietary polishes were available, and when furniture was made out of real wood, people made their own furniture polishes and pastes. Of these, beeswax polish is still popular today, although it is more often bought than mixed at home.

LINSEED OIL

Linseed oil, also famously used on cricket bats, was once commonly used to treat mahogany furniture:

Polish for Dining Tables,
Is to rub them with cold-drawn linseed oil, thus: put a little in the middle of a table, and then with a piece of linen (never use woollen) cloth rub it well over the table; then take another piece of linen, and rub it for ten minutes, then rub it till quite dry with another cloth. This must be done every day for several months, when you will find your mahogany acquire a permanent and beautiful lustre, unattainable by any other means ... and when once this polish is produced, it will only require dry rubbing with a linen cloth for about ten minutes twice a week, to preserve it in the highest perfection.
William Kitchiner, *The Cook's Oracle; and Housekeeper's Manual* (1830)

If you need quicker results (and don't have time to spare every day for several months) then a furniture paste, such as one made with beeswax, is recommended. Linseed oil (which protects and moisturizes the wood, just as beeswax does) can also be used to make a good furniture polish:

Furniture Polish.
INGREDIENTS.—*Equal proportions of linseed-oil, turpentine, vinegar and spirits of wine.*
Mode.—When used, shake the mixture well, and rub on the furniture with a piece of linen rag, and polish with a clean duster. Vinegar and oil, rubbed in with flannel, and the furniture rubbed with a clean duster, produce a very good polish.

Mrs Isabella Beeton,
Beeton's Book of Household Management (1861)

Linseed oil, linseed and flax flowers
© *Bon Appetit / Alamy*

BEESWAX

Furniture Paste.

INGREDIENTS.—*3 oz. of common beeswax, 1 oz. of white wax, 1 oz. of curd soap, 1 pint of turpentine, 1 pint of boiled water.*
Mode.—Mix the ingredients together, adding the water when cold; shake the mixture frequently in the bottle, and do not use it for 48 hours after it is made. It should be applied with a piece of flannel, the furniture polished with a duster, and then with an old silk rubber.

Mrs Isabella Beeton, *Beeton's Book of Household Management* (1861)

A very simple beeswax polish can be made by mixing beeswax with turpentine. The beeswax is melted in a bowl set over a pan of simmering water. Then the turpentine is added, and mixed well, before the polish is poured into a jar and left to cool before use.

HOUSEHOLD ODOURS

In medieval households, bad odours were countered by laying rushes on the floors and strewing them with sweet-smelling herbs and flowers. Walking on the herbs crushed them, allowing their fragrant essential oils to be released. Such strewing herbs fulfilled a dual purpose – not only did they help to mask the many odours associated with a household of this time, some also helped to repel pests such as fleas, and even acted as an antiseptic. While rush- and herb-strewn floors would not be desirable in the modern home, strewing herbs can still be used to make sachets for the linen closet, or be added to pot pourri, and there are a number of other natural remedies for unpleasant everyday pongs.

Pot pourri
© Andrew Newey / Alamy

TWENTY-ONE STREWING HERBS

Many herbs were popular as strewing herbs, including rosemary, sweet cicely, sweet woodruff, lavender and tansy. In his *Five Hundred Points of Good Husbandrie* (1557), Thomas Tusser lists 21 herbs which he recommends as suitable for strewing: basil; balm; camomile; costmary; cowslips; daisies of all sorts; fennel; germander; hyssop; lavender; lavender spike; lavender cotton; marjoram; maudeline; pennyroyal; roses of all sorts; red mints; sage; tansy; violets; and winter savory, although a 19th-century edition of his work also includes this cautionary footnote:

When domestic cleanliness was less regarded, strong or sweet scented herbs and flowers were liberally strewed in passages and apartments. This practice is highly improper, and is justly discontinued, as the smell of some is deleterious, and the effluvia of very few, indeed, can be conducive to health.

Thomas Tusser and William Mavor, *Five Hundred Points of Good Husbandry* (1812)

THE ROYAL HERB-STREWER

The post of 'royal herb-strewer' was created in the 17th century, after the English Civil War. The first royal herb-strewer was one Bridget Romney, apparently appointed to this newly created role in thanks for the loyalty and sacrifice shown by her family during the previous troubled years. She received a salary for her work, and kept the royal household supplied with deodorizing herbs. The post became increasingly ceremonial, with herb-strewers appearing in coronation processions, and now exists as an honorary title alone.

SMELLS IN THE KITCHEN

There are many ways of dealing with strong smells in the modern kitchen:

- Half a lemon can be used to rub down and freshen a wooden chopping board, or a pan that has retained a fishy aroma after cooking.
- A smelly fridge or kitchen cupboard can be rectified with a bowl of either bicarbonate of soda (also known as baking soda, or sodium bicarbonate) or charcoal, both of which will remove unwanted aromas – simply replace the bicarbonate or charcoal every three months.
- Unwanted cooking odours can be eradicated by simmering a little vinegar in water (but make sure the pot doesn't boil dry). The addition of spices, such as a cinnamon stick, will replace the cooking odour with a pleasant aroma.
- To freshen up a microwave, place a bowl of water with slices of lemon in it, and cook for 30 seconds or so.
- To remove the odour of onions from your hands after you have been chopping, wet your hands, rub in some salt, then rinse. Alternatively, wet your hands, then rub them on the side of a stainless steel sink, before washing them as normal.
- Smelly lunchboxes can be renewed by soaking them in a solution of bicarbonate of soda and water, before washing as normal.

- A kitchen drain that is smelly (but not blocked) can be freshened by pouring vinegar down the plughole, letting it stand for half an hour or so, then flushing it away with cold water.

To prevent disagreeable Smells from Sinks, &c.
The disgustful effluvia arising from cabbage-water, and the various ungrateful
odours which arise from the sink of kitchens, drains, &c., are not only an unnecessary
nuisance to the good folks of the second table, but we believe such miasm is not an
uncommon cause of putrid fevers, &c. &c.
It cannot be too generally known, that a cheap and simple apparatus has been
contrived for carrying off the waste water, &c. from sinks, which at the same time
effectually prevents any air returning back from thence, or from any drain connected
therewith. This is known by the name of Stink Trap, and costs about five shillings.
No kitchen sink should be without it.

William Kitchiner, *The Cook's Oracle; and Housekeeper's Manual* (1830)

ROOM ODOURS

- Make your own pot pourri from any combination of dried herbs, flowers, bark, seeds, fruit and berries. Flowers and leaves are dried by tying them in small bunches, and hanging them upside down somewhere dry and airy. Essential oils are often used to give the mixture extra fragrance, or to renew its fragrance once it has become stale.
- Place a thin layer of bicarbonate of soda in the bottom of a clean ashtray, replacing it each time the ashtray is emptied.
- Place bowls of vinegar in a freshly painted room to help remove the smell of the paint.

PET ODOURS

To remove the lingering odour left by pets on a carpet, sprinkle the offending area with bicarbonate of soda ten minutes or so before vacuuming. The same procedure will also work on a pet's bedding between washes, or on upholstery.

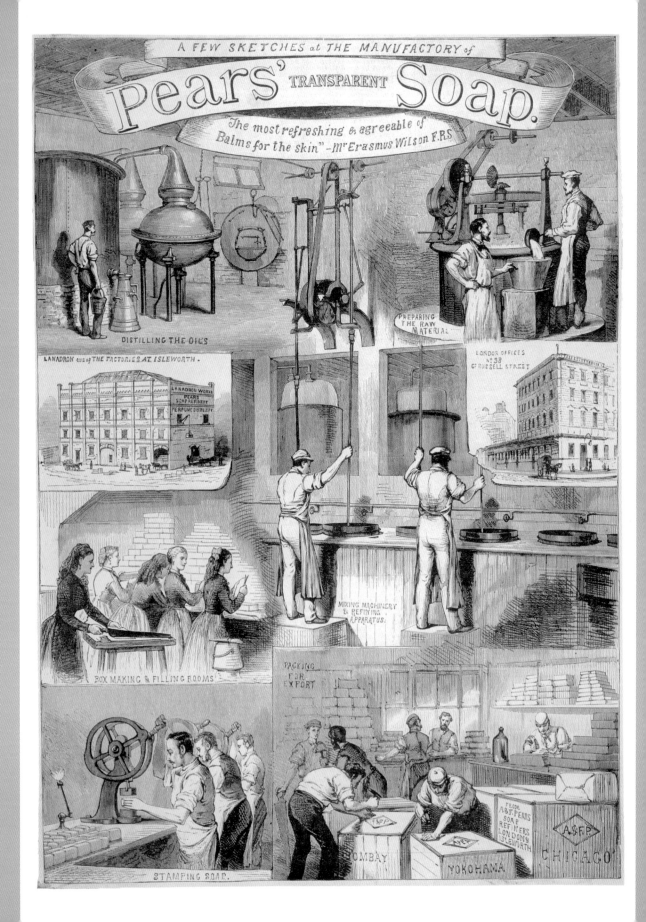

Soap Making

SOAP

Soap is a cleansing agent which, chemically speaking, is made of salts of fatty acids. Soaps were originally made from animal fats or vegetable oils mixed with ashes, an alkali which when combined with fat causes the chemical reaction which creates soap.

SOAP HISTORY

The word soap (sapo) occurs first in Pliny. He informs us that it was an invention of the Gauls, who employed it to render their hair shining; that it was a compound of wood-ashes and tallow, that there were two kinds of it, hard and soft (spissus et liquidus); and that the best kind was made of the ashes of the beech and the fat of goats. Among the Germans it was more employed by the men than the women.

Thomas Thomson, *The History of Chemistry* (1830)

While Pliny attributed the invention of soap to the Gauls, it is known that soap solutions were used by the Sumerians in 3000 BC. They used a mixture of ash and water to clean raw wool. Ashes are alkaline, and by mixing them with some of the natural grease and oil on the wool, a soap solution was formed, which dissolved the rest of the dirt. Realizing that the grease made the ash solution more effective, the Sumerians made soap solutions by boiling animal fats and oils with plant ashes and water.

Exactly when soap was first made in Britain is not known, but from the Middle Ages onwards soap in northern Europe was made by boiling animal fat with an extract of plant ashes (lye) and lime, while in

Mediterranean countries the animal fat was replaced by olive oil. As early as 1192, the English chronicler and monk Richard of Devizes referred to the foul smells which the activities of Bristol soap-makers produced, and other large towns such as Coventry and London also became soap-making centres. Most soap was used in the cloth-making industry, and for centuries, soap in the domestic setting was a luxury item, as fat was needed for necessities such as candles and rushlights. Soap was also heavily taxed from an early stage, and the large pans used for boiling the mixture were fitted with padlocks in order to control the amount of soap that was made.

Dried soapwort roots
© *Geoffrey Kidd / Alamy*

ALTERNATIVES TO SOAP

Nature provides a number of alternatives to soap, exploited by individuals and used as soap substitutes for washing clothes. Soapwort (*Saponaria officinalis*) grows near streams. By crushing the roots and leaves and stirring them in warm water, a lathery liquid is produced which was once commonly used for washing woollen clothes. The roots of red campion (*Silene dioica*) have been used in the same way, and other so-called 'soap' plants have been exploited in various parts of the world at different times. In Scotland, bracken was used to make a soap substitute in a method which stopped just short of making lye, as described below:

In several places in the north the inhabitants mow it [bracken] green, and burning it to ashes, make those ashes up into balls, with a little water, which they dry in the sun, and make use of them to wash their linen with instead of soap.

John Lightfoot, *Flora Scotica* (1777)

The fruit of the *Sapindus* tree that grows in India and Nepal, soap nuts, has become a popular Western-world alternative to washing powder or liquid, having been used by Indians for centuries. The shells of these nuts contain saponin and are a very effective, non-chemical detergent.

HOME-MADE LYE

Because lye is an alkaline solution, it loosens grease and dirt in clothes and linen, and long before the introduction of soap powder, many homes made their own lye. This was done by making water seep through wood ash. The ash was placed on a cloth in a 'lye dropper' (a wooden bucket with holes in the bottom). The water was poured onto the ashes and dripped through the holes into a tub placed below. Washing with lye solution was known as 'bucking with lye', the procedure taking place in a large bucket known as a buck. If the lye water was to be used to make soap, it was concentrated by boiling it down until a fresh egg (in its shell) would float on the mixture. It was then simmered with melted fat or oil for a number of hours, before salt was added as the mixture cooled. The salt hardened the soap, but settled to the bottom of the mixture, so was left behind when the soap was poured into moulds. Herbs could then be added to the moulds to improve the soap's scent. Lye making was a difficult procedure, and more unpleasant than it sounds when you consider that it is caustic.

Receipt to make Soap without boiling.
Boston, New England, May 1, 1791.
Put 20 lb. of grease into a kettle with two pails full of strong lye, set it over the fire until the grease is well melted; then take a barrel, placing it in the yard or any other open place, where the sun may come to it, and fill it two thirds full of strong lye, and put the melted grease and lye into it, boiling hot, stirring it well together with a stick, and put in a pail full of weak lye every day, continuing the stirring until the barrel is full, and in about a week's time you will have excellent soap. (The above method has been tried in this town of Boston, New-England, and found to exceed any common soap hitherto made by boiling, and will not be subject to any disagreeable smell by keeping; besides it will ease many worthy families from the confusion and vexation which usually attends the making of soap.)
The Annual Register, or a View of the History, Politics, and Literature, for the
Year 1791 (1800)

SOAPY SUPERSTITION

Everyone knows that soap is slippery, and as such is liable to slip from the hands. Nevertheless, in the 19th century some people considered this extremely unlucky, and likely even to lead to death. In the following report, a woman called Kate Elshender goes to a quarry hole in the Scottish Highlands to wash her clothes. She buys soap from a village shop, but it slips from her hands. She buys more, but it slips from her hands again:

She returned for a third half pound of soap. This time the old woman in the shop was thoroughly frightened, and begged and prayed her not to go back again; but she would go, in spite of everything that could be said to her. Shortly after the old woman, being quite unable to rest in her shop, went away to the quarry, she found no one there, and the clothes lying on the side of the hole. She gave the alarm, and, on search being made, the said Kate Elshender was discovered, drowned, at the bottom of the quarry hole.

Notes & Queries (1876)

MODERN SOAP MAKING

Fat and alkali are still needed to make soap. While in the past fat was obtained from slaughterhouses, soap-makers now use either fat that has been processed into fatty acids or vegetable fats such as olive oil, coconut oil and palm oil. The alkali used is commonly sodium hydroxide (for hard soap) and potassium hydroxide (for soft soap). Additives are used to provide the soap with colour and scent. Hobbyist soap-makers still make soap on a small scale at home, but generally use ingredients from specialist suppliers rather than saving up animal fat and mixing it with home-made lye.

Eradicating Pests and Vermin

BODY LICE

Of all the pests people in earlier times had to deal with, lice might seem the worst from a modern perspective. In addition to head lice, our forebears also had to contend with pubic lice and, when they started wearing clothing about 9,000 years ago, body lice. Infestations could be considerable. A student in 1499, one Thomas Platter, recorded that 'the scholars young and old, as well as some of the common people, crawled with vermin'. A mixture of ashes and oil was one remedy and the powdered seeds of stavesacre (a larkspur), still used in modern products, were recommended by Nicholas Culpeper in his *Complete Herbal* of 1649. But the normal treatment was to remove the lice by hand, which, according to contemporary accounts, could be a sociable activity, much like helping someone dye their hair or paint their fingernails today.

RATS AND FLEAS

The brown rat with which we are all familiar (there are now thought to be more rats in Britain than people) only arrived in England around 1730. People then called it the Norwegian rat in the mistaken belief that it came from Norway, but it almost certainly originated in China. The black rat, on the other hand, no longer present in the British Isles, arrived hundreds of years earlier and the fleas it carried were responsible for spreading bubonic plague. No one at the time understood how the plague was transmitted but, even so, nobody wanted fleas:

Some laies the hearbe called Fleawort, in Latin pulicaris, which if ye lay it in your chamber, no flea will breede, some takes brimstone and perfumes therewith ...

Anon, *A Profitable Booke* (1605)

The last rat-borne plague in Britain began in London early in 1665, killed 100,000 people and spread terror. 'Great fears of the sickenesse here in the City,' wrote Samuel Pepys in his diary. 'God preserve us.' Since there was no cure, the only solution was to run. The novelist Daniel Defoe was only five years old in the plague year, but his subsequent book was no doubt based on the memories of older people he knew:

... nothing was to be seen but wagons and carts, with goods, women, servants, children &c.; coaches filled with people of the better sort, and horsemen attending them, and all hurrying away ...

Daniel Defoe, *A Journal of the Plague Year* (1722)

Engraving from 1823 showing terriers hunting rats
© The Print Collector / Alamy

The Great Fire of 1666 coincidentally brought the plague to an end, but bubonic plague is a disease that a few Westerners still catch each year.

By Victorian times, rat-catching was a profitable profession, partly because live rats could be sold for rat-baiting. According to one contemporary account of a rat pit at Cambridge Circus, London, 'a hundred rats were put in it, large wagers went back and forth on whose dog could kill the most rats within a minute.' Jack Black was the rat-catcher by appointment to Queen Victoria, his favourite weapon being his black-and-tan terrier Billy. As he told a writer at the time, 'As rat-killing dogs, there's no equal.' But ratting could also be a sport for gentlemen:

It is the middle of October – just the nicest time of the year and the very best for ratting, for the vermin are yet out in the hedges, fine and strong from feeding in the corn, and with few young ones about. Come, Jack, we'll get the ferrets first; and off I go with the boy to the hutch, while the dogs in the kennel, having heard our steps and perfectly understanding what is up, bark and yap at the door, jump over each other, tumble and topple about like mad fiends.

H C Barkley, *Studies in the Art of Rat Catching* (1896)

Even in Victorian times, rats could also be pets. Queen Victoria was said to have two, and the writer of children's stories Beatrix Potter had a pet rat called Samuel Whiskers.

Nowadays, you can put down poison to kill rats, but there is always the risk of poisoning something else, including dogs, as well as the rat dying somewhere inaccessible and creating a bad smell. Traps, then, are better but rats are quite intelligent and will quickly learn to avoid them. The solution is to put down and bait several traps but leave them unset. Only set the traps after a few days, once you see the baits are being taken, and in that way you may catch the whole community.

MICE

Cats are the traditional mice exterminators and can be good 'mousers' but, quite often, they bring mice in from outside and then lose them, thus making the situation worse. Here's how to make your own, very effective humane mousetrap. Take the cardboard tube from inside a toilet roll and flatten a strip to create an n-shaped tunnel. Put a dob of some attractive sticky food (try peanut butter) at one end of the tunnel. Balance the tunnel at the edge of a kitchen surface or table so that the end with the treat sticks out directly above a deep container on the floor, such as a wastepaper basket. When the mouse enters the tunnel it will tip up, depositing the mouse in the basket. Take it at least a mile from your home and release it.

FOXES

It seems that fox hunting with hounds dates only from 1534 in Norfolk. Most hunts thought it beneath their dignity to chase 'vermin'. Instead they hunted deer until the building of new roads and canals had, by the 1830s, broken up the huge tracts of open land that previously existed. Fox hunting, as we now think of it, was created by Hugo Meynell, Master of the Quorn Hunt between 1753 and 1800, who set about breeding hounds especially for the purpose. According to one early account, 'Mr Meynell's hounds are uncommonly fleet, [but] they do not appear to draw well'. Later, his hounds excelled at both picking up the scent and running. For Meynell and those who copied him, hunting was far more about entertainment than controlling foxes:

> *The veriest tyro must have heard of, if he have not witnessed, the effect of a tally-*
> *ho as soon as a fox puts his nose out of covert; and, with all due allowance for*
> *exuberance of delight, he has no business out hunting if he have not learned to view*
> *the animal in respectful silence till he is clean 'gone away'. A view halloo given then*
> *to the full extent of the utmost capability of lungs, can do no harm ...*
> Frederick Radcliffe, *The Noble Science* (1839)

Now that fox hunting with hounds has been made illegal in Britain (although other methods can still be used) it seems that the 'tally-ho' has gone for ever.

INSECTS

> *The flying moathes will bee in the beginning of June, and continue till August ... The*
> *running moath hee will continue in your Chests all the yeare long ... For the flying*
> *moathe, take the pouder made of drie Orange Pilles, and the pouder of Elecompane*
> *rootes mixt together, and so cast it among your cloths.*
> Anon, *A Profitable Booke* (1605)

All kinds of commercial traps and poisons are now available for moths and most other insects including cockroaches. But there are quite a few natural things you can also do to reduce problems.

Against *moths*, vacuum regularly and use a dehumidifier – moths are most comfortable in high humidity.

For *flies*, old-fashioned flypapers are very efficient. A good trick for killing flies is to position your hands a little way apart just above a fly that has settled. Then clap. The fly, disturbed by the movement, takes off – straight into the clap. A bowl of vinegar (cider vinegar works particularly well) left out is also effective.

To reduce *mosquito* populations, eliminate standing water wherever possible. If you have a pond, stock it with goldfish or minnows, both of which eat mosquito larvae. Eucalyptus oil is quite good at keeping the adults away.

Lots of things are effective against *ants*. Try sprinkling them, their trail, and the point where they enter the house, with baby powder, cinnamon, black pepper, cayenne pepper or chilli powder. A paste of chilli powder is effective in any small holes or cracks by which they enter. Vinegar squirted and left to dry also deters them.

Despite modern technology, insects are probably more of a nuisance in many places than in former times. It is believed that the percentage of the medieval crop lost to pests was 30 per cent, whereas today the figure is put at over 35 per cent, partly because more than 500 species have developed resistance to pesticides. Possibly the best way of dealing with insects is to eat them (see the section on dining).

See the gardening section for advice on eradicating slugs and snails.

Insects trapped in a plastic bottle containing vinegar
© Per Karlsson - BKWine. com / Alamy

SWEET WILLIAM, Rainbow Mixture

BEES' SEEDS
THAT GROW
1ᴰ

NIGHT-SCENTED STOCK

BEES' SEEDS
THAT GROW
1ᴰ

SCARLET FLAX

BEES' SEEDS
THAT GROW
1ᴰ

CRESS

BEES' SEEDS
THAT GROW
1ᴰ

Gardening

SEVEN WONDERS

Early humans were far more concerned with growing food than flowers, but the famous Hanging Gardens of Babylon, one of the Seven Wonders of the World, were certainly for pleasure and were probably built around 600 BC. The Greek historian Diodorus, writing in the 1st century BC, described them as 'ascending terraces ... planted with every kind of tree'. Indeed, for hundreds of years such grandiose conceptions, built by the aristocracy or public authorities, were the only gardens. Being a gardener was a profession and only became a hobby in recent times. In Britain, the earliest discovered garden is at Fishbourne Roman Palace in Sussex. The first handbook on British gardening is thought to be the verse-form *The Feate of Gardening*, written by 'Mayster Jon Gardener' in c.1440.

TOOLS

Of course, until recently, everything in the garden had to be done by hand and, indeed, many gardeners even made their own tools:

A Good husband hath his forks and rakes made ready in the winter before, and they would be got between Michelmas and Martylmas, and baked, and set even, to lie upright in thy hand: and then they will be hard stiff and dry. And when the husband sitteth by the fire, and hath nothing to do, then may he make them ready, and tooth the rakes with dry wethywood, and bore the holes with his wymble, both above and under, and drive the teeth upwards fast and hard, and then wedge them above with dry wood of oak ...

John Fitzherbert, *Boke of Husbandrye* (1523)

FERTILIZER

All kinds of fertilizers were used in Georgian and Victorian gardens, including horse and cattle dung, rotted fish, seaweed, soot, blood from the slaughterhouse and guano, vast quantities of which were imported from South America. There was lively debate about the merits of salt. Every gardener, it seems, had his own special 'recipe':

Raise a platform of earth ... On the first stratum of earth lay a thin stratum of lime, fresh from the kiln. Dissolve this into the earth with brine from the rose of a watering can and immediately add another layer of earth. Lime and brine as before, carrying it to any convenient height. In a week, it should be carefully turned over ... This compost has been used in Ireland, and it has doubled the crops of potatoes ...
Charles McIntosh, *The Practical Gardener* (1828)

Most gardeners nowadays would disagree with the routine use of lime. The accepted system in vegetable plots is to divide them into three and rotate root crops, brassicas and other plants, only liming the land for brassicas – which means each third gets limed once every three years.

One place you can use lime systematically is the compost heap, the inexpensive way to create manure from kitchen and garden waste. The first step is to dig two intersecting trenches in the form of a cross for aeration. Make them about two to three good paces in length, the depth of a hand and the width of a foot, and lay some scraps of wood over them to prevent the compost falling in. Then gradually pile on your material. Every foot or so alternate layers of animal manure and dustings of lime, until the heap, tapering in, is as high as it can safely be. Don't cover the ends of the trenches. To keep moisture and heat in, an old carpet or some plastic sheeting will speed things up enormously.

NEW PLANTS FOR THE GARDEN

As enthusiasm grew for creating ever more original gardens, so owners demanded new plants, and they came from two sources: hybridization and imports from abroad. Many gardeners, like Richard Bradley, author of the early 18th-century *New Improvements of Planting and Gardening*, had benefited from what he called 'accidental coupling', but when Thomas Fairchild (1667–1729) used a feather to transfer pollen from a sweet william to a carnation he created the first deliberate hybrid – a pink (*Dianthus*).

In the modern garden, most flowers owe their existence to Thomas Fairchild, including roses, peonies, poppies, marigolds, petunias, tulips, daffodils and azaleas. He, himself, agonized over what he had done, just as we do now about genetically modified crops. As a sort of penance, he left money to his parish church for an annual sermon on 'the wonderful works of God' and the sermon is still preached today, every Whitsun, at St Giles, Cripplegate.

The other source of new species was exploration. In 1771, Joseph Banks brought back 1,300 plant species from Botany Bay and unwittingly created the profession of plant hunter. But there was the problem of how to transport the most delicate specimens. The solution was provided by Dr Nathaniel Ward and, as is so often the case, it came by accident. In 1829, Dr Ward saved the pupa of a moth in a sealed jar. What happened to the moth isn't known but a fern and some grasses flourished. In 1833, Dr Ward successfully sent plants to Australia in the 'natural environment' of his terrarium or 'Wardian case' and two years later received back some delicate Australian plants. Within a few years, thousands more species new to Britain had been successfully shipped back, including the rhododendron, discovered in Sikkim by Sir Joseph Hooker.

Even today, new species of plants are still being found but the golden age of plant hunting ended with Frank Kingdon-Ward (1885–1958) whose journeys into Tibet, China and Burma spanned 45 years.

HOTBEDS

As more and more exotic plants were imported so it became increasingly necessary to protect them with hotbeds. Horse manure was often used to generate heat, but the best was tanner's bark – crushed oak bark used in the process of converting raw hides into leather:

Dig a trench in the earth, about three feet deep, if the ground be dry: but if wet, not above six inches, at most, and raise it in proportion above ground, so as to admit of the tan being laid three feet thick ... [The bark] should be laid in a round heap for a week or ten days, before it is put into the trench, that the moisture may the better drain out of it. Then put it in the trench, and gently beat it down ... put on the frame over the bed, covering it with the glasses, and in about a fortnight, it will begin to

heat; at which time may be plunged into it, pots of plants or seeds, observing not to tread down the bark in so doing ...

Duncan MacDonald, *Garden Almanac* (c.1800)

With the development of electric heating for greenhouses and frames the traditional ways gradually died out.

OUT, DAMNED SLUG

Although slugs do have a beneficial role to play in the garden by breaking down decaying plant matter, these perennial pests have been the bane of gardeners' lives for centuries. The traditional method to deter them (and snails too) is to create a barrier around your plants from material that they don't like. Popular ingredients include crushed eggshells, soot, ash, lime, salt, seaweed and hair clippings.

If the barrier doesn't work, then a trap might. Sinking a container into the ground and filling it with beer is another method that has long been used. The slugs are attracted by the smell of the beer, fall in and can't get out. If you don't want to waste good beer, however, you could follow an age-old practice of simply getting yourself some ducks or geese, which find the slimy pests palatable.

GARDENING BY THE MOON

The astronomical information given in *Old Moore's Almanack* was long used as guidance for when to plant and harvest crops, and it seems there is a sound basis for this belief. Planting is best done when the moon is waxing or full, because the moon exerts a pull on the water in the soil in the same way as it does on the sea. The water rises and can so promote growth in the young plants or seeds which are better able to take it up. When the moon is waning, there is a decreased gravitational pull – a good time to harvest but not to plant.

The signs of the zodiac also play a role in when to do your gardening: water signs are meant to be good times to plant and, for example, Leo – a fire sign – is meant to be a good time to weed.

Starting a Car

GREEN FIRST, BLACK SECOND

The motor car was in use much earlier than most people realize, and its origins were potentially greener than the machine it has become today. In 1806, a Swiss inventor called François Isaac de Rivaz designed a primitive but environmentally friendly engine fuelled by hydrogen and oxygen, and in 1881, the French inventor Gustave Trouvé unveiled a three-wheeler powered by electricity. If either had succeeded in perfecting their ideas the history of the planet might have been very different. But it was the four-stroke petrol engine built in Germany by Karl Benz that, in 1888, was first into production. The first British production car was a Daimler in 1896, but it was the American Henry Ford who saw the advantages of the assembly line, and by 1914 his cars were being made so fast that only the paint known as Japan black could dry quickly enough – giving rise to the famous remark, 'any colour as long as it's black'. The first Ford cars were imported into Britain in 1903 and in 1911 an assembly plant was opened in Manchester to make the Model T, the market leader.

THE MODEL T

From 1909 to 1927, the Ford Motor Company built more than 15 million Model T cars and until 1919 they, like all cars, had to be started using 'hand cranks'.

The first step was to make sure that the handbrake lever was fully applied because, on the Model T, it also held the clutch in neutral. If the car started without the handbrake being on then it would drive away on its own, probably running over whoever was using the starting handle.

The steering wheel on the Model T had two levers, much like the modern controls for windscreen washers or lights. On the Model T they had different functions. One was the spark lever and the other was the throttle:

... the spark lever should usually be put in about the third or fourth notch. The throttle should usually be placed in about the fifth or sixth notch ... Care should be taken not to advance the spark lever too far, as the engine may 'kick back'.

Anon, *Ford Owners Manual* (1922)

The 'kick back' could actually be quite dangerous. It meant that the engine was running in reverse, taking the crank or starting handle with it.

The result could easily be a broken thumb or wrist. The way to avoid it was to make sure the spark was sufficiently 'retarded' by using the spark lever.

After inserting the key and turning on, the proud owner was nearly ready for the difficult part. But if the weather was cold there was one more thing to do:

Controls of a 1910 Ford Model T showing spark lever and throttle
© Tom Wood / Alamy

When the engine is cool it is advisable to prime the carburetor by pulling on the small wire at the lower left corner of the radiator ...

Anon, *Ford Owners Manual* (1922)

The handle now had to be pushed firmly in until it engaged with the crank ratchet and the engine given 'two or three quarter turns with the starting handle'. However, if the engine was warm, all that was necessary, according to the manual, was to push home the handle and 'lift upward with a quick swing'.

There's always an easier way

For those with sufficient skill, the engine could sometimes be tricked into life by rotating the crank with the ignition off until the piston was just past top dead centre (TDC). Turning the ignition on at that point could sometimes start the engine, as if by magic, if you were lucky enough that the continuous spark ignited fuel in the combustion chamber. The easiest method, though, was simply to remember to park on a hill and 'jump' start.

THE STARTER MOTOR

The starting handle was fairly obviously a problem that needed a solution and Charles Kettering was the man who provided it, patenting a successful starter motor in 1911. Cadillac were the first to install them in 1912 and by 1920 most manufacturers offered them as an option.

THE STARTING HANDLE TODAY

Starting handles continued to be a back-up on cars well into the second-half of the 20th century, but as compression ratios increased so it became harder and harder to turn them. Nowadays, your best chance of seeing them in use is the London to Brighton Veteran Car Run (www.lbvcr. com) which commemorates the 1896 Emancipation Run celebrating the increase in the speed limit from 2 mph to 14 mph.

Superstitions

ALL IN THE MIND

The place to search for the origin of superstitions is not, according to scientists, in the history books but in the human mind. When Japanese psychologist Koichi Ono asked people to try to control a randomly flashing light, without knowing that it was random, they very quickly developed 'superstitions' about what worked. They convinced themselves the 'secret' was in pulling a special combination of levers, or banging on the walls, or even jumping in the air. In the same way, if someone happened to be wearing a particular dress or ring when something good or bad happened, that item became 'lucky' or 'unlucky'.

Some such charms or amulets could take on very specific powers:

There was a superstition to the effect that the cross-bone of the head of a Bollan-fish would prevent anyone from straying from the most direct road to any place to which he wanted to proceed, either by day or night. Manx sailors seldom went to sea without one of these bones in their pocket to direct their course at night or in hazy weather.

A W Moore, *Folk-Lore of the Isle of Man* (1891)

SYMPATHETIC MAGIC

Sympathetic magic is the idea that if something resembles something else then there must be some kind of magical connection that could be exploited:

Ruptured children are expected to be cured by being passed through a young tree, which has been split for the purpose. After the operation has been performed, the tree is bound up, and, if it grows together again, the child will be cured of its rupture.

Robert Chambers, *Book of Days* (1869)

Similarly, if someone was shaking with ague (malarial fever) it was believed that giving them a severe fright would cure it.

Probably the most widely practised form of sympathetic magic in the world was, and still is, homeopathy. The word was coined by the German physician Samuel Hahnemann and first appeared in print in 1807, although he had been writing about the 'law of similars' for a decade previous to that. The idea behind it was that if a substance produced symptoms in a healthy person that resembled those associated with a disease, then that substance, extremely diluted, could be used to treat the disease. It did not need modern science to point out that homeopathy ran contrary to the laws of physics, and Sir John Forbes, physician to Queen Victoria, called the idea 'an outrage to human reason'.

Why does belief in homeopathy persist in the face of science? In the first place, people recover from about 80 per cent of ailments without any treatment. So, someone taking a homeopathic remedy is likely to have got better anyway. And, because of the placebo effect, any treatment at all, provided it is harmless, is better than no treatment.

But sympathetic magic was not only confined to medical matters:

At table, no one will turn a Herring; but, when one side is eaten, the bone is taken away, so that the rest can be eaten: for to turn the Herring would be tantamount to overturning the boat into which it was drawn from the ocean if it then chanced to be at sea.

A W Moore, *Folk-Lore of the Isle of Man* (1891)

Some sailors actually held the unfortunate belief that it would be fatal to save a drowning man. In Sir Walter Scott's *Pirate*, Bryce, the pedlar, justifies his inaction. 'Are you mad?' said the pedlar. '... to risk the saving of a drowning man? Wot ye not, if you bring him to life again he will be sure to do you some capital injury.' The thinking was that if the gods intended that someone should be drowned then the rescuer would be drowned in his place.

THE UNKNOWABLE

Not unnaturally, some people have always wanted to know things beyond the possibilities of science. The mirror has long been thought to be a means of seeing into the future, which is why it's bad luck to break one. The forked twig is another form of divination:

I sent for a labouring man in the village who would 'work the twig,' as the divining rod is called here, and he came and cut a blackthorn twig out of my hedge, and proceeded around the field, and at one spot the twig became so violently affected that it flew out of his hands ...
     T Sharper Knowlson, *The Origins of Popular Superstitions and Customs*
                          (1910)

Believers never seemed to ask why the twigs never moved on their own. The reason for the success of dowsers is simply that there is water everywhere. Under London, for example, it is as little as ten metres down and, before the Industrial Revolution, was even closer to the surface. Nevertheless, dowsers are still used by some well-drilling companies today.

THIRTEEN

The idea that the number 13 is unlucky stems, of course, from the Last Supper when 13 were present. At one time, there were clubs of people who deliberately flouted that superstition as well as several others:

... the diners sat at tables thirteen to each ... As soon as the company was seated a new mirror was broken. The ices were served in the form of a skull reposing in a coffin ...
     T Sharper Knowlson, *The Origins of Popular Superstitions and Customs*
                          (1910)

However, it was reported that 'fate had revenge'. At the head of each table an open umbrella had been placed (to flout yet another superstition) and a waiter, carrying a full soup tureen, tripped on it, throwing soup over the diners.

  Still, other people's superstitions can have their benefits. The novelist Ernest Hemingway liked to relate how, when he was still a poor and unknown writer, the actress Marlene Dietrich entered the restaurant where, in a borrowed tuxedo, he was eating. Seeing that there were already twelve at her table she refused to sit down. Gallantly, the struggling novelist came over and offered to make the party up to fourteen. And they remained friends till his death.

TO RID YOURSELF OF SUPERSTITIONS

Most people only take notice of the times that a superstition seems to be borne out. In order to make a balanced judgement, you also need to take account of the times that nothing at all happens, as well as the times that something happens *without* the conditions of the superstition being met. You also might like to see www.skepdic.com.

Outdoor Life

Weather Forecasting

FORECASTING BY NUMBERS

The British mathematician Lewis Fry Richardson (1881–1953) was one of the first to develop a scientific system of weather forecasting based on equations. But so complicated were the calculations that it took him several months to produce one six-hour forecast – and it was wildly wrong. Undaunted, he published a book on his method, confident that, given sufficient manpower, accurate forecasts could be produced. The problem was that the number of mathematicians necessary was 64,000.

His dilemma illustrates the problem of making accurate forecasts. In fact, it wasn't until recently that computers became powerful enough to crunch all the data in time. And they can still be wrong. No wonder our forebears relied on their own observations and superstitions.

OLD MOORE'S ALMANACK

First published in 1697 as *Vox Stellarum* ('Voice of the Stars') by astrologer Dr Francis Moore, this annual publication that is still in print today gives, amongst other predictions, weather forecasts based on the phases of the moon and tide timetables. It was widely used by farmers and gardeners, as is its American cousin *The Old Farmer's Almanac*, published continuously since 1792. Its precise weather forecasting formula is kept secret and locked in a box in its offices in Dublin, New Hampshire, but is believed to use solar activity and historical weather patterns in addition to astronomical data.

ANIMAL FORECASTERS

Country folk have always had a high regard for the wisdom of animals. At least, in certain respects. Anyone who owns dogs, cats or horses will almost certainly have observed their pets becoming agitated some significant time before they themselves have become aware of an approaching storm. And the evidence that animals can predict earthquakes has convinced scientific writers as far back as Pliny the Elder 2,000 years ago. He wrote that earthquakes were preceded by 'the excitation and terror of animals with no apparent reason'. So in the era before weather satellites and computers, turning to animals made sense:

Storms will ensue when Seagulls come inland and Rooks fly to the mountains; when Cattle and Sheep seek shelter, and when the Porpoise ... is seen gambolling round ships at sea. Rain will follow when Sparrows chirp, when Rooks and Herons fly low, when Rats and Mice are rest-less, and when many Bees return to the hive and none leave it. Fine weather is certain when Bats fly about at sunset, when Rooks, Herons and Larks fly high, when Seagulls fly out to sea, when Bees are seen far from their hives, and Spiders spin their webs in the open air.

A W Moore, *Folk-Lore of the Isle of Man* (1891)

Possibly the most intriguing rhyme concerning animals is this one:

If a cat washes her face o'er her ear,
'Tis a sign the weather will be fine and clear.

The explanation for this one may be static electricity which builds up in fur when it's dry. Licking the fur would help prevent it.

THE WIND

Winter
North winds send hail, South winds bring rain,
East winds we bewail, West winds blow amain:
North-east is too cold, South-east not too warm,
North-west is too bold, South-west doth no harm.

Thomas Tusser, *Five Hundred Points of Good Husbandry* (1557)

The easiest way to understand wind is to think of it as a river. Just as a river flows one way, so the prevailing wind in Britain also flows one way, from south-west to north-east. But in the same way as there can be whirlpools in a river, so wind can also circulate as it moves along. As a result you feel it coming from a succession of different directions.

The direction of circulation, and the strength of the wind, both depend on the air pressure.

PRESSURE

The first person to realize that changes in air pressure were related to changes in the weather was an Italian scientist called Evangelista Torricelli (1608–47). Filling a metre-long glass tube, closed at one end, with mercury (then known as 'quicksilver') and inverting it in a dish of mercury, he discovered it fell to around 76cm (leaving a vacuum above). This was the approximate height of mercury the atmosphere could support – but, as he noted, the exact level is constantly changing. Today, pressure is measured in millibars (mb) and, at sea level, normal pressure is considered to be 1013mb, with a range of 950–1050mb.

By the late 17th century, these quicksilver barometers began to appear in wealthy homes and helped create their own weather lore:

> *When the glass falls low,*
> *Prepare for a blow;*
> *When it slowly rises high,*
> *Lofty canvas you may fly.*

What causes the 'blow' (usually but not always) is a sudden change of pressure. Again, using the analogy of a river, it means there are two very different 'levels' and that can only result in violence – a waterfall in the case of the river, a gale in the case of the atmosphere.

Some people say they have more aches and pains when the pressure is low:

> *A coming storm your shooting corns presage,*
> *And aches will throb, your hollow tooth will rage.*

High pressure means the air is descending and therefore becoming warmer so that the sky is clear and blue; any wind, meanwhile, will be circulating clockwise (in the northern hemisphere). Low pressure, on the other hand, means air is circulating anticlockwise and ascending, as a result of which it cools and clouds form. Not surprisingly, most people will feel better in a high.

CLOUDS

Clouds are one of the most obvious weather indicators and, not surprisingly, a good deal of lore surrounds them:

Mackerel sky and mares' tails,
Make lofty ships carry low sails.

A 'mackerel sky' refers to altocumulus (lines of clouds between 2,000 and 8,000m) and cirrocumulus clouds (like altocumulus but higher - between 5,000 and 13,000m – and more delicate), while 'mares' tails' are cirrus clouds (long high wisps).

Mackerel sky
© *Joan Gravell / Alamy*

The pattern of clouds

In reality, only a limited amount can be told from clouds at any given moment. To make an accurate prediction you need to watch the unfolding pattern of clouds over several hours:

If clouds are gathering thick and fast,
Keep sharp look out for sail and mast,
But if they slowly onward crawl,
Shoot your lines, nets and trawl.

Every weather system is different (otherwise forecasting would be easy), but the typical pattern is as follows. You see cumulus and stratocumulus clouds and it's relatively cold. Then the cloud thickens, it rains and it becomes warmer – a warm front is passing through. The rain stops for a while but the clouds soon coagulate into towering cumulonimbus which drop 'stair rods'. Finally, it becomes colder once more – a cold front is passing – and there are occasional showers from cumulus once again.

AND THOSE RED SKIES?

Everyone knows this rhyme:

> *Red sky at night, shepherd's delight;*
> *Red sky in the morning, shepherd's warning.*

Is there any truth in it? Yes, there is. A red sky at night can be caused by the setting sun shining through dry dust particles in the west. The weather normally comes from the west, which suggests it will be dry. But modern observations show the rhyme is right on only about 60 per cent of occasions.

Telling the Time

IN SUNLIGHT

The sky is itself a clock by which you can tell the time if you know how to read it. The sun rises from an easterly direction (not necessarily due east), reaches its highest point at 'solar noon' (not necessarily the same as noon by the clock), and sets in the west (not necessarily due west). If every day was exactly the same length it would be easy to tell the time by the sun, but in London, for example, it varies between 7 hours 49 minutes on 21 December and 16 hours 38 minutes on 21 June. However, provided you have a rough idea of the times of sunrise and sunset you can deduce the time simply by dividing the sky up in your mind by the number of daylight hours and noting in which sector the sun is.

For more accuracy, you can improvise your own sundial, a concept which must have been known well over 2,000 years ago:

Your only cares will be to scent yourself, and to go and dine, when the shadow of the gnomon is ten feet long on the dial.

Aristophanes, *Ecclesiazusae* (393 BC)

The simplest form of sundial is a stick planted vertically in the earth. If you want to try it for yourself, hammer a thigh-high stick firmly upright into flat ground some time before the sun has reached its peak. Mark the tip of the shadow with a stone. Wait about a quarter of an hour and again mark the tip of the shadow with a stone. Draw a line between the two stones and extend it sufficiently that you can draw a second line at right angles going to the base of the stick. When the shadow of the stick falls precisely on that line it will be local noon. Divide the 90° angles as accurately as you can into six segments and each will then be approximately 15°, equivalent to one hour, enabling you to tell the time with reasonable accuracy throughout the day.

The stick has obvious limitations, one of which is that the sun's path is different every day of the year, so the lines would have to be redrawn fairly regularly. Early astronomers realized that the way to overcome the problem was to cast the shadow from a triangular gnomon designed with a slope parallel to the earth's polar axis. In other words, the style angle (the angle made between the slope and the horizontal base of the sundial) has to be equal to the latitude at which the sundial is to be used (see section on understanding longitude and latitude). In the London area the angle would have to be around 51°, but 56° for Edinburgh, while Aristophanes in Athens would have needed an angle of 38°. Such a sundial is reasonably accurate but, because the length of day as measured by the sun can be slightly more or less than 24 hours, there can be a difference of up to 16 minutes at certain times of the year between sundial time and clock time.

If you need to time things repeatedly day and night (such as, for example, periods on watch), you can use the ancient 'sinking bowl' method. You need two containers, one large, one small. Fill the large one with water. Make a tiny hole in the second and set it afloat. When it sinks, the time is up. Of course, you won't know exactly how long that period is, but if you've set up some kind of sundial you'll have a rough idea, and you can alter the length of the period by changing the size of the hole, or the floating container, or by putting a weight in it.

BY THE STARS

On a clear night, telling the time to within an accuracy of one hour or better is extremely easy because there is a group of stars that (with a little imagination) is in the shape of a clock hand. The keys are the seven stars known as the Plough (Ursa Major), the Pole Star (also known as Polaris), the date 7 March and the number two.

The first step is to locate the Plough. It's always visible in Britain from a good vantage point – although in autumn it's so close to the northern horizon that it might be partly obscured by hills. As you'll see, three of the stars form a sort of handle and the other four form a sort of square.

Starting from the handle, follow the shape along to the last two stars, Merak and, last of all, Dubhe. Now draw an imaginary line from Merak to Dubhe and continue it and you'll come (more or less) to the Pole Star.

The next bit seems a bit tricky at first but becomes easy with a little bit of practice. Facing the Pole Star (in other words, north), try to imagine the sky as a huge clock, with 12 at the top and 6 at the bottom, and that a line drawn from the Pole Star back through Dubhe and Merak and onwards is an 'hour hand'. If you watch intermittently over a couple of hours or so you'll notice that this 'hour hand' appears to move *backwards*. Let's say it's now pointing horizontally to the right, in which case it's indicating the number 3.

Unfortunately, that isn't the actual time (things are never that easy) unless it happens to be 7 March, because that's the only day of the year the 'star clock' is correct. However, by applying a little maths we can adjust for every other day of the year. That's where the number 2 comes in, because for every day before 7 March we have to subtract two minutes and for every day after 7 March we have to add two minutes (which amounts to one hour per month).

Let's say the 'hour hand' was pointing to 3 on 7 February. That's one month before 7 March, so we subtract one hour which gives the number 2. Now double that number (which gives 4) and subtract it from 24 (or 48 if the number is too big). In this case, that gives us the number 20 (20:00 on the 24-hour clock, 8pm on the 12-hour clock). We're now very close to the right time, but there are still two possible adjustments to make. The first is an adjustment for summer time – if the clocks have gone forward

The northern constellations of Ursa Major and Cassiopeia, showing how to find Polaris (the Pole Star), as seen from mid UK looking north.
© *Robin Scagell/Galaxy*

for 'daylight saving' then add one hour. In our example, the clocks are still on 'winter time' so there's no adjustment to be made. The other is for your position within your time zone. Theoretically, if you're towards the eastern edge of your time zone you should subtract half an hour, but if you're towards the western edge of your time zone you should add half an hour. However, for practical reasons time zones are never that neat and the boundaries meander with the shape of national borders, so you may find you should add or subtract a little more or less. Once you know the adjustment for your area then you'll always be correct. In our example, we'll assume the observation was made in London, right in the middle of the time zone, which means the time was, indeed, 8pm.

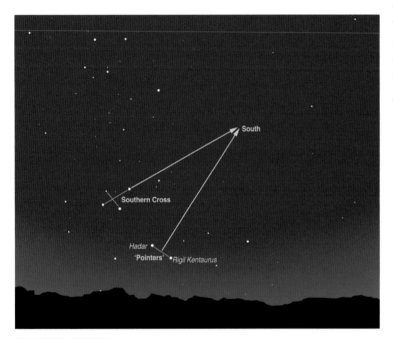

Method of finding the South Celestial Pole in the southern hemisphere using the Southern Cross. Project its length about 4¹/₂ times. Use Alpha and Beta Centauri to identify the Southern Cross.

© Robin Scagell/Galaxy

Working with the Moon and Tides

OCEANS INTO THE MOON

The earliest-known reference to a connection between the moon and the tides occurs in the *Samaveda*, one of the four ancient Hindu scriptures, probably dating from around 3,000 years ago. In the Mediterranean, where tides are less obvious, Aristotle, the 4th-century BC Greek philosopher, nevertheless noted that the 'ebbings and risings of the sea always come around with the moon and upon certain fixed times'. Pytheas of Massalia (Marseilles), the first Mediterranean sailor to reach Britain, in around 310 BC, was astonished to encounter 'tidal differences of 50 feet', large even by British standards, suggesting he must have visited the Bristol Channel.

Various theories were advanced to explain the link between the moon and the tides, including the idea that the moon somehow compressed invisible matter between itself and the earth. It wasn't until the 17th century that scientists began to pin the phenomenon down. The German astronomer Johannes Kepler (1571–1630) correctly suggested the moon attracted the water of the oceans, although he rather exaggerated when he proposed that, if it wasn't for the earth's own gravity, the oceans 'would flow into the moon'. It was left to Britain's Isaac Newton (1642–1727) to fully unlock the secrets. He calculated the moon's motion on the basis of his theory of gravity, explained why there were two tides for every transit of the moon, and worked out why there were springs and neaps.

HOW TIDES WORK

In fact, tides are not the work solely of the moon but also, to a lesser extent, the sun. The waters of the oceans are attracted towards these bodies by gravitation and thus form a sort of 'bulge' underneath them. At the same time, on the opposite side of the earth, centrifugal force keeps things in equilibrium by creating a 'bulge' there as well. High water therefore occurs simultaneously at places which have a difference of longitude of 180° (see the section on understanding longitude and latitude), while places halfway between will have low water. As a result, any point on the ocean would have two high tides and two low tides every day, if it were not for the moon's own motion. In fact, it takes rather more than 24 hours for the moon to return to the same station above the earth, with the result that each tide is roughly 54 minutes later each day (and the time between one high tide and the next, or between one low tide and the next, is approximately 12 hours 27 minutes).

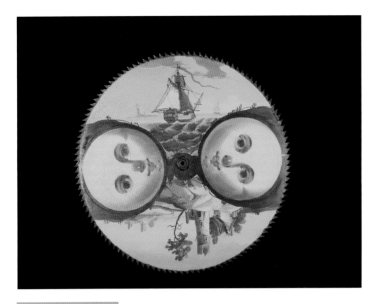

But things are a little more complicated than that. The moon and sun are only in alignment and pulling in exactly the same direction when there's a new moon and when there's a full moon. If you see the first quarter or the last quarter of the moon (that is, half the face) it means the sun and moon are acting at right angles to one another or, effectively, in opposition. The moon always wins, because its gravitational effect is some two and a half times greater than the sun's. But the effect of the sun being at right angles is to reduce the influence of the moon and, therefore, the rise and fall of the tide. It's this that explains neap tides (when the difference between high and low water is relatively small) and spring tides (when the difference between high and low water is relatively great).

Spring tides, then, have nothing to do with springtime. But, just to confuse things, the alignment of the moon and sun does produce the highest tides of the year, known as equinoctial tides, in March – and, again, in September (whilst solstice tides in June and December have the lowest range).

THE TWELFTHS RULE

Sea level doesn't rise and fall at a constant rate. The change is slowest around high and low water and fastest three to four hours later. Navigators can consult 'tide curves' for a fairly precise picture but, for most sailors, the 'twelfths rule' is good enough. It says that during the first hour the water will rise or fall by one-twelfth of its range, during the second hour two-twelfths, during the third hour three-twelfths, during the fourth hour three-twelfths, during the fifth hour two-twelfths and during the sixth hour one-twelfth. It's easy to remember – 1,2,3,3,2,1.

TIDAL STREAMS

The rising and falling of the tide causes tidal streams, as the water rushes 'in' and 'out'. Although the average tidal stream runs at a maximum of three knots, around Britain there are places, such as the Pentland Firth and the Race of Alderney, where they can reach up to ten knots. No small yacht, whether under sail or power, can make headway against a powerful tidal stream. Sailors therefore have to know how to work the tides. On Admiralty charts the rate and direction of tidal streams are given for several places (identified by a diamond enclosing a letter) so mariners can time their passages so as to have the tidal streams flowing *with* them rather than against them. Quite often yachts will have to anchor and 'wait for the tide'. Tidal streams are strongest at springs.

Tidal streams don't necessarily run with or against a boat's intended course but are often *sideways* to it. As a result, the boat may not go where it's pointed. The navigator therefore has to take tidal streams into his calculations (together with the 'leeway' caused by the wind) and steer a 'heading' that, after taking everything into account, results in the correct 'track' being made.

Note that tidal streams do *not* obey the twelfths rule above and *may* be at their weakest when the tide is rising or falling at its fastest rate:

The turn of the tidal stream off shore is seldom coincident with the time of high and low water on shore. In open channels, the tidal stream ordinarily overruns the turn of the vertical movement of the tide by three hours, forming what is usually known as tide and half-tide, the effect of which is that at high and low water by the shore the stream is running at its greatest velocity.

Anon, *Lloyd's Seaman's Almanac* (1897)

WAXING OR WANING?

When the moon is just a crescent, how do you know if it's getting bigger (waxing) or smaller (waning)? French sailors have long had a simple way of remembering and, if you know French, you can use it as well. The French for 'first' is 'premier', while for 'last' the French word is 'dernier'. When you look up at the night sky, mentally draw a line down the edge of the moon. If it makes the moon into a 'p' then you know it's in its first quarter (waxing), but if it makes it into a 'd' it's in its last quarter (waning).

Navigating by Nature

NAVIGATING WITHOUT A COMPASS

Before the introduction of the compass, and long before the use of global positioning systems, man was able to navigate using the stars and sun. Modern technology has led to a decline in the craft of natural navigation, but such simple skills are still known to save lives, and can be enjoyable to learn for the most or least adventurous.

STAR LIGHT, STAR BRIGHT

To the mariners of old these constellations were of essential importance. The polar star, in particular, was their great guide, when leaving sight of land they ventured to embark upon unknown seas. The magnetic compass has enabled the mariners of the present day to steer their course over the pathless ocean with unerring certainty, even in the darkest night; and astronomical science has furnished them with other means of determining their position on the earth's surface; yet the polar star may still be regarded as the great celestial compass of the northern half of the world.

Robert Sullivan, *Geography Generalized* (1859)

For thousands of years it has been known that in the night sky of the northern hemisphere, north is indicated by the Pole Star, or Polaris. (With a little celestial knowledge, it is nearly as easy – and obviously just as important – to find south in the southern hemisphere, as described below.) The Pole Star travels in a tight circle above the north pole, so remains a relatively fixed point in the sky, making it invaluable in navigational terms. Early navigators could also estimate how far north they were by the position of the Pole Star in the sky – the further north, the higher it appears, the further south, the lower, until you reach the equator and it disappears from view.

Finding north in the northern hemisphere

(See illustration on p. 259) The Pole Star (which indicates north) is the final star in the constellation Ursa Minor, also known as the Little Bear or the Little Dipper. The key constellations you will need to learn to be able to identify it in the night sky are Ursa Major, also known as the Plough, the Big Dipper and the Great Bear (one constellation, many names), and, for times when that is not visible, the constellation of Cassiopeia. Ursa Minor lies between these two.

Ursa Major is often thought of as a pot with a long handle. A simple way to find the Pole Star from this is to look at the side of the 'pot' opposite the handle, made up of two stars. Imagine a line that goes through these two stars, but then extends beyond it for five times the distance between them. The end of this line should put you at or very near the Pole Star (be warned, the Pole Star is not that bright, so you may overlook it at first, especially if there is any light pollution). If you prefer things to sound more technical, the stars on the end of the pot are called Merak and Dubhe.

To find the Pole Star when Ursa Major is not visible, look for Cassiopeia. This constellation is shaped like a squashed letter W, and you can find Polaris by looking away from the first 'V' of the 'W'.

Once you know you are facing the Pole Star, you are also facing north.

Finding south in the southern hemisphere

To find south in the southern hemisphere is slightly more tricky as there is no one star to guide you. Instead, you need to find the Southern Cross, then two stars next to this called Rigil Kentaurus and Hadar (these are known as the pointers). Imagine a line that comes from between the pointers, and another line that extends from the long arm of the Southern Cross. The two imaginary lines will cross above south. See illustration on p. 260.

ALL IN THE SUN

During the day, when the stars are not visible, the navigator can use the sun to reliably find his way. In both hemispheres, the sun rises in the east and sets in the west – at its zenith (its highest point, when it appears directly overhead) it is due south in the northern hemisphere. The simplest way to track the movement of the sun, and therefore find a line of east to west and your way, is to place a stick upright into relatively flat ground. Mark where the stick's shadow falls over a period of time, and you will find a line that gives you east to west.

Navigating Using Traditional Maritime Instruments

EARLY NAVIGATION

Early navigators used celestial navigation (the position of the sun and stars in the sky, as described in the section on navigating by nature) to find their way across the seas. As well as finding north in the northern hemisphere, for example, by finding the Pole Star, they could also estimate how far north they were by the position of the Pole Star in the sky – the further north, the higher it appears, the further south, the lower, until you reach the equator and it disappears from view. While this worked for very rough estimation, later seafarers needed to know not only where north is (and from that, where east, south and west are), but also to gain a more accurate idea of their position in latitude (ie angular distance from the equator), ascertained through the use of traditional maritime instruments, some of which are described below.

QUADRANTS, ASTROLABES AND CROSS-STAFFS

To establish latitude at sea, it is necessary to measure the angle of the sun or a star above the horizon, then to convert this to a latitude position. The earliest instrument commonly employed for this task was the seaman's quadrant – a quarter circle, often carved from wood or made of brass, with sights at each end of one straight edge, and a plumb line hung from the point where the two straight edges met. The sights were lined up on a known celestial body, and the position of the plumb line at this point noted. The curved edge of the earliest quadrants was often marked with the names of places where the latitude had already been established, while they were later marked with the degrees from 0 to 90 – the altitude could then be read as an angle, and the angle checked against the tables of latitude published in navigation manuals. Portuguese explorers were using seaman's quadrants in the 15th century, initially, it seems, to measure the altitude of the Pole Star, and therefore keep track of how far south they had travelled from their point of departure. The quadrant later evolved into the sextant, again used for measuring angles at sea.

The seaman's, or mariner's, astrolabe performed the same function as the quadrant, measuring the altitude of celestial bodies when at sea. Often made of brass, these were simplified versions of the astrolabes used by early astronomers. A seaman's astrolabe consisted of a circular ring, with degrees marked around the edge, a sighting device at the centre, and a rotatable sight rule called the alidad. To use it, the seaman's astrolabe was suspended from the thumb, so that it hung vertically. At night it would be held at eye level, the alidad turned until the star was sighted and the angle read. During the day, the astrolabe would be held below eye level, the alidad again turned until a ray of sunlight was sighted and the angle read. Such astrolabes were also in use by the Portuguese in the 15th century.

CROSS-STAFF. *An instrument used by navigators.*
The crosse staffe is an artificiall quadrant, geometrically projected into that forme as an instrument of greatest ease and exactest use in navigation, by which in any naturall disturbance of weather (the sunne or starres appearing) the poles height may be knowne, when the astrolabe or quadrant are not to be used. Hopton's Baculum Geodæticum, 1614.

Robert Nares, *A Glossary* (1859)

The cross-staff is another early maritime instrument, in use by the 16th century. Made of wood, the cross-staff consisted of a long wooden staff – square-cut and with scales marked on its sides – and a cross-piece at right angles to it which slid up and down its length. It was held rather like a crossbow with the far end of the staff pointed at the celestial body in question and its butt held against the measurer's cheek. The cross-piece was then moved so that the top of it aligned with the sun or star, and the bottom of it aligned with the horizon. A reading from the staff could then be taken. Later cross-staffs had three or four cross-pieces.

MAPS AND CHARTS

The earliest-known maps were carved into clay tablets in Babylonia about 4,000 years ago and showed such things as settlements, crops, rivers and hunting grounds. Naturally, early maps were quite crude and not always of much practical use – one by Hecataeus in the 6th century BC showed the world as an island with Greece at the centre. But within a few hundred years all educated people understood that the Earth was a sphere. The first surviving map to show it that way was by the 2nd-century AD Egyptian astronomer Ptolemy. Sea charts came later, simply because people travelled by land before they travelled very far by sea. The Portolan charts are the first-known and were produced by Italian draughtsmen in the 14th century.

Reading maps

Maps contain vast amounts of information, if you know how to read them. The first thing to do before setting off anywhere is to spread out a map and commit a simplified version to memory. For hiking, a scale of 1:25,000 (in which 1cm on the map represents 250m on the ground) is ideal, but 1:50,000 will do. Put the map on the table so north is at the top. Locate your start point and the place you intend hiking to and then try to relate that route to the map. For example, if the route heads north, the sun will be to your right first thing in the morning (since the sun rises in the east) and on your back at midday. If there's a river, take note of whether it's to the right or left of your path. And pay particular attention to any features that could be used as landmarks:

Every old scout on first turning out in the morning notices which way the wind is blowing. Then you should notice all landmarks for finding your way ... If you notice your landmarks going out you can always find your way back by them, but you should take care occasionally to look back at them after passing them, so that you get to know their appearance for your return journey.

Robert Baden-Powell, *Scouting for Boys* (1907)

ORDNANCE SURVEY "ONE-INCH" MAP

Hertford & St. Albans
Mounted in Sections
Price Four Shillings & Sixpence.

Published by the Ordnance Survey Office, Southampton.

Cover of an Ordnance Survey map of Hertford and St Albans, 1931
© The British Library / HIP / TopFoto

Some of the most valuable information on the map comes from the contour lines – lines that connect points having the same altitude. On hiking maps they're normally drawn every 20 metres with an extra thick line every 100 metres. Contour lines quickly tell you if your intended route is uphill, downhill or flat. For example, where your path runs more or less *along* a contour line it will be flat, but if it cuts *across* the contour lines it will be sloping. If the contour lines are close together the terrain is very steep. But how do you know whether you'll be going up or down? The altitudes are marked here and there, but a quick way is to look for the rivers and streams – they'll be flowing in areas of lower altitude.

To calculate the distance, lay a piece of cotton along your route, following all the wiggles, then measure it off against the scale printed on the chart.

Reading charts

Compared with maps, charts can seem pretty empty. After all, there aren't any features to draw in the open sea. But they contain everything the mariner needs.

Like maps, charts have contour lines, in this case for the seabed, and they show the depth of the water, usually in metres, when the tide is at its lowest predicted level. In other words, there should never be less water than shown on the chart, although, depending on the tide, there could be considerably more. If you have a boat that draws 2m and you see from the chart that the depth is 1.5m and the tidal range is 3m then you know that you will have plenty of water at high tide, but will run aground at low tide. Numbers with a line drawn under them are 'drying heights'. In other words, the ground is covered at high water but sticks up at low water. Charts give no information about inland areas but plenty of details about the coast, especially cliffs, beaches, harbour entrances, and, most of all, lights used for navigation.

THE COMPASS

When clouds prevent sailors from seeing Sun or star, they take a needle and press its point on the magnet stone. Then they transfix it through a straw and place it in a basin of water. The stone is then moved round and round the basin faster and faster, until the needle, which follows it, is whirling swiftly. At this point the stone is suddenly snatched away, and the needle turns its point towards the Stella Maris. From that position it does not move.

Thomas of Cantimpré, *Liber de Natura Rerum* (c.1244)

The 'magnet stone' or 'lodestone' was magnetic ore, the name possibly coming from the town of Magnesia, in Asia Minor, where the mineral was found in ancient times. As for the Stella Maris, that was what we now know as the Pole Star. Just to complicate things, magnetic north is not exactly under the Pole Star, nor is it the same as true north, but in those days it was good enough (and remains so today for most hikers).

The modern hiker's compass looks almost as simple as Thomas of Cantimpré's description, but is deceptively sophisticated. It consists of a magnetized needle which, of course, points at magnetic north, housed within a rotating bezel, divided into 360°. The needle and bezel are mounted on a transparent oblong base which has a direction arrow printed on it, and it's this that makes the design so ingenious.

In order to use the compass for simple direction-finding, make sure that north as printed on the rotating bezel is lined up with its mark. We'll call this the 'basic position'. Now, holding the compass with the direction arrow on the base pointing in front of you, turn around until the red end of the compass needle points to north. East will now be to your right, south will be behind you, west will be to your left, north will be straight ahead, and all the in-between directions will be as shown on the bezel. But if you have a map as well as a compass you can do a lot more than that.

USING THE MAP AND THE COMPASS TOGETHER

In order to use the compass to follow a bearing, you first have to know what bearing you want. Unfold your map to the relevant part, put it on a flat surface and place the compass on it (in the basic position as described above) so that the direction arrow on the base and north on the bezel both point to the top of the map. Now rotate the map, with the compass on it, until north as indicated by the needle is lined up with north on the bezel. If you've done that correctly your map will now be orientated with the real world and, as a result, you can read off the bearing of any route by referring to the compass.

Having noted the desired bearing, this is how you walk it. Let's say your course is 120°. Hold the compass in front of you so the direction arrow on the base is pointing away from you. Rotate the bezel until 120° is lined up with the direction arrow on the base. Rotate yourself until the red end of the needle lines up with north on the bezel. You will now be facing 120°. You won't want to walk with the compass in your hand all the time, so just note a landmark along the bearing and head for that.

Compass with grid lines aligned with map grid lines
© Cordelia Molloy/Science Photo Library

FINDING OUT WHERE YOU ARE

If you have a map and compass you can always work out your exact position. First of all, look around for a landmark which you can also identify on the map – a distinctive mountain peak, a pass, a church spire or whatever it may be. Point the direction arrow of your compass at the landmark and rotate the bezel until north as indicated by the needle lines up with north on the bezel. Put the map on a flat surface and place the compass on it, with one edge touching the landmark and with the grid lines of the compass parallel with the grid lines of the map. Draw a pencil line along the edge of the base-plate starting at the landmark and going in the direction that you are from the landmark. You must be somewhere on that line. To find out *exactly* where, repeat the procedure for a second landmark and you will be at the point where the two lines intersect. To be absolutely certain, you can always check with a third landmark if you want. Exactly the same procedure was used on sea charts, taking bearings from coastal features, lights or radio transmitters, until the era of satellite navigation.

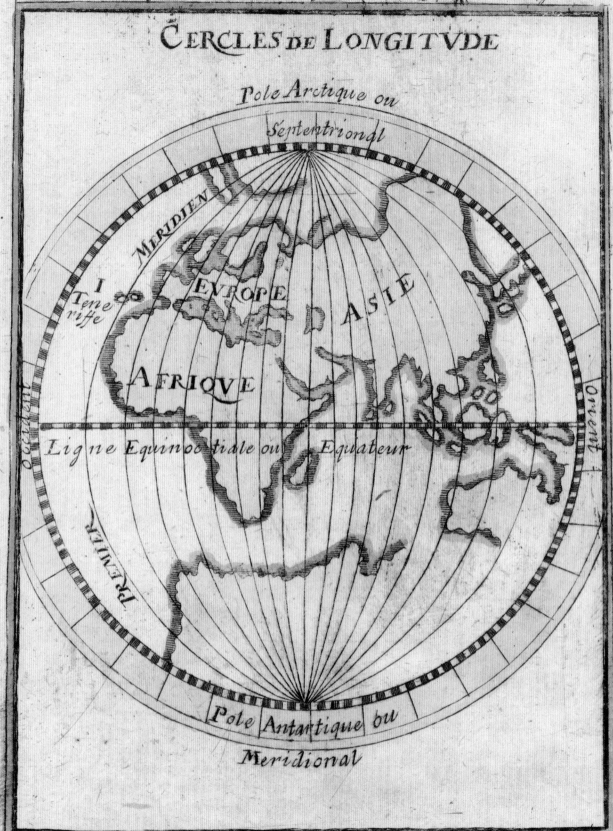

ČERCLES DE LONGITVDE

Pole Arctique ou

Sentrional

MERIDIEN

I Tene riffe

EVROPE

ASIE

AFRIQVE

Occident

Orient

Ligne Equinoctiale ou Equateur

PREMIER

Pole Antartique ou

Meridional

Vogel fec.

Understanding Longitude and Latitude

LATITUDE

Latitude denotes where a place is north or south of the equator. The equator is 0°, the north pole is 90° N and the south pole is 90° S. Degrees can be subdivided into 60 minutes which in turn can be subdivided into 60 seconds. London, for example, lies at 51° 30' N – and, roughly speaking, so do Calgary in Canada and Kiev in Ukraine. The key lines of latitude are the Arctic Circle at 66° 33' 39" N, the Tropic of Cancer at 23° 26' 21" N, the Tropic of Capricorn at 23° 26' 21" S and the Antarctic Circle at 66° 33' 39" S.

The number of degrees of latitude north or south corresponds with the angle of the sun. If you were to draw a line from the centre of the earth to the sun, and another line from the centre of the earth to the equator, then the angle between those two lines would be the latitude – and that's exactly the principle by which the early navigators did, indeed, work it out.

The first instrument for measuring the altitude of the sun – and other celestial bodies – was the astrolabe, in use on land from about 150 BC but not, it seems, used at sea until a man called Martin Behaim tried it in 1480. Basically, the astrolabe was a flat circle of metal, graduated in degrees, with a pointer equipped with sights. The celestial body was observed through the sights and the angle read off.

It wasn't easy to use an astrolabe aboard a rolling ship and the cross-staff soon came to be preferred for its simplicity. It was nothing more than a length of wood with a scale marked on it, on which another piece of wood could be slid backwards and forwards. The navigator held the staff to his eye and moved the cross-piece until its top edge coincided with the

French map showing lines of longitude, 1683
© *Mary Evans Picture Library / Alamy*

heavenly body and its bottom edge with the horizon. The angle was then read off on the scale. Over the years, the design was, of course, improved, culminating in the modern sextant.

LONGITUDE

As to longitude, I declare that I found so much difficulty in determining it that I was put to great pains to ascertain the east-west distance I had covered. The final result of my labours was that I found nothing better to do than to watch for and take observations at night of the conjunction of the moon with the other planets, because the moon is swifter in her course than any other planet. I compared my observations with an almanac.

Amerigo Vespucci, *Letter to Lorenzo di Pier de' Medici* (1500)

Longitude denotes where a place is east or west of Greenwich. The Greenwich meridian (line of longitude) is 0° and the far side of the earth from Greenwich is 180°. For example, Melbourne in Australia is 145° E while New York is 74° W.

The principle of longitude is quite simple. Since there are 360° in a circle and 24 hours in a day, so a place where the time is one hour ahead or behind the place you are must be 15° away from you (360 divided by 24 = 15). However, in practice, there were two problems.

The first was simply a political problem – *where* to measure longitude from. Every country wanted the 0° meridian to run through its own capital. The Russians therefore opted for Saint Petersburg, the Italians for Rome, the French for Paris, and so on. It wasn't until 1884 that the International Meridian Conference agreed on Greenwich as 0° longitude.

The second problem was scientific and much harder to solve. Given that longitude corresponds to time difference, so it only requires an accurate timepiece to calculate it. But the motion of a ship meant that a pendulum clock could gain or lose as much as 15 minutes a day, equivalent to anything up to 250 miles. Amerigo Vespucci had no chance. It was one of the great challenges of the era and in 1714 the Board of Longitude went so far as to offer a prize of £20,000 – a fortune in those days – to anyone who could develop a method of calculating longitude accurately. Many thought it impossible:

The World has long been perplexed about an intricate affair which some have promised mankind they shall one time or other be much better for ... I mean the Longitude, or the settled distance of East and West; we shall in the process of this work endeavour to put an end to the importance of that search, by setting two things in a clear light about it. I. That it can never be fully and finally ascertained ... II. That it is not so very essential to the World as some would have us believe.

Daniel Defoe, *A General History of Discoveries* (1726)

In the age of the cheap digital watch, it's difficult to comprehend the engineering problem that an accurate timepiece posed in the 18th century. John Harrison, the son of a carpenter, was one of those who accepted the challenge. It took him 30 years to succeed. To test Harrison's chronometer, it was sent on a voyage to Jamaica, reaching the island aboard the *Deptford* in 1762 and returning aboard HMS *Merlin*. After enduring five months at sea, storms and tropical temperatures, the chronometer was accurate to just under two minutes, equivalent (in the latitude of Portsmouth) to about 18 nautical miles. It was a tremendous achievement – and Harrison went on to better it, although it took many years before the Board of Longitude parted with all the prize money.

John Harrison's H5 chronometer, 1770
© *Science Photo Library*

Nowadays, we only have to switch on a GPS unit to know our latitude and longitude to an accuracy of three metres, something Daniel Defoe could not even dream of (see the section on navigating using a map and compass).

st belua ī marī que grece aspido delone dicūr Aspido til
Latine ū aspido testudo. Cete etiam dicta. ob ℔ete.
inmannitatē corporis. est enī sicut ille ꝗ excepit

Seafaring

ST BRENDAN

The first boats were almost certainly rafts (see section on raft-making) followed by dugouts and coracles. Early seafarers would have stayed within sight of land – unless blown off course – but long voyages were nevertheless made. The Babylonians traded by sea with India 6,000 years ago and there's good evidence that, in 1493 BC, the Egyptians sailed down the Red Sea and Indian Ocean as far as present-day Mozambique. By 310 BC, at least one Mediterranean sailor, Pytheas of Massalia (Marseilles), had sailed to Britain:

The people of Britain are simple in their habits and far removed from the cunning and knavishness of modern man …

Pytheas (c.310 BC)

The first great voyage *from* the British Isles was possibly made by an Irish curragh – a square-sailed vessel of animal hides over a framework of wood and wicker – to America and the Caribbean in the 6th century. That, anyway, is one interpretation of the *Navigatio*, probably written by an Irish monk in the 8th century but purporting to describe the voyage of St Brendan 200 years earlier. Certainly the work gives a reasonably good impression of the handling of such craft. For the first 15 days, the *Navigatio* tells us, the wind was fair and the crew had little to do as the curragh ran before it, but after that they were forced to row 'until their strength failed'.

The square rig, efficient only for downwind sailing, was a problem, but it was also an opportunity for those who knew how to exploit it. At the Battle of Cape St Vincent in 1797, the Spanish fleet, sailing downwind, had carelessly allowed itself to break up into two groups. The smaller British fleet under Sir John Jervis, sailing with the wind abeam, went right into the gap, effectively cutting the nine leeward ships out of the action and securing an important victory.

SCURVY

The greatest challenge to seamen was not the Atlantic but the Pacific. Antonio Pigafetta, one of the survivors of the first circumnavigation from 1519 to 1522, under Magellan, described how during the 'three months and twenty days' it took to cross, 'the gums of most part of our men swelled above and below so that they could not eat'. This, of course, was scurvy and it was to kill many. Magellan's crew ate 'old biscuit … full of worms', ox hides soaked in the sea then cooked on embers, and rats which they traded with one another for 'half an écu apiece'.

Captain James Cook was the first to criss-cross the Pacific from 1768 to 1780 without any crew members succumbing to scurvy, partly because he carried plenty of sauerkraut. And soon afterwards, the Royal Navy developed its own preventative, issuing the men with a dash of lemon juice mixed with three gills of water, a little sugar … and one gill of pure navy rum. This was known as 'the sailor's sheet anchor' and was made available once the beer had run out.

CLUBBING

Britain's old seafaring traditions are maintained by a handful of tall ships as well as thousands of yachting enthusiasts all around the coast. But, with modern technology and equipment, some techniques have become so redundant that only a few still know about them:

Drifting with the tide with an anchor down; a vessel clubbing will therefore be taken stern first. This method of dropping down on a tide is only employed when the tide runs very strong, and it is necessary to keep the boat under command of the rudder. It may be seen daily at Yarmouth; the sailing wherries coming in from the rivers on an ebb tide drop their anchors short, and by this means club down to their quays.

Without some such method of opposing the strength of the current, they would be swept past their landing places.

A Ansted, *A Dictionary of Sea Terms* (1898)

A variation of the technique was used when a boat was in danger of running aground on a lee shore during a storm. The lee anchor would be let go, thus helping the ship onto a new tack in a very short distance. This was known as 'club-hauling' – but the cable would then have to be cut to allow the ship to sail away.

BEFORE ELECTRONICS

Nowadays, thanks to modern electronics, the yachtsman knows not only his exact position to within a few metres, but the ship's speed, the depth of the water and much more. In the old days, it wasn't quite so easy.

The most basic way of calculating speed was for a seaman to drop a piece of wood into the water by the bow and then run with it until reaching the poop. Slightly more sophisticated was to have a log line with a float at one end. The float was dropped into the water at the stern. The line was marked with knots at intervals and timed by a special sandglass. The number of knots paid out by the time the sand had run through was the speed of the ship. This was the origin of the knot or nautical mile.

Depth was determined by lead and line (known to Anglo-Saxon seamen as 'sund-gyrd'). That's to say a lead weight attached to 20 fathoms of line (a fathom is 6ft), marked at intervals with pieces of leather and bunting of different colours. The lead was swung out well forward and as soon as the seaman felt the attached line jerk he stopped it running through his fingers and checked the nearest mark.

SPLICING

Every old seadog would have known how to splice traditional three-strand hawser-laid rope and especially how to put an eye in it. Here's how to do it. Unlay the three strands a little way. We'll call the central strand 'B', the left-hand strand 'A' and the right-hand strand 'C'. Curling the rope around to form the eye, the central strand 'B' should be tucked back into the rope first, after opening up the lay at the chosen point with a 'fid' or spike. 'A' should then be passed *over* the strand under which 'B' has been tucked and pushed *under* the next. Finally, to complete the first set, turn the eye over. 'C' will now be on the left. Take it over to the right and tuck it, from right to left, under the remaining strand. Go through the whole procedure twice more and you have an eye splice.

By the way, the order to 'splice the mainbrace' had nothing to do with ropes, but meant there would be an extra allowance of spirits to combat the cold and wet.

ROWING

In the age of the outboard motor, hardly anyone knows how to row properly. Feathering the oar, as when rowing on smooth water, is impossible at sea:

... the blade of the oar being kept at pretty much the same angle throughout both stroke and recovery; not at right angles to the water, but at an angle of something like 45 degrees. At sea ... the oar goes into the water at an obtuse angle, which, directly pressure is put on it, causes it to dip itself somewhat deep; the rower then puts his weight upon it and pulls down (not along), thus lifting the oar instead of actually pulling it. This, indeed, is the only way in which the long, heavy oars used by fishermen can be handled.

A Ansted, *A Dictionary of Sea Terms* (1898)

COLLISIONS

In the days when everyone at sea was a professional of some sort, the collision regulations posed no problem. For those amateurs whose knowledge is incomplete, or perhaps too complete, the following traditional rhyme is worth remembering:

Here lies the body of Michael O'Day
Who died maintaining the right of way;
He was right, dead right, as he sailed along,
But he's just as dead as if he'd been wrong.

Raft-making

KON-TIKI

Rafts were probably the earliest boats and could have been in use more than 10,000 years ago. The concept, after all, is ingeniously simple. Take some things that naturally float, such as wooden logs, tie them together until you have a platform large enough for a person, or several people, to stand on and you have a way – albeit not a very good one – of travelling about on water.

Rafts tend to behave just like any flotsam, which is to say they're fine for travelling with the current, but useless for travelling against it. Nevertheless, rafts can travel vast distances, as Norwegian Thor Heyerdahl proved in 1947 when, with five others, he sailed 4,400 miles across the Pacific aboard *Kon-Tiki*, a raft built to Native American designs from nine balsawood trunks lashed together with hemp ropes. The average speed was 1.5 knots. Heyerdahl thus proved that people from South America *could* have settled in Polynesia in pre-Columbian times.

A TRADITIONAL LOG RAFT

Assuming you have an axe and there's some suitable dead wood lying around, then you can make a simple raft. For a craft that will support the weight of two people, seek out half a dozen or so dry logs about 30cm in diameter and cut them equally to a length of about four good paces. The combined weight is going to be too much for one or two people when it comes to launching, so the construction site has to be considered very carefully.

If you have access to the calm waters of a lake or the protected inlet of a riverbank, then assembling in the water will be your best course. Alternatively, you could assemble your raft on rollers *overhanging* the bank of a river, from which it could be tipped in, using levers. A bigger raft will obviously be even more of a problem – think in terms of about six tons for a raft measuring 6m x 9m.

Cut notches about a hand's length in from the ends of the logs, making sure the notches line up when the logs are also in line. The notches should be about 5cm deep and wider at the bottom than at the top. Now seek out two good poles that, when trimmed with the axe into a roughly triangular shape, can be pushed through the lines of notches to hold the logs together. That having been done, it only remains to tie everything in place with anything you have available – seaweed, strips of leather, rope or whatever it may be.

Kon-Tiki, *on display in the Kon-Tiki Museum, Oslo, Norway*
Frits Solvang © Dorling Kindersley, Courtesy of the Kon-Tiki Museet, Oslo, Norway

A BARREL RAFT

If you're making your raft where you have access to modern tools and materials things will be much easier. First get hold of some plastic barrels, completely fill them with scrap foam (polyurethane is best but Styrofoam will do) and seal the lids on to make floats. The number of barrels will depend on their size and the load to be carried so you'll have to experiment – but you'll need at least four. Make a deck frame from four pieces of wood – twice as long as it is wide – and attach it to your floats. A quick way to do this is to use heavy-duty luggage straps equipped with ratchets – at least three per barrel and make sure the ratchets can be accessed once afloat, as you may need to tighten them. Screw or nail your floor to the frame. As a refinement, it would be a good idea to add some extra beams to prevent the barrels from twisting.

SAFETY

Everyone should always wear a life jacket.
Tow a canoe or inflatable behind a raft as a precaution.
On a raft you'll need long steering poles to guide it.
If there's any doubt about the conditions, don't go.

Foraging for Wild Food

WILD FOOD

For hunter-gatherers the knowledge of which wild foods were edible and beneficial was essential, passed from generation to generation. As soon as people settled in one place and started to farm and grow crops, such knowledge was gradually lost – wild plants were cultivated, and became the vegetables we know today, their often unrecognizable antecedents ignored as weeds. However, this was a slow process – our Elizabethan ancestors still knew the medicinal values and culinary virtues of many wild plants and herbs, but such widespread knowledge later dwindled with increasing industrialization and urbanization. Pockets of wild-food foraging persisted – in Britain, obvious sources of wild food, such as brambles covered in blackberries in late August or early September, are still exploited – but with the exception of times of food shortage, such as during the two World Wars, as a whole foraging for wild food is a craft that has died and has had to be relearnt. It is currently undergoing something of a revival.

PRINCIPLES OF FORAGING

Most of the principles of foraging are commonsense. Never eat anything that you have not positively identified. Many plants are toxic, and while these are relatively rare, you should always double-check before you eat wild food, especially as a beginner – if this makes you nervous, simply stick to very obvious foods until you have built up a knowledge of what's good to eat. Never pick foods from busy roadsides – these will be too heavily polluted by the passing traffic to be good eating. If you are picking food in an area popular with dog walkers, harvest from above dog level, for obvious reasons. A very important principle of foraging is never to pull up a whole plant – you want that plant to be there next year, providing you with another harvest (and such behaviour is in any case often illegal). Similarly, never harvest too much from one plant or bush; it should be left healthy and growing. Finally, forage from your own land and open-access land, but don't forage on private land without permission.

FRUIT

In country places, besides the ordinary fruits of the garden, many of the wild products of the woods and fields are made use of in the manufacture of preserves. The bilberry or blueberry, the barberry, and above all the bramble, are largely employed for this purpose; while in the Highlands and moorland districts, the cranberry ... and even the harsh and unsavoury berries of the rowan or mountain-ash are made into jam ... Bramble-gathering forms a favourite ploy amid the juvenile members of a Scottish family, and we have a very distinct recollection in connection therewith, of wild brakes where the purple fruit grew luxuriantly, amid ferns, hazel-nuts, and wild raspberry bushes, with the invigorating brightness of a September sun overhead, and the brilliant varieties of a September foliage. Faces stained with livid hues, hands scratched with thorns and briers, and shoes and stockings drenched with ditchwater, are among the reminiscences of the joyous days of bramble-gathering.

Robert Chambers, *Book of Days* (1869)

Late summer and early autumn, when numerous fruits and berries become ripe, is an important time for the wild-food forager (and jam maker). Remember that some berries are poisonous, but with a field guide (or an expert friend) it is very easy to learn to recognize the good from the bad, and some of the more common ones such as blackberries and wild strawberries are unmistakeable. Some berries are delicious eaten straight from the bush, while others need a little more work to become palatable – there really is no other use for the sour sloe (fruit of the blackthorn tree) than in making warming sloe gin.

Blackberries

The prickly blackberry or bramble bush (*Rubus fruticosus*) grows in hedges, woods and on waste ground. Its berries are widespread and abundant, making them the most popular of wild foods. The juicy dark purple fruits are made up of a cluster of drupelets, and are delicious raw or cooked – simply avoid those infested with insects. Blackberries can be picked from August to early October, although traditionally you must pick them before Michaelmas, 29 September, as on this date the Devil, or witches, are said to urinate on them. The origins of this piece of folklore might lie in the fact that blackberries become watery and sour after the first frost.

Bilberries

The wild British bilberry (*Vaccinium myrtillus*) is closely related to the North American blueberry, now a popular imported fruit. While the fruit of cultivated blueberries is larger and sweeter, bilberries (also known as whortleberries, whorts, blaeberries, hurtleberries and wimberries) are more often overlooked than they deserve. The bushes grow low on heath and moorland, with bright green leaves, and the berries (from July to September) are small and nearly black. If you find the berries too sour, cook them in pies or crumbles or make jam.

Bilberries
© *Arco Images GmbH /*
Alamy

Crab apples

The wild crab apple (*Malus sylvestris*) is the ancestor of the many modern cultivated varieties of apple, and is an ancient source of food. Crab apples can be found on their small trees in woodland and hedgerows and the fruit can be picked from July to December. Beware however, they can be extremely bitter (especially if they truly are wild, without having crossed back with cultivated forms). Use to make crab apple jelly, add to savoury dishes, or try your hand at making lamb's wool, a drink made from mixing up the pulp of roasted apples, hot ale and spices such as nutmeg:

The ingredients put into the bowl, viz. ale, sugar, nutmeg, and roasted apples, were usually called Lamb's Wool. I am of the opinion that the custom was very ancient; but from whence it arose, or why the mixture

Crab apples
© *FoodStock / Alamy*

was called Lamb's Wool, I do not at present pretend to account. Shakespeare certainly alludes to it in his 'Midsummer Night's Dream,' where he makes Puck, or Robin Goodfellow say:

> And sometimes lurk I in a gossip's bowl,
> In very likeness of a roasted crab,
> And when she drinks, against her lips I bob.
>
> *A Selection of Curious Articles from the Gentleman's Magazine* (Volume I, 1811)

Rosehips

Rosehips (*Rosa canina*) are the fruit of the wild rose, and have long been prized as a foodstuff, and more recently (particularly during World War II) appreciated as a good source of vitamin C. Rosehips are a bright orange-red, and can be found in hedgerows from late August onwards. Some people are put off by the work involved in preparing rosehips – the seeds inside hips are covered in tiny stiff hairs, which, if ingested, will seriously irritate the gut. All the seeds must be removed by slitting the hips in half and cleaning each one out individually. The simplest way to enjoy rosehips is to make rosehip tea – after halving and cleaning the seeds away, steep the hips in boiling water for five to ten minutes. Strain, drink the tea, and (when they have cooled enough) you can eat the seedcases too.

NUTS

Hazelnuts

Nutting is the grandest amusement, after all, because you have to go into the great woods to get the prime ones, as it is there that the largest hazels grow, some of them as high as a two-storied house. It is of no use to go a-nutting without having a long hook of some kind or another, as the finest and ripest clusters grow at the tops of the hazels, the branches of which are too slender to be climbed, so must perforce be pulled down by the nut-hook, or you will never taste the richest of the creamy kernels.

Games and Sports for Young Boys (1859)

Hazels (*Corylus avellana*) can be found in woods and hedgerows throughout the British Isles and hazelnuts (also known as filberts or cobnuts) from August until September – but in August you might find them bland when you pick them green, and if you wait too late into October for them to fully ripen, squirrels will quite probably have got there first. Try to collect them in between these times. They hang in clusters of two or three, and are encased in thick green husks. When ripe they will readily drop from the bush. To store them, remove the husks, but keep them in their shells until you are ready to eat them – once shelled, they are delicious roasted in the oven, and eaten as a snack.

Sweet chestnuts

The sweet, or Spanish, chestnut (*Castanea sativa*), is found in woods and parks throughout Britain, although it does best in southern England. The trees are tall, and have distinctive leaves with serrated edges. The chestnuts are ready from around October, with two or three small nuts contained in cases which are densely covered with very long spikes (you might want to wear gloves). They can be collected from the ground, or helped on their way with a well-aimed stick. They are best roasted. Simply make a small nick in the brown shiny case (to prevent the nut from exploding, and to make them easier to peel) and place in the oven. Do not confuse the sweet chestnut with the unrelated horse chestnut – conkers are not edible.

Beech nuts

Beech nuts, or beech mast, are the three-sided nuts of the beech tree (*Fagus sylvatica*). Beech trees are both common and widespread in the British Isles, and beech nuts are ready in September or October (although again you will be battling with squirrels to get them), forming inside a prickly brown husk. Unfortunately, if you find a tree with a plentiful harvest one year, do not rely on it the next – good crops are only to be had every few years as a general rule, although you will usually find another tree nearby. It is possible to extract very good oil from beech mast, but rather time-consuming. A simpler option is to warm the husks gently, till they open and reveal the nuts inside, which can then be peeled and eaten. Be warned, the nuts are rather small, so it can take some time to prepare a reasonable number.

GREENS

Nettles

The stinging nettle (*Urtica dioica*) is possibly the most abundant and widespread of all wild foods, and some people will still be amazed that once cooked it will not sting your mouth. Nettles are best in spring and early summer, before they become too bitter (and laxative), and you should only pick the tops of the stems and the young leaves that grow there – it is best to wear gloves while doing this. You can treat your harvest in a number of ways, but they are commonly boiled (add plenty of butter and seasoning when they have been drained) or made into soup.

Jack-by-the-hedge

Jack-by-the-hedge (*Alliaria petiolata*), often known as hedge garlic, grows, surprisingly enough, in hedgerows and on the edges of woods. It tastes strongly of garlic, and the leaves are used, in small quantities, as a flavouring in sauces, or finely chopped in salads.

Jack-by-the-hedge
© Chris Gomersall / Alamy

Fat hen

Fat hen (*Chenopodium album*) was once a very commonly used vegetable, but today it is generally treated as an anonymous weed. It is widespread and abundant in Britain, and has lance-shaped leaves on plants that grow to around 60 centimetres to 1 metre in height. Archaeologists have revealed that it was known as a foodstuff to Neolithic man, and the seeds of fat hen were among the stomach contents of the Iron Age Tollund Man. Pick young, tender leaves in spring and treat them as you would spinach.

Flowerhead of fat hen
© Richard Becker / Alamy

Good King Henry

As with fat hen, good King Henry (*Chenopodium bonus-henricus*) was popular from Neolithic times until the last century. The plants grow to around 60 centimetres in height, and the leaves can again be treated in the same way as spinach. The plant takes its name not from an English king, but from Henri IV of Navarre (1553–1610) – the 'good' distinguishing this edible plant from the poisonous bad Henry (*Mercurialis perennis*).

Good King Henry
© Arco Images GmbH /
Alamy

1 et 2 *Chanterelle comestible* t*antharellus cibarius.* 3. *Agaric alutacé* *Agaricus alutaceus.* Alim.

4. *Agaric sapide* *Agaricus sapidus.* Alim. 5. *Agaric styptique* *Agaricus stypticus.* Venen.

Hacquart del.

A. Hacquart sculp.

Mushrooming

MUSHROOMS

So many fatal accidents happen every season from the use of poisonous mushrooms,
and it is so difficult to distinguish between the edible kinds and those that are
deleterious, that we would advise our readers either to eat none that they have not
examined for themselves, or to be contented with what are raised in artificial beds,
though the flavour of these is as inferior to that of the wild mushrooms as a coop-fed
chicken is to the heath-cock.

Mistress Margaret Dods, *The Cook and Housewife's Manual* (1824)

There are thousands of species of fungi growing wild in the British
Isles, but extreme caution must be taken before enjoying any of them
as a meal. Some are deadly poisonous – there is no antidote to the toxins
of the death cap (*Amanita phalloides*); you might feel fine for up to a day
after you have eaten it, but within a week you will be dead – and many of
the poisonous varieties closely resemble some of the tasty, edible ones.
In France, you can enlist the help of a local pharmacist in identifying
your finds (although some are obviously more helpful than others) but
if you are without expert help you should never eat anything you are
even slightly unsure of. Buy a very good guide that shows lots of detail,
and always collect the whole mushroom (don't just cut off the top) as
you will need all of it to make a proper identification – the best way to
pick a mushroom is to twist it gently until it comes away in your hand. If
at all possible, you should attend a course on mushroom identification
before you begin collecting your own, and start by learning to identify the
deadly varieties, so you know what to avoid. Also, remember that you may

be intolerant to certain mushrooms even if they aren't poisonous. The mushrooms described below have not been chosen simply for flavour, but because they are among the safer ones for the beginner to forage for, as they each possess a combination of features which makes them more readily recognizable from poisonous or inedible forms (but great care should still be taken, and there is not space here to provide all the details necessary for safe identification).

There are some general rules for mushrooming – try to avoid wet days, when the mushrooms will have soaked up a lot of water; avoid anything that has started to decay; remember where you picked the different specimens you collect, as knowledge of habitat will help with identification; avoid immature fungi as these will be more difficult to identify; collect your mushrooms in an open basket (they will keep better this way); if you are unsure about some of the fungi you collect, keep the species separate (don't mix poisonous and edible up together, as the poisonous ones might contaminate the edible); don't handle the specimens too much, as any damage will hinder identification; go through the mushrooms carefully before you cook them, double-checking in your guide that they are good to eat; clean your mushrooms by wiping them with a cloth, rather than washing them; use any foraged mushrooms which you are sure of within 24 hours of picking.

GIANT PUFFBALL

The giant puffball (*Langermannia gigantea*) is one of the most easily identified species of edible fungi. It is large, spherical, white and around the same size as a football. It grows in fields, gardens and woods, and can be found from summer to autumn. Only firm white specimens should be picked. When sliced, the inside of the giant puffball should be firm, smooth and creamy white (if this is not the case, discard it). Giant puffballs can be cooked very simply – slice into 'steaks' and fry the steaks in butter.

CEP

The cep (*Boletus edulis*), also known as the penny-bun (because of its brown cap), or by its Italian name, porcini, is a highly prized wild mushroom. It is found in any type of woodland from summer to late autumn. It has a brown cap, 8–20 centimetres across, which is glossy in wet weather. The stem is thick and bulging toward the base, and cream or beige in colour. Rather than gills, the cep has a spongy layer under its cap, made up of tiny tubs. When cut, the flesh should be firm and white (other *Boletus* fungi change colour when cut, but not *Boletus edulis*). Commercially, cep are often dried, as this intensifies the flavour, and they are often used in 'wild' mushroom soup.

PARASOL MUSHROOM

The parasol (*Lepiota procera*) is a distinctive species, easier to spot than many other mushrooms as it grows on open pastures and has a tall stalk and frilly cap. Its season is summer and autumn, and it is not common, but has an excellent flavour if you do find it. Its cap is 10–25 centimetres across, and is pale with darker shaggy scales. It starts off egg-shaped, before expanding to an open parasol shape (some people say parasol mushrooms are best picked between these two stages, before they are fully opened). The stem is tall, slender, and slightly bulbous at the base, with snake-like markings, and a double 'ring' which is movable, and will slide on the stem. To cook, remove the stems and either slice and fry, or leave the caps whole and stuff them and bake them. The shaggy parasol (*Lepiota rhacodes*) is also edible, but is known to cause stomach upsets in some people. It is smaller than the parasol, and easy to distinguish as its flesh becomes red when cut.

Cep mushroom
© Holmes Garden Photos
/ Alamy

HORN OF PLENTY

The horn of plenty (*Craterellus cornucopioides*) is funnel-shaped, and dark brown to black in colour. It is fairly common in the leaf litter found in deciduous woods from late summer to late autumn. The outer edge of the cap (2–8 centimetres across) is crinkled or wavy, and its underside is continuous with the stem. They can be gritty, so need careful cleaning, but have an earthy flavour and dry well.

WOOD HEDGEHOGS

The wood hedgehog (*Hydnum repandum*), or hedgehog fungus, can be found in any type of woodland from late summer to late autumn. The cap is irregularly shaped, and 3–17 centimetres across. Its 'gills' take the form of distinctive whitish 'spines', 2–6 millimetres long. Far more popular in mainland Europe than in Britain, it is good eating, but has a slight bitterness that is best removed by blanching.

SUMMER TRUFFLE

The English summer truffle (*Tuber aestivum*) is very rare, and very difficult to find without a specially trained animal, but it does exist and can sometimes be found in the southern counties of England. The truffles grow underground, are 3–7 centimetres across, of an irregular globular form, and are blackish brown in colour. They are occasionally found in beech woods growing on chalky soils, and can fetch a premium price from top restaurateurs or be used to great effect at home in risotto or on eggs. England's last professional truffle hunter, one Alfred Collins, retired in the 1930s.

[The truffle is] one of the best of the edible funguses ... and occurs on the downs of Wiltshire, Hampshire, and Kent. Truffles are generally discovered by means of dogs, which are taught to hunt them by scent; and wherever they smell one of them, they bark, and scratch it up. In Italy they are hunted, in a somewhat similar manner, by pigs.

William Bingley, *Useful Knowledge* (1831)

Cooking Alfresco

COOKING WITH POTS AND PANS

The only thing better than a camp fire is a camp fire over which a tasty meal is cooking. But cooking on a camp fire is a skill that has to be learned, especially using small lightweight camping pots. With these alone it's difficult to produce a sufficient quantity of food, so you may need to utilize other methods as well (see below). If you can take standard kitchen saucepans, do so. For a large group, make a long fire between two logs or two rows of stones and heat several pots at once.

Soot, smoke and ash are the enemies of nice-tasting food so things may go better if you can improvise some kind of enclosed wood stove, leaving the open fire for heat and entertainment. An upturned metal wastepaper basket is ideal. Cut away enough metal at the base to be able to light and feed a fire inside, and make a second hole near the top to let the smoke out. You then have a flat 'hotplate' on which to place your pan or pans.

COOKING WITHOUT POTS

In a survival situation it may be that you have no pots. Nevertheless, you can still toast, roast, bake or steam food, using traditional methods – and it's fun at any time. To toast or roast simply impale suitable foodstuffs on an improvised spit over the fire. You could, for example, set up two Y-shaped sticks either side of the hearth and run a straight stick between them. Alternatively, you could use a single Y-shaped stick, trapping the outside end of your spit with a small rock to balance it. Or you might

301

simply like to hold one end of the spit in your hand, happily anticipating your meal as you turn it just above the flames.

To bake or steam food you'll need to dig a pit. The size will depend on the number of people to be fed but, as a rough guide, when you put your foot in the bottom of the hole the ground should be level with the top of your knee. The diameter should be similar. Now set a fire in the pit with a good pyramid of logs (see the section on making fire without matches) interspersed with solid fist-sized stones (avoid any that are fissured or flaky). The idea is to get the stones hot. Once that's been achieved remove any remaining embers, wrap all the items of food individually in foil or in some good-sized leaves (for example, maize, sycamore or hazel), or in bundles of grass, and place them on the stones. Cover the food with more leaves and on top shovel back enough earth to retain the heat. You can now get on with other things leaving the food to cook itself over the next hour or two.

Food placed on heated stones in a pit
© *Dan Santillo / Alamy*

As a variation, you can insert a straight stick into your pit before arranging the food. When all is finished as described above, withdraw the stick and pour some water down the hole. That will turn to steam and give you steamed food instead.

BAKING BREAD

Most campers content themselves with making flat bread if they make any at all but real bread is quite possible, as John Muir (1838–1914), the Scottish-born conservationist, discovered when he worked as a shepherd:

Sheep-camp bread ... is fermented with sour dough, a handful from each batch being saved and put away in the mouth of the flour sack to inoculate the next. The oven is simply a cast-iron pot ... After the batch has been mixed and kneaded in a tin pan the oven is slightly heated and rubbed with a piece of tallow or pork rind. The dough is then placed in it, pressed out against the sides, and left to rise. When ready for baking a shovelful of coals is spread out by the side of the fire and the oven set upon them, while another shovelful is placed on top of the lid ... With care good bread may be made in this way ...

John Muir, *My First Summer in the Sierra* (1911)

AN ALFRESCO MENU

Let the three Ss be your guide to alfresco menus – keep it Simple, be Systematic and choose Strong flavours (things that have a delicate taste indoors seem to have none in the open air). Here's a menu suggestion:

First course

Leeks make an excellent starter. Roast them over the fire or bake them in the embers, then just peel away the burnt outer layer, dip in a sauce (such as garlic mayonnaise, curry or tomato) and eat. Red peppers and chicory can be dealt with in a similar way. Asparagus can be carefully skewered, wrapped in foil or cooked in a frying pan, just brushed with oil, as if on a grill.

Main course

While you're preparing and eating your first course, potatoes should be cooking in their skins, wrapped in foil in the embers or baking in the pit. The first course over, everyone takes their own personal skewer or 'spit' and uses it to roast their own food – perhaps sausages, a steak, a piece of chicken, a whole fish or, for vegetarians, a parasol mushroom. As an accompaniment, a pot of ratatouille could be bubbling away over the flames.

Dessert

The easiest way to create a hot alfresco pudding is to leave bananas or chestnuts in the embers.

Making Fire
without Matches

FIRE

We cannot know when man first discovered how to make fire, but fire has always existed, started, for example, when lightning strikes a tree, or in the vegetation at the edge of a lava flow. Archaeologists have found burnt sediment and charcoal at sites in Kenya dating back around 1.4 million years, perhaps showing the controlled use of fire, although it is generally thought that if fire was being used at this time it would have been 'borrowed' from naturally occurring fires, rather than started. Fire is a source of warmth and protection and provides the means for cooking, essential to the survival of modern man, and as the safety match was not invented until 1827, a number of methods existed for making a fire without matches.

PLAYING WITH FIRE

Fire can, obviously, be dangerous. If you want to try some of the methods described below for starting a fire, do so in sensible surroundings (ie outdoors), and perhaps keep a bucket of sand or water handy in case your beginner's attempts at the craft of fire-making are a bit too successful (especially important if the weather has been dry, when fire can spread rapidly). Keep the fire small, and always make sure it is out before leaving it (douse it with water if necessary). Ideally, try the craft on your own bonfire site in the garden, or at least do it somewhere fires have been lit before (to avoid damage to wild vegetation).

NO SMOKE WITHOUT FIRE

The most obvious source of igneous action with which mankind has always been familiar, is undoubtedly the orb from whence our earth is indebted for light and heat. It is not, indeed, probable that the earliest fires kindled by the progenitors of the human race were derived immediately from this luminary – as they could not be acquainted with the method of collecting its rays by the burning glass, nor of concentrating them by concave mirror: it is now, however, well known, that in some parts of the world vegetable and other matters may be in a state of dryness and inflammability, sufficient to allow them to become ignited by the mere action of the solar heat upon them.

John Holland, *History and Description of Fossil Fuels, the Collieries, and Coal Trade in Great Britain* (1835)

On a sunny day, it is possible to start a fire by focusing the sun through a magnifying glass, or similarly, onto dry tinder. Unfortunately, just as sunny days are not reliable, neither is this method of making a fire without matches.

DRILL METHODS

I have certainly made a thousand fires with rubbing sticks, and I have made at least five hundred different experiments. So far as I can learn, my own record of thirty-one seconds from taking the sticks to having the fire ablaze is the world's record.

Ernest Thompson Seton, *Woodcraft and Indian Lore* (1912)

Some of the oldest, but most reliable, methods of starting a fire without matches rely on friction. Perhaps the best of these is the drill-and-bow method, said to be efficient even in bad weather.

In this method, the drill (a spindle of wood) is held upright under the palm of one hand. A bearing block (a piece of wood with a notch in it into which the drill comfortably fits) protects the palm from the drill. The base of the drill is pressed into a board of wood (sometimes referred to as the hearth) which has a notch cut out of it (drill a shallow hole, then cut a notch in this before you start drilling to make the fire). The notch allows dust created by the friction to collect and form an ember (which can be transferred most easily by placing a piece of bark or the blade of a knife under the notch before you start). The final piece of equipment is the bow. The string of the bow is twisted around the drill, and with one hand pressing down on the drill, and the hearth held in place by a foot, the other hand is free to move the bow backwards and forwards, causing the drill to bore into the hearth. Once you have a good ember you should transfer it to a grapefruit-sized bundle of tinder (dry combustible material, such as dry grasses, or fine wood shavings). Place the ember in the bundle (without squashing it and putting it out), and blow on it gently (but carefully) to encourage the tinder to burn. Once it is burning, place the tinder among some kindling (small dry pieces of wood). Once the kindling is burning, you can gradually add pieces of firewood (collect this in advance, selecting wood that is dead and dry). It is said that for the most reliable results you should make your drill and hearth from the same wood, which should ideally be dead and dry (ie seasoned, and not rotten). For maximum efficiency, shape your drill into a shallow point at the bottom (where you want most friction) and a narrower point at the top (where you want least).

The hand-drill method is similar to the bow-and-drill method, but requires fewer pieces of equipment (no bow or bearing block), and is somewhat less dependable. Again, the foot holds the hearth in place, but the drill is twisted backwards and forwards between the palms of the hands, rather than with a bow.

Finding Water

FOLLOW THAT TORTOISE

Assuming that you have a map, that's the place to begin. Rivers, streams, lakes, ponds and springs will all be marked (look at the key on the map). However, if nothing is shown near you, or you don't have a map, then you'll have to 'read' the terrain as best you can. Obviously, you're more likely to find water at the bottom of ravines and valleys than on the tops of hills. Useful signs are areas of lush vegetation (look out for willows, alders, reeds and palms), birds heading for water at dawn or dusk (herons, pigeons and grouse are good indicators), and animal paths. It was the paths of tortoises that led early explorers, such as Charles Darwin, to the few wells on the Galapagos Islands:

The tortoise is very fond of water ... The tortoises, therefore, which frequent the lower districts, when thirsty, are obliged to travel from a long distance. Hence broad and well-beaten paths radiate off in every direction from the wells even down to the sea-coast ... When I landed at Chatham Island, I could not imagine what animal travelled so methodically ...

Charles Darwin, *Voyage of the Beagle* (1839)

If there simply is no surface water then you may have to dig for it. Again, look for areas of lush vegetation or signs of dried-up streams or ponds and get busy with a spade, a piece of wood or your hands.

DOWSING

There is evidence that dowsing has gone on for thousands of years. Traditionally, dowsers have used Y-shaped twigs, usually of hazel. But some modern dowsers use metal rods, wire coathangers or pendulums. In fact, dowsers do no better than chance and dowsing is not an effective method of finding water (see section on superstitions).

MAKING A SOLAR STILL

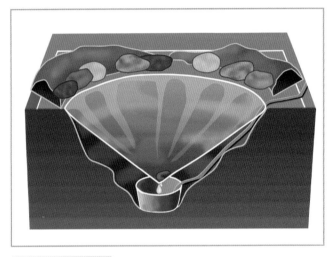

An improvised solar still
© Kate McLelland

If you haven't been able to find water you still have the possibility of 'making' it in a solar still, although the quantity made will rarely be great. (A variant can also be used for purifying dirty water.) Dig out a hole about as deep as your arm and a little bigger in diameter and in the middle place a container. Cover the hole with a sheet of plastic, preferably clear, and secure it with stones and earth or sand all around the edge, so that no air can escape. Place a small stone in the middle of the plastic to weigh it down into a V-shape, with the point of the V just over the container. That's it.

The sun's rays will evaporate water in the ground which will then condense on the underside of the sheet and run down into the container. A still like this could make from half a litre up to one and a half litres a day.

As a refinement, put a plastic tube into the container so you can suck the water up without disturbing the still.

A variation is to encase a small bush in plastic to collect the moisture it transpires.

RAIN

In Britain, rain is a fairly reliable source of fresh water for anyone living in the wilderness for any length of time. Collection is easy. Just stretch out a sheet of plastic horizontally between, say, the trunks of four trees, let it gradually fill with rainwater, then scoop it out and store it safely in containers. On a boat, rainwater can easily be collected from the sails – but make sure the salt from spray has been washed away before you begin.

SEAWATER

Because the body cannot tolerate the concentration of salt in seawater it is *never* safe to drink, no matter how thirsty you are. You would end up excreting *more* water than you drank in order to eliminate the salt. However, seawater can be desalinated using the principle of the solar still (see above).

If you're adrift at sea there are, however, unexpected sources of fresh water. According to Dougal Robertson, who in 1972 spent 37 days adrift with his family in a tiny boat, two pounds of fish contain a pint of water which can be extracted by sucking out the eyes and spinal fluid. The blood of turtles is another source of liquid low in salt:

In order to allay his thirst, he killed a turtle and drank of the blood, which gave him great reliefe ...

Captain James Cook, *The Journals of Captain Cook* (1777)

MAKING WATER SAFE TO DRINK

Purification of water collected in the field is advisable unless it's from a clear stream in a remote area, with no upstream habitation and devoid of livestock.

The first step is to filter the water. You can make a filter by part-filling a sock or the arm of a shirt or blouse with clean sand or charcoal. Suspend your filter from a framework of branches, place a container underneath and tip the dirty water slowly in at the top. By the time it emerges from the bottom of the sand/charcoal it will be free of particles. Another way of clearing water is to put it into a solar still (see above). If you have no method of removing impurities then, at the least, leave the water to stand for a few hours so the debris settles out at the bottom.

The fact that water is clear doesn't make it safe, so the final step is to boil it for five minutes or to put in a purification tablet (such as iodine, which is available from chemists and outdoor shops).

Measuring Ice

ICE PLANET

Although the last Ice Age ended more than 8,000 years ago, ice remains a substantial, if diminishing, feature of the earth. At the peak of that Ice Age some 20,000 years ago, the ice cap covered just about all of the British Isles and had a maximum depth of four kilometres, lowering the sea by 120 metres. Of the southern ice, some 17 million square kilometres remain in summer (14 million square kilometres of the Antarctic continent and 3 million square kilometres of sea ice) while the extent in winter is something like 34 million square kilometres (nearly four times the size of the USA). Of the Arctic sea ice, only just four million square kilometres remain at the end of summer, although in winter the total reaches around 15 million square kilometres.

We know all this and a great deal more but very little was known until the satellite era.

ICE HOLES FOR FISHING

The only reasons the earliest explorers wanted to know the thickness of sea and lake ice were, firstly, to make sure they didn't fall through and, secondly, to be able to make holes for fishing.

The traditional Inuit method of checking was to use an ice chisel. The chisel, usually flat on one side, would be fixed to a long handle and struck repeatedly into the ice with a throwing motion. For ice less than one foot thick the chisel is quick and still preferred by many ice fishermen today, rather than the more recent ice auger.

But measuring ice could be a dangerous pastime, especially if there were killer whales around:

A lizard-like head would show while the killer gazed along the flow with wicked eyes. Then the brute would dive, to come up a few moments later, perhaps, under some unfortunate seal reposing on the ice ... Wordie, engaged in measuring the thickness of young ice, went through to his waist one day just as a killer rose to blow in the adjacent lead. His companions pulled him out hurriedly.

Sir Ernest Shackleton, South (1919)

Clear ice is surprisingly strong. In the journal of his expedition to the south pole, Robert Scott (1868–1912) described nine inches of ice as 'very solid' but conceded that 12 inches was desirable for the ponies. In fact, modern opinion holds that a thickness of just 10cm (4in) is enough to walk on, while 20cm (8in) will support a small car and 30cm (12in) a pick-up, always provided, of course, the ice is not at all rotten.

From the point of view of safety, a single measurement is not enough because ice is seldom a consistent thickness. Currents can eat it away underneath, so take several. If you're on the ice with a vehicle, park at least 20 paces from the next one and move it every two hours. A tip is to make a hole next to the car. If water starts to overflow from the hole then it's time to get off the ice.

THE MODERN ERA

Making a hole in floating ice is one thing. Finding the depth of ice over land is quite another. At the end of the 19th century and early part of the 20th century, scientists argued over the thickness of the Antarctic ice cap. Because mountain peaks stuck through in places, many argued that the ice must be quite thin. In the opposite camp were those who argued in terms of miles (24 miles or 39km was one serious suggestion). But the technology to settle the argument just didn't exist until seismic techniques were introduced. The Norwegian–British–Swedish expedition of 1949–52 fired 80 seismic shots on an inland traverse and established beyond doubt that the ice sheet was at least 2,400m thick. In fact, we now know it's as thick as around 4,500m in places.

As regards sea ice, devices such as radar altimeters mounted on board satellites have reduced the need to risk killer whales and other dangers.

The altimeter fires pulses of electromagnetic waves down onto the ice and by measuring the time taken for the reflections to arrive at the onboard receiver, the height of the ice above sea level can then be calculated. As the depth of the ice under water is nine times the height above water so the total thickness of the ice can be worked out.

However, neither satellites nor submarines have been able to make the crucial distinction between the ice and the snow on top of it and complete accuracy still requires people on the floes, like Pen Hadow and his team in 2009 who dragged a sledge equipped with Surface Penetrating Radar for Ice Thickness Establishment (SPRITE).

THE AGE OF THE ICE

When light is shone through an ice core, alternating bands of light and dark snow can be seen. The light layers are summer snow and the dark layers are winter snow so every pair represents one year. Counting the bands, rather as with trees, therefore gives a quick indication of the age of the ice before more detailed tests are carried out in the laboratory. For now, the age of the oldest ice on the planet remains controversial. Some scientists put it at a mere 80,000 years, others at half a million and some at several million. Bringing up ice cores from the maximum depth will be fascinating but for the moment science can only scratch the surface, penetrating just around 60m a day, equivalent to a mere 200 years, with a maximum depth of 200m.

INFLORESCENCES.

1, Umbel of Ivy ; 2, Raceme of Wild Hyacinth ; 3, Catkin of Hazel ; 4, Corymbose raceme of Wallflower ;
5, Dichasial cyme of Pink ; 6, Head of Daisy ; 7, Panicle of Horse-Chestnut ; 8, Spike of Plantain ;
9, Spadix of Lords-and-Ladies.

Identifying Plants

CAROLUS LINNAEUS

The Greek philosopher Aristotle (384–322 BC) was the first to devise a system of classifying life forms, now obsolete, and over the centuries many others developed things further. In England, the most notable was John Ray (1627–1705), the son of the blacksmith in the village of Black Notley, Essex, who invented the word 'species', and whose *Historia Plantarum*, classifying plants according to the similarities he observed, was published in 1686.

But the man known as the father of modern taxonomy (the classification of organisms) was the Swedish scientist Carolus Linnaeus (1707–78). The first edition of his *Systema Naturae*, printed in 1735, contained just eleven pages, but by the time of the tenth edition of 1758 it classified almost 8,000 species of plants (as well as over 4,000 species of animals) and was considered one of the most important books in the world. It sounds a dry way of approaching nature, but for Linnaeus everything about it was a passion. 'The actual petals of a flower,' he wrote, are 'precious bed-curtains ... perfumed with so many sweet scents in order that the bridegroom and bride may therein celebrate their nuptials'.

BINOMIAL NOMENCLATURE

In his *Letter on Botany* (1882) the would-be botanist Ernest Bersot complained that it was impossible to identify a plant 'without the scalpel and the microscope, and without having at one and the same time the flower and the fruit'. But given that over 400,000 species of plants have now been named (sometimes two or three times over), no system could ever be easy. What Linnaeus had done was to group plants according to shared characteristics, such as the number of stamens, and to give them Latin names, in which the first word (always written with a capital) represented the genus and the second the species. This is known as 'binomial nomenclature' or 'binary nomenclature' and its great advantage is that botanists all over the world, whatever language they speak, can be certain which plant is being referred to. For example, in the Latin name for the tufted vetch, *Vicia cracca*, *Vicia* is the genus to which every other vetch also belongs, and *cracca* is the word that distinguishes the species from the other members of the genus.

This system is still used but many groupings have now been changed and, with the arrival of DNA sequencing, biological classification will keep evolving and some plants will undoubtedly be grouped in new ways.

SPOT THAT PLANT

A system of naming plants is one thing, but an easy way of identifying them is quite another. One creditable attempt was made by Gaston Bonnier, a professor of botany at the Sorbonne, who published his 'Simple Way' in English in 1917. It led the would-be botanist to a conclusion via a series of questions such as 'Flower composite/Flower not composite?' But the system still wasn't simple enough, involving a total of more than one thousand questions, although most plants could be identified from a dozen or so.

In Britain, there are well over one thousand species of wild flowers. This selection is provided by Edward Jesse, who in 1835 wrote a popular and charming little book called *Gleanings in Natural History*. In it he described a walk through a meadow and named the plants he saw.

The dog rose

The rose goes back 35 million years. At Knossos, Crete, is the earliest-known European painting of a rose, dating from around 1500 BC. The Romans would strew their floors with the fragrant petals, and also their guests when entertaining. In Britain, there are four wild species, the burnet, field, downy and dog rose, of which the dog rose (*Rosa canina*) was the one spotted by Edward Jesse on his walk. It is identified by its typical thorny stem and delicate pinky-white flowers.

The tufted vetch

A member of the pea family, the tufted vetch (*Vicia cracca*) is a clambering plant with tendrils and six to fifteen pairs of leaflets. The little bluish-violet flowers are in clusters along the stems.

Cuckooflower

The cuckooflower (*Cardamine pratensis*), also known as lady's smock and milkmaid, grows in marshy areas to a height of about 60cm and has cruciform pale lilac flowers from April to June.

Honeysuckle

Like the rose, the common honeysuckle (*Lonicera periclymenum*) is extremely fragrant, so that country folk would perfume their houses with it in summer. The scent is particularly strong at night, attracting moths to the nectar. Common honeysuckle is identified by its clusters of creamy to reddish-white flowers, which appear to split into two halves, and by its red berries.

Great Burnet

Another lover of damp meadows and growing up to 1m tall, the fascination of Great Burnet (*Sanguisorba officinalis*) is that its browny-red flower-heads turn out, on closer inspection, not to be a single flower but an agglomeration of tiny individual flowers.

Primrose

This is one of the flowers Edward Jesse would have seen in abundance, but nowadays the pale yellow primrose (*Primula vulgaris*) has become more difficult to find, partly due to herbicides and partly due to picking and collecting. The crinkly, rather elliptical leaves, are a distinguishing feature. The flowers appear generally from March to May, but also occasionally in autumn and winter.

1 to 4 Oak. 5 to 13 Elm. 14 Ash.

Identifying Trees

THE RISE AND FALL OF THE WILDWOOD

Once the last Ice Age had ended, the British Isles were soon totally recolonized by trees. Aspen, birch and sallow were followed by hazel and pine, then alder and oak, then elm and lime, then ash, beech, holly, hornbeam and maple. Yet nothing at all of the wildwood remains. Exactly how our prehistoric ancestors cleared the forest is something of a mystery. Of the native trees, only pine will burn where it stands and felling the others would simply have resulted in more shoots from the stump (see the section on choosing and using wood), while pulling out the roots would have been a staggering task with primitive tools. An explanation once popular was that the forests were cleared by the Romans:

The Romans, when the Britons fled, always pursued them into the fortresses of low woods, and miry forests: in these the wild natives found shelter; and when opportunity offered, issued out and fell upon their invaders without mercy. In this manner the Romans were at length so harassed, that orders were issued out for cutting down all the woods and forests in Britain.

Oliver Goldsmith, *History of the Earth* (1774)

In fact, archaeologists estimate that half of Britain's wildwood had already been destroyed 500 years before the Romans arrived. However it was done, just about all the woods that now exist in Britain, even those of natural origin, have been managed by people.

THE OAK

No tree seems more quintessentially English than the oak, nor more vividly illustrates the enormous task prehistoric hunter-gatherers faced when they began clearing the land. One example, famous in its time as the Golynos Oak, grew near Newport until it was sold in 1810 for 100 guineas:

Five men were twenty days stripping and cutting it down, and two men were employed one hundred and thirty-eight days sawing it ... The main trunk of the tree was nine feet and a half in diameter, and consequently no saw could be found long enough to cut it down; two saws were therefore brazed together.

Edward Jesse, *Gleanings in Natural History* (1835)

In fact, there are several species of oak in Britain. The Golynos was undoubtedly the English oak (*Quercus robur*) with deeply lobed leaves and, of course, acorns. But the durmast or sessile oak (*Quercus petraea*) is very similar and easily confused. The trick is to check the stems on the leaves and acorns. The English oak has stems on the acorns but only the tiniest length on the leaves; the durmast has no stems on the acorns but stems on the leaves.

The red oak (*Quercus rubra*) comes from North America and is identified by its leaves which turn red in autumn and have pointed lobes. Turkey oak (*Quercus cerris*) is identified by the long narrow filaments around its leafbuds. Holm oak (*Quercus ilex*), common around the Mediterranean, has become naturalized in southern England and has long, narrow evergreen leaves. The cork oak (*Quercus suber*) has also been planted in southern England and is easily distinguished by its thick cork bark.

THE CHESTNUT

Chestnuts are surprising for two reasons. Firstly, the two principal species aren't related, as the Latin names make clear – *Castanea sativa* for the sweet chestnut and *Aesculus hippocastanum* for the horse chestnut. Secondly, neither is a native species. The famous game of conkers certainly couldn't have been played earlier than the 16th century in Britain, when the horse chestnut was introduced from Albania. The sweet chestnut is more controversial. John Evelyn in his famous 17th-century book *Sylva* considered it an indigenous species, but in 1769 the Royal Society began to debate the issue, some arguing that sweet chestnuts had been boundary markers 'from the first introduction of private property into this kingdom' while the zoologist Daines Barrington maintained that sweet chestnuts did not stand up to his four tests. Only recently has the argument been settled on the basis that no prehistoric chestnut pollen has been found in Britain. Almost certainly the species was introduced by the Romans.

The two species are most easily told apart, firstly by the leaves – the sweet chestnut has long, narrow, sharply-toothed leaves, while the horse chestnut has clusters of oval leaflets – and, in autumn, by the fruits. The fruit of the horse chestnut has a shell with only a few short spines and, inside, the inedible conkers. The fruit of the sweet chestnut has a shell completely covered by long spines and the nuts inside are edible.

THE ASH

In spring, the ash (*Fraxinus excelsior*) is unmistakeable on account of its large black buds. It is also one of the last native trees to come into leaf, revealing three to seven pairs of notched leaflets. In the autumn, it can be identified by its keys or winged fruits which hang singly, unlike those of the sycamore which are in pairs.

THE BEECH

From a distance, the beech (*Fagus sylvatica*) might be confused with the oak, but up close the pointed oval leaves are quite different. Writers in the 17th century described them as 'glistering' because in the spring they're a silky and almost translucent yellow-green (when they're good to eat in salads) becoming shiny dark green later.

THE HAZEL

The hazel (*Corylus avellana*), usually more of a bush than a tree, had a multitude of uses, including, according to John Evelyn, 'divinatory rods for the detecting and finding out of minerals':

... by whatsoever occult virtue, the forked-stick (so cut, and skilfully held) becomes impregnated with those invisible steams and exhalations; as by its spontaneous bending from an horizontal posture, to discover not only mines, and subterraneous

treasure, and springs of water, but criminals, guilty of murther ...
John Evelyn, *Sylva* (1664)

The hazel is easily recognized at all times of the year – in the spring by its long yellow catkins, in summer by its ragged, rounded, pointed-tipped leaves, in autumn by its nuts and in winter by its bushy shape.

THE WILLOW

Several species of the *Salix* genus grow in Britain, generally recognized by their fondness for riverbanks and their long, thin leaves. The osier (*Salix viminalis*) is the most extreme, with leaves 15 times longer than they are broad, while the white and crack willows (*Salix alba* and *Salix fragilis*) are somewhat less distinctive. The sallow or pussy willow (*Salix caprea*) is unmistakeable in the spring on account of the large yellow catkins on the male trees and the long greenish-yellow catkins on the female trees (although the leaves are more oval and pointed). But probably the most easily recognized tree in Britain, near or far, is the weeping willow (*Salix* × *chrysocoma*).

Tracking Animals

TRACKING ANIMALS

The most obvious way to track an animal is to follow its actual tracks (ie its 'footprints') in either snow or soft ground. Less obvious methods include identifying an animal's droppings (or 'scats'), or looking for more subtle signs – the telltale damage to vegetation that some animals cause (for example, bark stripped from trees by deer) or the food remains that they leave behind (such as the exceptionally neat small round holes that dormice leave in discarded hazelnut shells). For our Mesolithic ancestors, the ability to track animals was a vital part of hunting, and before the widespread cultivation of crops, meat was essential to survival. Now the craft of animal tracking is more often a hobby, used to identify the wildlife present in an area.

FOSSILIZED FOOTPRINTS

Animal tracks are of interest not only to the hunter or the wildlife enthusiast. The fossilized footprints of a number of extinct creatures, including dinosaurs, have been found in various parts of the world. The study of these may not lead to the animal, but can provide information on the size and the gait of the creature and the speed at which it moved (calculated from the distance between prints). The discovery of fossilized footprints in Dumfriesshire in the 19th century caused the geologist (and Dean of Westminster) William Buckland to wax philosophical:

The historian or the antiquary may have traversed the fields of ancient or of modern battles; and may have pursued the line of march of triumphant conquerors, whose armies trampled down the most mighty kingdoms of the world. The winds and storms have utterly obliterated the ephemeral impressions of their course. Not a track remains of a single foot, or a single hoof, of the countless millions of men and beasts whose progress spread desolation over the earth. But the reptiles that crawled upon the half-finished surface of our infant planet, have left memorials of their passage, enduring and indelible ... Centuries and thousands of years may have rolled away between the time in which those footprints were impressed by tortoises upon the sands of their native Scotland, and the hour when they were laid bare and exposed to our curious eyes. Yet we behold them, stamped upon the rock, distinct as the track of the passing animal upon the recent snow; as if to show that thousands of years are but as nothing amidst eternity—and, as it were, in mockery of the fleeting, perishable course of the mightiest potentates of mankind.

Chambers's Edinburgh Journal (Volume XVII, January–June 1852)

Roe deer tracks
© *Juniors Bildarchiv / Alamy*

TRACKS

A good place to start when you are trying to identify the tracks of British animals is to count the toes. The track left by a badger is quite easy to recognize – badgers have five toes, and a large kidney-shaped pad behind the toe pad. Otters also have five toes, but the large pad is almost round, and in very soft mud you might be able to distinguish the webbing between the toes. Hares and rabbits have five toes on their forefoot, but the inner toe is very short and rarely leaves a mark. Rabbit prints can look very similar to those of a hare but are much smaller. Foxes have four toes, but unfortunately, dogs do too. However, fox prints are more compact. Deer are cloven-hoofed, so their prints show only two toes – sheep are also cloven-hoofed, but the toes are shorter, so deer prints are easy to distinguish.

DROPPINGS

To help you to confirm the identifications you have made from tracks, the following are the distinguishing features of some British mammal droppings. Badgers deposit their droppings in specific areas, known as latrines – these are communal, and can often be found either near the sett or at the edge of the feeding range used by the group. Badgers dig out a pit for this purpose, but do not cover over the droppings. Otter droppings are called 'spraints', and are often found in a prominent position, such as on top of a rock. They vary in accordance with the otter's diet (as all animal droppings do) but are often black or dark green and have a very distinctive odour, which has been described as being like everything from new-mown hay to lavender. Fox droppings are often left in the same place each night (sometimes somewhere prominent) and are pointed and twisted. Deer droppings can be confused with those of rabbits (which are small and round, approximately 10 millimetres in diameter) and hares (not so small but also round, approximately 15 to 20 millimetres in diameter) but are generally more oval in shape.

TRACKING HUMANS

First of all you must be able to distinguish one man's foot-mark from that of another, by its size, shape, and nails, etc. And, similarly, the prints of horses and other animals. From a man's track, that is, from the size of his foot and the length of his stride, you can tell, to a certain extent, his height ... It is very puzzling for a beginner to tell the difference between a lot of footmarks of bare feet [but] when measuring the footprint of the man you are after draw a line from the tip of the big toe to the tip of the little toe, and then notice where the other toes come with regard to this line ... All people vary a little in the position of their toes.

Robert Baden-Powell, *Scouting for Boys* (1908)

When tracking a human the tracker must remember to be as wily as the person being tracked:

A man walking puts the whole of his foot on the ground, each foot a little under a yard from the other. In running, the toes are more deeply dug into the ground, and a little dirt is kicked up, and the feet are more than a yard apart. Sometimes men walk backwards in order to deceive anyone who may be tracking, but a good scout can generally tell this at once by the stride being shorter, the toes more turned in, and the heel marks deeper.

Robert Baden-Powell, *Scouting for Boys* (1908)

Identifying Birds

BIRDWATCHING

Birdwatching as a hobby in Britain dates back only to William Turner, Dean of Wells in the 16th century, and there wasn't a bird identification book until *Ornithology* by Francis Willughby and John Ray was published in Latin in 1676 and two years later in English. Even in the 18th century, the famous naturalist and curate Gilbert White (1720–1793) had to resort to sending specimens to the zoologist Thomas Pennant for identification, as when he found a dead 'falco':

… it weighed two pounds and eight ounces, and measured, from wing to wing, thirty-eight inches. Its cere [at the base of the upper beak] and feet were yellow, and the circle of its eyelids bright yellow.
Gilbert White, *The Natural History and Antiquities of Selborne* (1789)

Even if he wasn't quite certain which member of the Falconidae family the dead bird was, White clearly knew which would be the significant features and Pennant duly identified it as a peregrine falcon (*Falco peregrinus*), the wingspan being too large for the hobby, merlin or kestrel. 'It gave me no small satisfaction,' White wrote, 'that the *falco* turned out an uncommon one.'

As recently as the 19th century, birdwatching was still considered an eccentricity and few were more out of step than Charles Waterton (1782–1865). He had a wall built all around the grounds of his home, Walton Hall in Yorkshire, partly to keep out foxes but mostly to keep out poachers, a project that took ten years. He put up nesting boxes and excavated holes for sand martins. 'The chief way to encourage birds,' he wrote, 'is to forbid the use of firearms in the place of their resort'. His own gamekeeper found it hard to accept that the order also applied to birds of prey, with the result that Waterton 'threatened to strangle him if ever, after this, he molested either the old birds or their young ones'. Unfortunately, an estimated 500 million birds are still shot and trapped around the Mediterranean every year, significantly reducing the number that return to the UK in the spring.

Before birds were killed for food and entertainment it was much easier to go birdwatching than it is now. When Charles Darwin reached the Galapagos aboard the *Beagle* in 1835, it was the sort of paradise that Britain, too, must once have been:

I must describe more in detail the tameness of the birds ... There is not one which will not approach ... One day a mocking-bird alighted on the edge of a pitcher ... which I held in my hand whilst lying down. It ... allowed me to lift it with the vessel from the ground.

Charles Darwin, *Voyage Of The Beagle* (1839)

BIRD SONGS AND CALLS

Novices try to identify birds by their markings but it's not always easy to see clearly enough, even with binoculars. Song provides a way of identifying birds even if they can't be seen at all. Oliver Goldsmith in his *History of the Earth* (1774) wrote of how while walking by 'the sedgy sides of unfrequented rivers' he could distinguish the 'scream of the wild goose, the croaking of the mallard, the whining of the lapwing and the tremulous neighing of the jack-snipe'.

Gilbert White was one of the first to use song to distinguish between three summer visitors, the chiffchaff, the willow warbler and the wood warbler. The chiffchaff has a rather monotonous song, which indeed, sounds like 'chiff-chaff', whereas the willow warbler has a very musical and liquid warble – hence the names. The wood warbler's song is different again – a series of accelerating 'sip' notes.

There is no universally agreed distinction between songs and calls but, generally, songs are considered to be longer, more complex, more melodious and associated with courtship and mating, whereas calls tend to be shorter and associated with such things as sounding an alarm. Once upon a time you would have accompanied a countryman to learn the different songs and calls but nowadays you can buy recordings or listen online (for example, www.bbc.co.uk/nature/programmes/radio/dawn_

chorus). If you're awake early enough to hear the first bird of the dawn chorus then it will probably be a blackbird, followed by the song thrush, robin, wren, great tit and chaffinch – and, then, many others.

BIRDS THAT ARE OFTEN CONFUSED

Some birds look very similar and are easily confused. Here's some lore for telling them apart.

Owls

Eagle owl: huge – twice the size of any other British owl.
Long-eared owl: ear tufts sometimes visible but half the size of the eagle owl.
Short-eared owl: no visible ear tufts; yellow eyes within black patches.
Barn owl: only owl with heart-shaped facial pattern; white face; does not hoot.
Tawny owl: black eyes.
Little owl: the smallest.

Birds of prey

Kestrel: pinky-brown, long tail, often hovers; male has blue-grey head and tail.
Sparrowhawk: barred under-parts; male slate-grey above; female grey-brown above.
Goshawk: larger, heavier-looking version of sparrowhawk.
Merlin: pointed wings; flies fast and low; male blue-grey above; female brown above.

Far left: Kestrel
© Nic Hamilton / Alamy

Left: Sparrowhawk
© Arco Images GmbH / Alamy

Peregrine: broad 'moustachial streak', sometimes soars, usually solitary.

Hobby: long, narrow but clear 'moustachial streak'.

Hen harrier: white on rump; male has grey wings with black tips; female is brown.

Marsh harrier: no white on rump; male has grey on wings; female is brown.

Red kite: forked tail, acrobatic flight with angled wings.

Osprey: flies slowly 10m above water.

Buzzard: perches on poles or branches; high-pitched mewing call in breeding season.

Golden eagle: enormous wingspan up to 3m; wingtips tasselled.

Crows

Rook: pale around base of bill, bluish sheen.

Carrion crow: greenish sheen.

Hooded crow: light grey and black.

Jackdaw: dark grey and black.

Chough: red downwards-curved bill and legs.

Raven: huge; remote areas.

Garden birds

Goldcrest: smallest European bird; yellow on head.

Goldfinch: red stripe on head, yellow stripe on wings.

Redstart: red tail; male has black face and red breast; female light brown.

Black redstart: red tail; male has black face and chest; female dull brown.

Robin: red breast and face.

Song thrush: spotted chest; solitary except during migration.

Mistle thrush: larger than song thrush; dry rattling call.

Redwing: red on wings and flanks.

Fieldfare: reddish-brown breast, grey head and rump.

Marsh tit: black cap with tiny bib.

Willow tit: black cap with large bib.

Coal tit: black cap and bib but white on nape of neck.

Great tit: black cap and bib; black chest stripe on yellow.

Blue tit: Blue cap, blue on wings, yellow breast.

Long-tailed tit: long tail.

Birds around water

Cormorant: white chin.

Shag: no white chin.

Mute swan: orange-red bill with black knob.

Whooper swan: long yellow and black bill.

Bewick's swan: short yellow and black bill.

Canada goose: white patch on cheeks.

Barnacle goose: sides of face and forehead white.

Brent goose: tiny white patch on neck.

Greylag goose: orange or pink bill.

Far left: Canada goose
© William Leaman / Alamy

Left: Brent goose
© Mike Lane / Alamy

SEMAPHORE ALPHABET

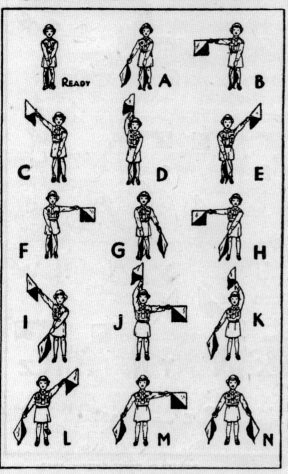

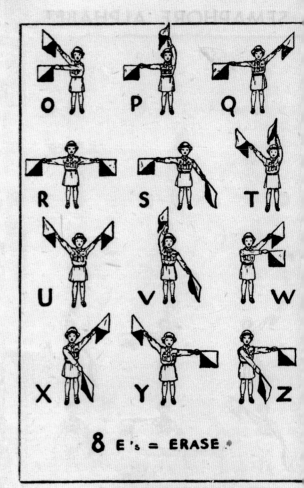

8 E's = ERASE

PRINTED IN GREAT BRITAIN 1947.

Signalling with Semaphore

SEMAPHORE

Semaphore is a system of visual communication, originally using a machine with movable arms, and later simplified to two hand-held flags. It was invented by the French brothers Claude (1763–1805) and Ignace (1760–1829) Chappe in the 1790s. In their original system, a set of arms pivoted on a post, with the position of the arms determining the meaning of the message. The posts were placed some miles apart, and a telescope was used at each of them to read the message from the previous post and then pass it on. This ingenious method was soon adopted outside France, and a semaphore system using hand-held flags was developed for signalling at sea. Stationary semaphore links (such as the first one established by the Chappes, covering the 230 kilometres (143 miles) between Lille and Paris) were eventually superseded by the electric telegraph in around 1850.

LEFT HAND DOWN A BIT

Semaphore signalling, which is done by waving your arms at different angles to each other, is even easier to learn [than Morse code]. Here you form the different letters by putting your arms at different angles. Be sure to make these angles correctly ... Once you know the Semaphore alphabet, all you need is practise. A Scout is not asked to send long sentences, or to send over long distances, or at high speed. All that is expected of you is that you should know your alphabet and read and send simple sentences or words really well. Do your best, so that when it comes to sending across a big field, or from hill to hill, your message will be easy to read ... If you want to write a dispatch that will puzzle most people to read, use the Semaphore letters in place of the ordinary alphabet. It will be quite readable to any of your friends who understand signalling.

Robert Baden-Powell, *Scouting for Boys* (1908)

Modern semaphore flags are generally square, and divided diagonally into yellow and red sections, with red appearing uppermost, although in an emergency anything which makes the position of the arms visible would be adequate for the task (providing you are facing someone who knows the semaphore alphabet, and can decipher your signalling). The reason for red and yellow flags being widely adopted is that these colours are highly visible. The flags are held with the arms fully extended in a series of positions, with a different position for each letter of the alphabet. The arms are held straight when changing between letters. Semaphore by hand-held flags is generally used for relatively short-distance signalling, although the distances covered can be increased by the number of signallers involved and by the use of telescopes in earlier times, and binoculars today.

SEMAPHORE SAINTS

The 'semaphore saints' were unveiled by artist Terry Hammill in 2004 as part of a large art exhibition held in York Minster. The saints consist of twelve headless statues spelling out a message ('Christ is here') using the semaphore alphabet (with haloes in place of the usual flags). Following the exhibition, the saints were donated to the Minster, and they now stand, arms outstretched, at the west end of the nave.

Signalling with Morse Code

MORSE

Morse is a method of signalling by a code in which each letter of the alphabet is represented by a combination of dashes and dots, originally sent as a series of long and short electrical pulses along a telegraph wire. The system was invented by Samuel Finley Breese Morse (1791–1872), a talented artist who also had a great interest in electricity. Morse developed an electric telegraph, and realized that by sending pulses of electricity which acted upon an electromagnet at the receiving end of the telegraph wire, a simple lever could be moved. A strip of moving paper under the metal point of this lever received the message as a series of indentations, which were then translated into words by the operator. The Morse method of signalling was soon internationally popular, and with some tweaks and additions to his original code, a standardized alphabet was accepted.

'WHAT HATH GOD WROUGHT'

Samuel Morse sent the first inter-city electric telegraph message on 24 May 1844, on an experimental line built between Washington and Baltimore. The message read 'What hath God wrought', a biblical quotation (Numbers 23:23) apparently chosen by Annie Ellsworth, the daughter of the Commissioner of Patents.

The code is based on a combination of dots and dashes. The dot is a very short signal. When the signal is made on a key, the lever is depressed for about one twenty-fourth of a second. A dash is about three twenty-fourths of a second. When signalling the letter, the space of time between the signals equals one dot. The space between the letters of a word is equal to one dash, and the space of time between two words is two dashes.

R Ewart Williams (editor), *Practical Information for All* (c.1939)

DIT DIT DIT, DAH DAH DAH, DIT DIT DIT

Every scout ought to learn the 'dot and dash' or Morse method of signalling, because it comes in most useful whenever you want to send messages some distance … and it is also useful in getting you employment as a telegraphist. It is not difficult to learn if you set about it with a will.

Robert Baden-Powell, *Scouting for Boys* (1908)

The best-known example of Morse code, and the most useful, is the international distress signal SOS, rendered as three dots followed by three dashes followed by three dots. The letters SOS are popularly held to stand for 'save our souls', but they are not in fact an abbreviation, and were chosen simply because they are easily transmitted and recognized. Morse can be relayed without recourse to telegraph wires, by sound (as simple as tapping on a wall if you are trapped) or light (using short and long flashes of torchlight, for example). One of the simplest methods of signalling for help is to reflect sunlight on a mirror (although any reflective surface can be employed in an emergency, such as the blade of a penknife, or a credit card).

A . _	J . _ _ _	S . . .	2 . . _ _ _
B _ . . .	K _ . _	T _	3 . . . _ _
C _ . _ .	L . _ . .	U . . _	4 . . . . _
D _ . .	M _ _	V . . . _	5 . . . . .
E .	N _ .	W . _ _	6 _ . . . .
F . . _ .	O _ _ _	X _ . . _	7 _ _ . . .
G _ _ .	P . _ _ .	Y _ . _ _	8 _ _ _ . .
H	Q _ _ . _	Z _ _ . .	9 _ _ _ _ .
I . .	R . _ .	1 . _ _ _ _	0 _ _ _ _ _

Morse code alphabet
© Dorling Kindersley

Signalling with Smoke or Fire

B'ACENS AND WEARDSETLS

Signal fires have probably been used for thousands of years. Certainly the ancient Greeks had developed a relatively sophisticated system by which different meanings were indicated by the number of fires lit side by side. The Romans in Britain had five signal stations on the Yorkshire coast, each about 20 metres high, at Hunt Cliff, Goldsborough, Ravenscar, Scarborough and Filey. Later, the Anglo-Saxons developed a network of beacons for defensive purposes and it's possible to work out where many of them were from place names. The Old English word for a beacon, for example, was *b'acen*, while *weardsetl* indicated a watch point. Other associated words were *tot* and *node*. So, all the many places in England called Beacon Hill, as well as Firebeacon in Devon, Warshill Top near Kidderminster, Totham in Essex, Node's Point on the Isle of Wight and probably Nath Point in Dorset, were places that signal fires would have been stationed.

In 1455, the Scottish Parliament adopted the Greek concept and established a bonfire signalling code. One bonfire meant 'The English are coming'. Two bonfires meant 'The English are here'. And four – so there could be no mistake – meant 'The English are here and there's an awful lot of them'.

Probably the most famous use of beacons was in July 1588 to warn of the approach of the Spanish Armada. The beacons ran all along the coast from Cornwall to Beachy Head, East Sussex, and then inland to London, so Queen Elizabeth would have known of the Spanish fleet's arrival within hours:

> *For swift to east and swift to west the ghastly war-flame spread.*
> *High on St Michael's Mount it shone: it shone on Beachy Head.*

Far on the deep the Spaniard saw, along each southern shire,
Cape beyond cape, in endless range, those twinkling points of fire.
Thomas Babington Macaulay (1800–59), *The Armada*

Another kind of signal fire was the lighthouse, warning of dangerous rocks or indicating a safe harbour. The Lighthouse of Alexandria, built on the island of Pharos in 280 BC, was one of the Seven Wonders of the World at between 115 and 135 metres high. In AD 46, the Romans constructed a pair of lighthouses either side of the Roman port of Dubris (Dover). One survives as part of Dover Castle. Like the Lighthouse of Alexandria, it would have been lit by a brazier on top, and that remained the method right up until the late 18th century when oil-fed wicks took over.

YOUR OWN SIGNAL FIRE

A signal fire is something that should only be used in an emergency, not least because of the danger of setting the countryside alight. To avoid that, clear the land around the fire site as much as you can.

After lighting the fire (see the section on making fire without matches), tweak it according to the situation. At night, try to produce as much bright flame as possible, but on a clear day it's smoke that you need, which means putting green vegetation onto the flames. On an overcast day, turn the smoke black by using oil or rubber on the fire.

There's no point in keeping a signal fire going if you know there's no one to see it. If you're marooned on an uninhabited island, for example, get your signal fire ready but don't light it until you see or hear a boat or plane. That

Roman lighthouse at Dover Castle
© Malcolm Fairman / Alamy

means constructing your fire with plenty of tinder at the base, followed by small twigs, then larger twigs then small logs, *all very dry*. And you'll have to find some way to keep it dry – by covering it with a tarpaulin, for example.

If, on the other hand, you're in an inhabited area where you know there's a good chance of your fire being spotted, your problem is how to make it clear that it's not a simple camp fire. Anything you can do to make it look different is a good idea. If you have the resources, light three fires in a triangular shape which, to those who know, is a sign of distress. Or you could try to produce a flashing light by holding something intermittently in front of the fire. Or set one end of a stick alight and wave it around.

At sea, special distress flares known as orange smokes are used to signal distress in the daytime, while red flares or stars are used at night.

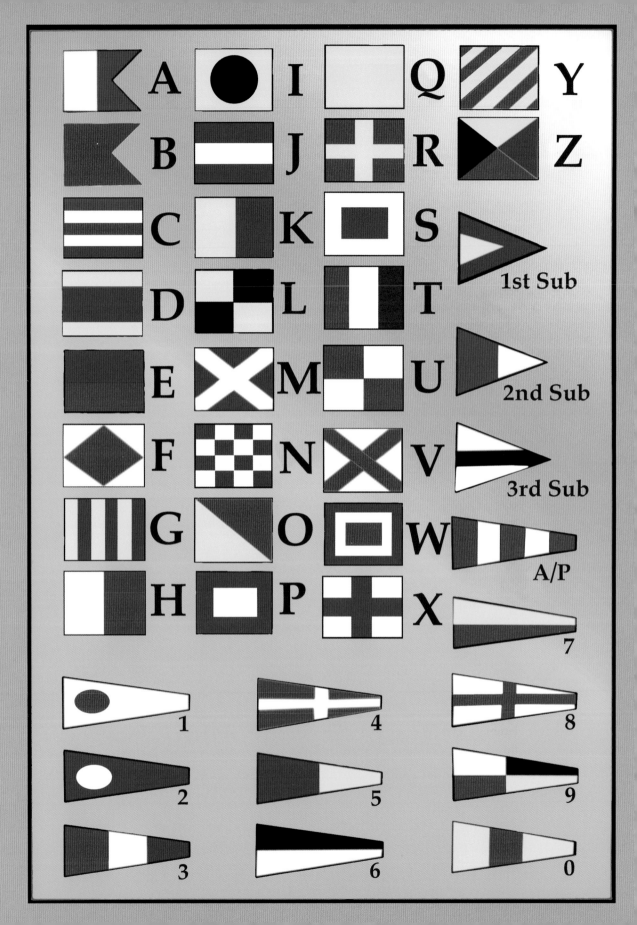

Signalling with Naval Flags

THE BATTLE OF TRAFALGAR

*The International
Code of Signals
© Steve Allen / Alamy*

ENGLAND EXPECTS THAT EVERY MAN WILL DO HIS DUTY.
Horatio Nelson, *Flag signal at the battle of Trafalgar* (1805)

In fact, Nelson had intended to signal to the fleet, 'England *confides* that every man will do his duty', but his Signal Lieutenant, Mr Pasco, pointed out that the word 'confides' would require the hoisting of seven flags. He suggested substituting the word 'expects' which, because it was in the Signal Book, would require only one flag. Nelson agreed and thus, with the help of Mr Pasco, sent what is probably the most famous signal in British naval history.

THE INTERNATIONAL CODE OF SIGNALS

The international code of signals may also be made by light or sound but, where flags are concerned, it comprises 26 flags for the letters of the alphabet, ten pendants (long triangles with their tips cut off) for the numerals zero to nine, three 'substitutes' (which will be explained in a moment) and the so-called Code Flag/Answering Pennant.

Obviously it would be extremely laborious to spell out the individual letters of every word using flags. To speed things up, single-letter flags flown on their own have special meanings.

A: I have a diver down; keep well clear at low speed.
B: I am taking in, or discharging, or carrying dangerous goods.

C: Yes, affirmative, or 'The significance of the previous group should be read in the affirmative'.

D: Keep clear of me – I am manoeuvring with difficulty.

E: I am altering my course to starboard.

F: I am disabled. Communicate with me.

G: I require a Pilot. When made by fishing vessels operating in close proximity on the fishing grounds, it means 'I am hauling nets'.

H: I have a Pilot on board.

I: I am altering my course to port.

J: I am on fire and have a dangerous cargo on board – keep well clear of me.

K: I wish to communicate with you.

L: You should stop your vessel instantly.

M: My vessel is stopped and making no way through the water.

N: No, negative, or 'The significance of the previous group should be read in the negative'.

O: Man overboard.

P: Flown in harbour it's known as the 'Blue Peter' and means 'All persons should report on board as the vessel is about to proceed to sea'. At sea, however, it may be used by fishermen to mean 'My nets have come fast upon an obstruction'.

Q: My vessel is healthy and I request free pratique.

R: The way is off my ship.

S: I am operating astern propulsion.

T: Keep clear of me as I am engaged in pair trawling.

U: You are running into danger.

V: I require assistance.

W: I require medical assistance.

X: Stop carrying out your intentions and watch for my signal.

Y: I am dragging my anchor.

Z: I require a tug. When made by fishing vessels operating in close proximity on the fishing grounds, it means 'I am shooting nets'.

There are also some two- and three-letter signals that have special meanings, but everyone at sea should at least know the meaning of single flags so immediate action can be taken.

For other messages, the red and white Code Flag is first flown to indicate that International Code is about to be used. On spotting a flag hoist, the other vessel should immediately also hoist the Code Flag (now known as the Answering Pennant) at the 'dip' (that's to say, halfway up the halliards). As soon as the full signal has been understood, the flag is hoisted 'close up' (all the way to the top).

Because most vessels would only carry one set of flags, the three 'substitutes' can be used to stand for letters that need repeating. For example, the first substitute repeats the first letter (the uppermost flag) of the hoist.

FLAG ETIQUETTE

There's a whole etiquette of ensigns and burgees that weekend sailors, as well as professionals, should observe.

Every British vessel should have a red ensign (or a special ensign if so entitled) and it should be flown on its own staff in the after part of the ship when at sea (unless out of sight of land or other vessels) or when entering or leaving a foreign port. The vessel should also fly its triangular club burgee at sea, either from the masthead or from the starboard yard arm, and keep it flying in harbour so long as the owner is aboard or in effective control.

Ensigns, burgees and house flags (if appropriate) should be hoisted at 08:00 in summer (09:00 in winter) and lowered either at sunset or 21:00, whichever is earlier. Many weekend sailors like to accompany the ritual with a 'sundowner'.

Surviving in the Wilderness

PSYCHOLOGY

Everyone who has survived an unplanned test of wilderness survival, from a plane crash, shipwreck or whatever, stresses the importance of psychology above all else. The will to live is essential, coupled with a strong sense of optimism:

Tuesday, January 16 ... The worst has happened, or nearly the worst ... The Norwegians have forestalled us and are first at the Pole. It is a terrible disappointment ... All the day dreams must go; it will be a wearisome return.
Robert Falcon Scott, *Journals – Scott's Last Expedition* (1913)

Many other reasons have been given for the deaths of Scott and his four companions on the way back from the pole but, undoubtedly, disappointment and demoralization played a part. As Scott revealed in his entry for Sunday 11 March, 'I practically ordered Wilson to hand over the means of ending our troubles ... We have 30 opium tabloids apiece ...'

Survivors need to know when to turn back and how to accept defeat with equanimity, even within a few hundred feet of the summit of Everest. Lt. Colonel Edward Norton, acting leader of the Third British Everest Expedition in 1924, and climbing without oxygen, was forced to turn back at 8,570 m (28,126 ft), less than 250m below the summit. Glory could have been his and yet, today, few people know his name even though he achieved a height not exceeded by anyone for the next 29 years. Yet, in his book, *The Fight For Everest*, he recorded that his feelings on opting for a safe return were simply 'relief' that the struggle of climbing was over.

Dougal Robertson, who in 1972 spent more than a month adrift with his family in an open boat after killer whales sank their yacht, wrote that 'comradeship' was vital because only the sharing of discomfort could maintain morale. But the single most important characteristic, he thought, was 'a well-developed sense of the ridiculous' because it helped overcome what he called 'the assassination of all civilised codes'.

EMERGENCY SHELTER

Everybody on a hike should be carrying a survival bag. In an emergency (such as hypothermia in the rain) the best way to deploy it is to sit on some insulation (such as a backpack) and pull the bag on *over your head*, not your feet. Just make a small hole for breathing. With your head completely protected you'll be considerably warmer. For more on this subject see the section on sheltering.

EMERGENCY DIRECTION FINDING

Elsewhere, we deal with compass work (see the section on navigating using a map and compass) and making a compass (see the section on making outdoor equipment). But supposing you have neither a compass nor the means of improvising one? In fact, there are still quite a few methods for finding your way. The most obvious, on a day you can see the sun, is to use it as a rough guide, since it rises in the east, reaches its highest point in the south, and sets in the west. You can be more precise at any time of day if you use the stick method. Plant a thigh-high stick vertically into some flat ground and mark the tip of the shadow with a stone. Wait about a quarter of an hour and again mark the tip of the shadow with a stone. A line drawn between the two stones will run east to west. Consequently if you stand with your toes touching the line, and the track followed by the sun passing behind you, you must be facing north.

If you have a watch with hands, you can use it in conjunction with the stick method to know direction as long as the sun is visible. Set up your stick before midday and mark your east-to-west line, extending it sufficiently to be able to draw another line at right angles going to the base of the stick. When the shadow of the stick falls precisely on the line it will be local noon. Set your watch by this. Whenever you now point the hour hand of your watch at the sun, south will be halfway between the hour hand and 12 on the dial, and north will be in precisely the opposite direction.

AT NIGHT

On a clear night in the northern hemisphere you can always find north (and consequently the other points of the compass) as long as you can identify the Pole Star (Polaris). For how, see the section on navigating by nature.

AN EMERGENCY PAINKILLER

Several trees and shrubs contain salicin or 'natural aspirin' in their inner bark, including the white, weeping, and crack willow (see the section on identifying trees). In an emergency, strip the outer bark from a young tree or from a limb of an older tree then peel away the inner layer and either chew it or make it into an infusion, simmering it in water for about ten minutes.

SURVIVING COLD

If you have any plastic bags you can use them as vapour barriers to contain body heat. On your feet, if you have two pairs of socks, slip the bags over the inner socks and then put on the outer pair. Similarly, you can cover your hands with plastic bags then put your gloves on.

Hypothermia can be a killer. The first signs are lethargy and irritability. Shelter and warm food will cure that. But uncontrollable shivering is a sign that the problem is becoming critical. Something must be done immediately and the best is to put the sufferer, stripped of wet clothes, into a sleeping bag with another bare-skinned person. Give hot sweet liquids as soon as the victim has recovered

Frostbite comes in three degrees. Gently warming your skin (for example, by putting your frostbitten fingers into your armpit) will deal with the first two. Third-degree frostbite means that not just the skin but also some flesh underneath has become frozen. The signs are pain followed by numbness and then by a sensation of warmth. Because of the numbness anyone with frostbitten feet will still be able to walk and should hike out to seek medical help before nightfall if possible. If not, the frostbitten part should be put into a bath of tepid water for 20 to 30 minutes – nothing hotter should ever be used.

SURVIVING HEAT

It takes about a week to acclimatize to heat, so avoid too much exertion at first. Wear loose, light-coloured clothing. If you're hiking in the desert you'll need to drink 10 litres of water a day *as a minimum* (see the section on finding water). But that, coupled with sweating, leads to salt deficiency, causing weariness and cramps, so extra salt needs to be taken – add about a third of a teaspoon per litre of water. However, *do not take salt if water supplies are low.*

There are two main kinds of 'heat disorder'. Heat exhaustion is faintness due to a sudden drop in blood pressure. The treatment is to get the head down between the knees and, when recovered a little, to drink water with salt. Heatstroke is far more serious because it amounts to the breakdown of the body's temperature control system and can be fatal. The treatment is artificial cooling – getting into the shade and covering the body with wet cloths, for example.

Sheltering

THE CAMPSITE

If you're not in an emergency situation, and you have a tent with you, you should be thinking in terms of environmental impact as much as comfort. Avoid pitching on grass or delicate vegetation, for example, because it can take a long time to recover. The best thing is to pitch on bare ground – perhaps in a wood (where the leaf mould will provide a soft bed as recompense). Nor should you pitch close to a water hole as you'll frighten away the animals that depend on it. In any event, cold air sinks so it's never a good idea to camp beside streams (or at the bottom of gullies) and far warmer to be on a protected shoulder.

THE PREHISTORIC SOLUTION

If you don't have a tent then, hopefully, you at least have a survival bag. Every hiker should carry one at all times, just in case. One style is the metallic thermal blanket that packs as small as a handkerchief and retains over 80 per cent of radiated body heat. Slightly more bulky is the orange plastic survival bag, but it has the advantage of high visibility when it comes to rescue. However, if you're not even carrying a survival bag, what can you do? The answer is to emulate the hunter-gatherers of prehistory.

The Stone Age hunters who came to Britain around 12,500 years ago across the 'land bridge' from the Continent weren't very interested in permanent settlements. They moved with the herds of mammoths, horses and reindeer, finding shelter or making it as they went.

Caves were not necessarily the first choice, partly because bears liked them. But bears aren't a concern today, so take a look at a map and see if any caves are marked. If not, start looking around for features that will help. Maybe there's an overhang that will keep the rain off, a wall that will act as a windbreak, or a big, old tree:

At length I came to a hollow tree with a hole at one side that I could go in at. I ... cut down all the dry, rotten wood I could get, and beat it small. With it I made a bed like a goose nest ...

James Smith, *An Account of the Remarkable Occurrences in the Life and Travels of Col. James Smith* (1799)

Shelter made from branches and twigs
© *mkNature / Alamy*

The 'Mount Sandel' design

Around 9,000 years ago, some of Ireland's earliest inhabitants built a handful of simple structures at what is now Mount Sandel, overlooking the River Bann in County Derry. Six were relatively large but the seventh, just about three metres in diameter, was exactly the kind of shelter you could improvise if necessary. Essentially it was a framework of saplings, pushed into the ground in a circle, then covered with animal skins.

When time is short and tools are lacking, look to see if you can make use of trees that are growing. A row of, say, four young trees could be bent over into hoop shapes and held down by cords or rocks to make a tunnel-shaped framework. That could then be covered in with a tarpaulin or plastic sheet, if you have one, or with a lattice of interlaced branches topped with turf. The top of a single larger tree can sometimes be pulled over with a rope; or, if you have an axe or a saw, cut through the trunk at about shoulder height until you can bend the top down to the ground. Incidentally, sleeping under a tree is a good way of keeping the dew off.

It's normally possible to improvise a lean-to. First, look for a wall, a rock or a big log, then find some pieces of wood or branches to lean against it for the roof. If you have some cord you can use this to make a lattice that will support bundles of plant material.

Where there are no trees but there's grass, if you have a shovel and the time, you can cut blocks of turf and pile them up into a shelter, emulating the pioneers on the Great Plains of America in the 19th century.

SNOW

The snow is seldom deep enough in Britain to excavate a snow shelter, but on those occasions that it's practical, a snow shelter beats a tent. In an emergency, a simple trench will suffice, which you can then roof over with whatever you have available – a tarpaulin supported on ski poles or branches, for example. But you'll be much more comfortable in a proper snow cave. Correctly constructed, it's dependable, draught-free and can be surprisingly warm, even too warm, as members of Shackleton's *Endurance* expedition to the Antarctic discovered:

We have already excavated a fair sized chamber big enough for eight men to sleep in, but it is much too wet for anyone to try to experiment yet.

Captain Thomas Orde-Lees, *Diary* (1916)

What the shipwrecked crew of the *Endurance* presumably hadn't allowed for was the melting of the snow by body heat. The solution is to create a raised and very slightly angled platform so that melt-water runs away. The traditional method is to excavate a tunnel for a metre or so, and then angle upwards to create a domed chamber with its floor well above the entrance. This will not only keep bedding relatively dry but also keep the cold air out and the warmer air, created by you, in. A faster but slightly more complicated way is to dig out a cave without bothering with the protective tunnel and then to create the tunnel afterwards from blocks of snow. Essentially you first excavate a slot in the snow bank in which to work. Having done that, you dig out your dome, the floor being horizontal at waist height. Once the dome is complete, you then close it off with your snow blocks, leaving enough of the initial slot as your entrance tunnel. One person, equipped with a proper snow shovel, can dig out a shelter in half an hour or so and then enlarge it at leisure. Don't forget to make a vent in the roof and to keep your shovel inside in case the entrance should be blocked by fresh snow. Mark the cave in some way when you go outside, to be sure of being able to find it again.

Making Outdoor Equipment

WALKING STICK

Ash is one of the best woods for a walking stick but you can also use oak, sycamore and hazel. Some country folk with plenty of patience used to actually 'grow' a walking stick in a coppice (see the section on choosing and using wood) by gradually forcing a shoot to take on the curved shape of the handle. From start to finish the process took about five years. Another method was to bend the wood over a heat source, which required considerable skill. But the easiest method is to carve out the handle. First of all, search out a suitable long, straight shoot in a hedgerow or coppice. It needs to be growing from a small trunk that has a diameter of around 12cm or more. Cut off the trunk about 5cm above the shoot and about 10cm below it. Trim the shoot to length. You should now already have a walking stick with the little bit of the main trunk as a crude handle. All that remains is to remove the surplus wood from the handle with a bow-saw and then finish off the shape with a knife and a file.

COMPASS

In an emergency there are several ways you can make a compass. The earliest was to stroke a pointer with a lodestone (see the section on navigating using a map and compass). You can achieve the same result today by stroking a needle, pin, nail or razor blade with a magnet – you'll find one in the loudspeaker of any audio equipment. Always stroke in one direction using the same 'pole' or end of the magnet. A second way to magnetize a pointer is to make a coil of insulated copper wire – as many turns as possible – and connect it between the terminals of a battery of at least six volts. Then slide your pointer into the 'tunnel' created by the coils and leave it for about half an hour. (If the coil gets too hot, disconnect it, let it cool, then reconnect it.) The third way to magnetize your pointer is simply to hammer it steadily while it lies on a north–south orientation. For how to find which way is north *without* a compass see the section on surviving in the wilderness.

Once you have your magnetized pointer you then have to devise a way in which it can swivel freely. Probably the most effective is to float it in a plastic, glass or china container of water by pushing it through a piece of cork or a matchstick.

BLUBBER STOVE

When Robert Scott's party spent the winter of 1911 in the Antarctic, the young engineer Bernard Day devised and built a blubber stove. Scott's journal described how it was done:

The blubber is placed in an annular vessel, A. The oil from it passes through a pipe, B, and spreads out on the surface of a plate, C, with a containing flange ... To start the stove the plate C must be warmed with spirit lamp or primus, but when the blubber oil is well alight its heat is quite sufficient to melt the blubber in A and keep up the oil supply ... With a satisfactory blubber stove it would never be necessary to carry fuel on a coast journey ...
Robert Falcon Scott, *Journals – Scott's Last Expedition* (1913)

Your own design could be different, depending on the materials and tools you have available. But the key to success is that the blubber container should surround the burning plate so that, once the stove has been ignited, the blubber in the reservoir melts and maintains the oil supply.

PRUSIK SLINGS

The Prusik sling was invented by the Austrian mountaineer Dr Karl Prusik and was made public in 1931. It provided a means for someone to climb out of a crevasse after an accident, for example, or to ascend a steep slope along a fixed safety rope. Nowadays, most climbers prefer to use ascenders or jumars which work on the ratchet principle, but Prusik slings are much lighter and it's always useful to know how to make and use them. The essence of the Prusik sling is that it can be slid up – or down – a standing rope when it's not under tension but that it jams in place by friction when weight is applied.

You'll need two loops to ascend a vertical rope, one to put your foot in and the other to attach to your climbing harness. If you don't have a climbing harness use three loops – one for each foot and the third to pass behind your shoulders to help keep you upright.

To create your loops you'll need mountaineering cord with a diameter that's about 70 per cent of the diameter of the standing rope. Create your loops using double fisherman's knots. A loop for standing in should be roughly a metre long, while for attaching to a harness about 20cm would be more comfortable, but it's a good idea to have several ready in different sizes.

The loops are attached to the rope when necessary by passing the knot around three times inside the loop and then pulling tight, making sure the spirals are neat and orderly.

To use the Prusik loops for ascending a vertical rope, stand in one and slide the other one (or two) up. Then transfer the weight and move the bottom Prusik up. If you're wearing a rucksack, attach it to the rope below you to relieve yourself of the weight and keep the rope taut. Practising your technique regularly before you get into a situation in which you might need your Prusik loops for real could save your life. Experts can climb 30m in as little as a minute this way.

HEAD COLLAR FOR A HORSE

If a horse should break its head collar it's possible to make a temporary replacement with some rope. Begin by making a loop in the end, secured by a bowline. Then put the loop over the horse's head just behind the ears and adjust the knot, if necessary, so the loop is comfortable. Next, make a second loop by twisting the free part of the rope twice around and push this second loop over the horse's nose, above the nostrils. Again, adjust the loop so it's snug. You can now lead the horse in the normal way.

FURNITURE WOODS.

1. Amaranth or Bois Violet (Copaïfera bracteata; South America). 2. Brazilwood (Caesalpinia; Africa). 3. Oak (Quercus; Italy). 4. Mahogany (Swietenia Mahagoni; Central America). 5. Ash (Fraxinus excelsior; Hungary). 6. Thuja (Thuja occidentalis; America). 7. Birds-eye Maple (Acer; South America, Java). 8. Walnut (Juglans; North America). 9. The "Rosewood" of Physocalymna scaberrimum; Brazil, Africa, East Indies. 10. "Iron-wood or Kingwood" of the Fragraea peregrina, East Indies. 11. Jacaranda brasiliana; Brazil.

W. & R. Chambers Ltd., London & Edinburgh.　　　　Printed in Saxony.　　　　J. B. Lippincott Company, Philadelphia. U.S.

Choosing and Using Wood

CHAIR BODGING

The art of wood-carving has also to fulfil its intellectual function, as an interpreter of the dreams and fancies of imagination. In this respect there is little encouragement to be looked for in the dull routine of a modern workshop.

George Jack, *Wood-Carving, Design and Workmanship* (1903)

According to H J Massingham, a prolific writer on the English countryside during the first half of the 20th century, few craftsman were more poetic and less in the workshop than Samuel Rockhall. Sam Rockall, who died in 1962 aged 84, was the last chair bodger in the Chiltern Hills. That's to say, the last of the men who set up summer camp in the beech forests to cut trees and then shape the 'billets' into the legs and stretchers of Windsor chairs. They used only hand tools and an improvised lathe driven in one direction by a foot treadle and in the other by the springiness of an ash pole. Beech was and is ideal for shaping on a lathe, as John Evelyn noted in his book *Sylva* in 1664. 'With it,' he wrote, 'the turner makes dishes, trays, rimbs for buckets, and other utensils, trenchers, dresser-boards, &c. likewise for the wheeler, joyner, for large screws, and ... chairs, stools, bedsteads.'

SOFTWOOD OR HARDWOOD?

When making anything in timber, the first decision is whether to use a softwood or a hardwood. Softwoods, such as pine, come from fast-growing coniferous trees and are relatively light (300kg–700kg per cubic metre) and open and, therefore, not well-suited to making anything delicate.

Hardwoods, like beech, come from slow-growing broad-leaved trees and are heavy (450kg–1250kg per cubic metre) and dense and, therefore, suitable for fine work. In John Evelyn's time, most timber in Britain came from broad-leaved varieties, but because coniferous trees grow faster and dry faster so most commercial timber today is softwood.

VARIETY AND ASPECT

Every timber has its own special qualities. According to John Evelyn, oak was favoured for shipbuilding, 'being tough, bending well, strong and not too heavy, nor easily admitting water', while elm was ideal 'where it may lie continually dry, or wet, in extreams; therefore proper for waterworks, mills, the ladles, and soles of the wheel, pipes, pumps, aquae-ducts, pales, ship-planks beneath the water line …'.

Many thought it important *where* the tree had grown. The Roman historian Pliny the Elder (c.23–79 AD) wrote that, 'the timber of those trees which grow in moist and shady places is not so good as that which comes from a more exposed situation, nor is it so close, substantial and durable'.

There was also the question of *when* the tree was felled. According to one school of thought, firewood should only be cut when the moon was waning, while timber for carpentry should only be felled when the constellations were in the right alignment, which happened only a handful of times a year. More logically, timber for most purposes is felled from October to March when there's less sap in the wood, unless it's 'green' wood that's required, as in the case of many coppice products.

Coppicing and pollarding

'Coppicing' means cutting a well-established hardwood tree to a stump so the new shoots can, in a few years, be used for a whole variety of woodland crafts, from handles for tools, to fencing and firewood. 'Pollarding' means cutting the tree higher up so the shoots are out of the reach of horses and cattle.

Here are some of the traditional uses of coppice produce:

Alder: Brush heads, clog soles.
Ash: Hurdles, tent pegs, tool handles, barrel hoops.
Birch: Besoms (the 'witch's broom'), spools, reels, brush heads.
Elm: Turnery, firewood.

Hazel: Wattle hurdles, thatching spars, sheep cribs, baskets.
Hornbeam: Firewood.
Maple: Firewood.
Oak: Fence posts, tanbark (for tanning leather).
Sweet chestnut: Walking sticks, hop poles, ladder rungs, fencing.
White willow: Gate hurdles.

SEASONING

For most purposes wood needs to be seasoned, that is, dried so its moisture content will be in equilibrium with the air where it's to be used. Otherwise, the wood will either shrink or expand. Traditionally, wood was dried in a cool, dry, shady place with good air circulation. For planks roughly 2.5cm thick, softwoods will dry to 20 per cent in six to twelve weeks in ideal conditions, while most hardwoods will take around nine months and oak a year. Out of doors in Britain, the moisture content will never go below 16 per cent, no matter how long the wood is left, so to get down to twelve per cent or less – the sort of level necessary for furniture indoors – the only solution is a kiln. (If you're drying your own timber you can simply keep it indoors for a while.)

Nowadays, there are special meters for calculating the moisture content of wood, but here's a way of doing it without one. Cut off a small cube of the wood and weigh it. Then place it in a warm oven for about 15 minutes and weigh it again. Continue the oven drying until the weight is stable. Then subtract the dry weight from the wet weight, divide the result by the dry weight and multiply by 100.

TIMBER MEASUREMENT

Anyone who wanted a long length of timber, perhaps for a roof beam or a mast, needed to know a tree was tall enough before going to the effort of sawing it down. Nowadays, there are hypsometers for calculating the heights of trees by triangulation, but this is how to do it the traditional way. Cut a stick to the exact distance from your eye to the tip of your thumb with your arm outstretched. Then, holding your stick vertically between thumb and forefinger and with your arm as before, walk backwards and forwards in front of the tree until you have the top aligned with the top of your stick and the base aligned with the bottom of your stick. Now pace out the distance from where you're standing to the tree and that's its height. For more precision, you can run a tape measure from the ground immediately below the stick to the centre of the base of the tree.

THE AGE OF A TREE

Counting the rings of a felled tree gives its precise age, but what about the age of a living tree? In fact, you can get a good idea by measuring the diameter of the tree in centimetres at breast height – known in forestry as dbh. A professional would use a special girth tape or callipers but all you need to do is place your hands either side of the tree, step back without moving your arms, and then have a friend measure the distance between your hands. Beech is one of the slowest-growing species while pine, spruce and larch are among the fastest.

Dbh (cm)	10	20	30	40	50	60+
Species	Age in years					
Beech	35	55	75	95	115	140
Oak	30	50	70	90	120	150
Ash*	20	30	40	60		
Alder/birch	15	25	35			
Pine	20	40	60	80		
Spruce	25	40	55	80		
Larch	15	30	45	70		

*Also good for sycamore, cherry and walnut

TREES AS FOOD

The inner bark of several species of trees is both edible and nutritious, especially in the spring. To harvest it, cut away the outer bark from a sapling or from the limb of an older tree and then peel off the white inner layer. You can eat it just as it is but it will be more palatable if you roast it or boil it into a jelly. It can also be dried and ground into flour. Trees with edible bark include: pine (which is very high in vitamin C), alder, birch and poplar. Willow is also edible but should only be consumed in small quantities because it contains the painkiller salicin (see the section on surviving in the wilderness).

Counting Sheep

HURDLES AND WATTLES

Sheep were first domesticated more than 10,000 years ago and by the Middle Ages some landowners had enormous numbers. It's recorded that in 1258, the bishops of Winchester had as many as 30,000 sheep, spread over several flocks. Counting them was enough to put anyone to sleep.

Until quite recently, sheep were often held within portable pens or 'folds' inside the fields, constructed from hurdles (usually in coppiced ash – see the section on choosing and using wood) or wattles of woven hazel. Ash hurdles had the advantage of strength and durability but were heavy and allowed the sheep to see out, which encouraged them to escape. Wattles, on the other hand, although less long-lasting, were easier to move around and prevented the sheep from seeing the grass on the other side. 'Genuine' wattles can be distinguished from garden fencing by the hole left in the middle to make it easier for the shepherd to carry them.

Every day the shepherd would add three new hurdles or wattles to the existing square, drive the sheep into the newly created area and then close off the new square, thus liberating three wattles from the old square to repeat the process the next day. This made it easier to keep a check on the sheep but also controlled their grazing and directed their dung where it was wanted – at one time it was said the dung was more valuable than either the meat or the wool.

But the only way to count the sort of numbers owned by the bishops of Winchester is to drive them through a handling pen or 'working race' sufficiently narrow to prevent the sheep from turning round and confusing the person doing the counting. For average-sized sheep a width of about

16in (0.4m) is about right. It's a good idea to build it going up a gentle slope since sheep will then move through it more happily. They also go better towards light and, of course, once one of the flock has gone ahead.

YAN TYAN TETHER

Until the end of the 19th century, many country folk had their own local systems of numbers for counting sheep, usually based on ten or twenty, to make it easy for those who used their fingers. The number for 'one' in much of the Lake District, for example, was 'yan' but in Eskdale it was 'yaena', while in other parts of Scotland it was 'yinty'. Here are the numbers for Keswick in the Lake District:

1	yan	8	hovera	15	bumfit
2	tyan	9	dovera	16	yan a bumfit
3	tether	10	dic	17	tyan a bumfit
4	mether	11	yan a dic	18	tether a bumfit
5	pimp	12	tyan a dic	19	mether a bumfit
6	sethera	13	tether a dic	20	jiggot
7	lethera	14	mether a dic		

It wasn't necessary to have names for numbers larger than 20. The shepherds would simply cut a mark in a stick every time they reached it. Another method of 'keeping score' was to transfer a pebble from one pocket to another. Finally, by counting the number of pebbles, they would know how many score of sheep there were. In Northumberland, the system was to use the fingers of one hand for keeping track of the scores while the fingers of the other hand would be used for the hundreds – making it possible to reach 600.

Penned sheep, from The Luttrell Psalter, 14th century
© HIP / The British Library / TopFoto.co.uk

Removing Stones from Horses' Hooves

SANDALS FOR HORSES

In their natural state, horses have few problems with stones trapped in their hooves. The issue only arose when, after perhaps 3,000 years of human experimentation with straw and leather sandals for horses, the Romans discovered that nailing bands of iron to the walls of the hooves stopped them wearing down on paved roads.

Once horses were shod, it became relatively easy for a stone to become trapped between the shoe and the part known as the frog, the rubbery protrusion in the middle of the sole towards the heels. But much worse is a sharp stone that actually becomes embedded in the frog.

The function of the frog wasn't understood in early times. Xenophon, the 4th-century BC Greek historian who wrote a treatise *On Horsemanship* considered that a 'high hoof' was preferable because it kept the frog off the ground, whereas contact between the frog and the ground caused a 'gait resembling that of a bandy-legged man'. The vital function of the frog was only discovered much later:

That portion of the hoof called the 'frog' ... is the spring at the immediate base of the leg, relieving the nervous system and joints from the shock of the concussion when the Race Horse thunders over the course ...

John E Russell, *Rational Horse-Shoeing* (1873)

The frog, then, *has* to make contact with the ground and damage to it from a trapped stone could be serious. What's more, the repeated concussion from the stone could bruise the sole, cause a corn in the angle between the wall and the bar, and generally make it painful for the horse to move.

TERMS OF ENDEARMENT

Removing a stone with a hoof pick is a simple matter – always provided the horse has been properly trained to lift its feet up on command. But if it hasn't, then things get more complicated. One early-19th-century horse-trainer recommended 'a somewhat loud and severe voice', while others were even more extreme:

Approach the horse firmly, fixing your gaze upon his eye. Have in your hand a six-chambered revolver, loaded with blank cartridges. The moment he attempts to savage you, fire …

Anon, *The Horsekeeper's Handbook of Tips and Wrinkles* (1922)

Fortunately for horses and riders alike, there were a few more enlightened horsemen in the 19th century. The best came to be known as 'horse whisperers' because it was believed they whispered 'magic spells' to horses that were difficult to handle. In reality they often did 'whisper', and one contemporary newspaper account of the legendary John Solomon Rarey reported on the 'extraordinary sounds of endearment' he made. But there were also very practical techniques, such as strapping up one hoof:

There is something in this operation of taking up one foot that conquers a horse quicker and better than anything else you can do to him, and without any possible danger of him hurting himself or you either, for you can tie up his foot and sit down and look at him until he gives up.

J S Rarey, *The Art of Taming Horses* (1858)

USING THE HOOF PICK

Wherever there is more than one horse owner or farrier there will be at least two different opinions on the best methods. But, broadly speaking, this is how it's done.

Approach the horse casually, with any tools hidden.

Make your actions slow but deliberate.

Face towards the rear of the horse and nudge him with your shoulder.

Slide your hand down the horse's leg, pat it just above the hoof and say 'Give' or whatever command you normally use.

If the horse doesn't then lift up his hoof for you, push with your shoulder to put the horse's weight onto the other three legs.

If the horse still doesn't respond, try pushing behind the knee.

As the leg comes up say 'Good boy' or something similar so the horse knows he's done the right thing.

Still facing the rear of the horse, you can now rest the hoof on your thighs.

For a front hoof, bring the hoof up between your thighs and then, with your legs bent, close your thighs so that the hoof is held just above your knees.

For a rear hoof, bring the horse's leg over your inner thigh and then, with your knees bent and your toes turned in, allow the hoof to rest just above your knees.

You can now remove the stone, along with any mud, and inspect the hoof for damage.

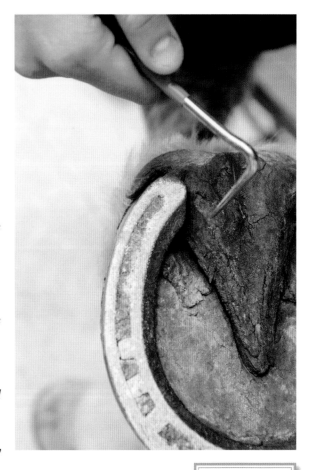

Cleaning a horse's hoof with a hoof pick
© Jupiter Images / BananaStock / Alamy

If it proves impossible to dislodge the stone with the hoof pick it may be necessary to tap it out with a small hammer, taking care not to bang it against the sole of the hoof.

If the horse is lame afterwards, or the frog is bleeding, the vet should be called.

DON'T USE YOUR SWISS ARMY KNIFE

Despite the long-running myth that the tool on a Swiss army knife that you never used was for getting stones out of horses' hooves, a hoof pick has only recently been added to specialized equestrian designs. Don't be tempted to use your mini-screwdriver.

How to Choose Livestock and Horses

COPERS

'There are at least five hundred fools born every day,' wrote a 19th-century horse dealer called Frederick Taylor, 'and ... in the population of the United Kingdom, indeed I may venture to say the whole human race, there are at least two rogues for one fool.'

Just as there are scams involving second-hand cars and agricultural machines today, so in Victorian times and earlier there were plenty of swindles involving livestock. The unscrupulous used all kinds of tricks to make the animals look sound, at least long enough for them to be sold, and for the crooks – known as 'copers' in the horse world – to get away before problems were discovered.

HORSES

Glanders, nowadays known as strangles, was a serious illness in horses before antibiotics, and the copers had an ingenious method of concealing the nasal discharge that was a symptom:

Glanders is a most malignant and highly contagious disease, so much so, that the law of our land justifies the destruction of a glandered horse ... It discloses itself by a constant discharge of a greenish yellow colour ... In horse coping slang, a glandered horse is designated a 'snitch'. ... a quantity of snuff and pepper is applied to the nostrils, which ... causes him to sneeze out any matter ... His nostrils are then carefully sponged and the tow (through which he can breathe) is thrust up ...
Frederick Taylor, *Confessions of a Horse Dealer* (1861)

A potential buyer was advised to fight cunning with cunning, also using cayenne pepper to make the horse sneeze a plug out, if there was one. Any mucous was then allowed to drip into a bucket of cold water. If it sank, the horse just had a cold, but if it floated it was a 'suspicious discharge'.

Of course, there were many other things to take into account besides the avoidance of horses with injuries and diseases. James Fillis, considered one of the outstanding horsemen of the Victorian era, liked a long, light neck, prominent withers, a short, strong back and long, oblique shoulders. But, above all, he emphasized temperament and few riders today would disagree:

The highest mental qualification of a horse is to be a free-goer; because such an animal, contrary to what is often thought, is neither irritable nor sulky ... such a horse is valuable, even if his make and shape are only moderate. If an animal has not the essential requirement of being always ready to go forward, he is useless, although he may be a perfect picture to look at.

James Fillis, *Breaking and Riding* (1902)

It's much easier to buy a horse than to sell one, so the first piece of advice is to take plenty of time. Never get on an unknown horse without first testing it on the ground. Caress the horse all over, see how quickly it moves away from the pressure of your finger, and try to back it up with light pressure on the nose. Ride the horse on at least two different occasions and, then, if interested, have it examined by a vet. If all that is positive, take the horse on trial.

CATTLE

In the 18th century, the only recognized 'breed' in Britain was the Longhorn, which considerably simplified the whole question of selection. Today, there are about 100 breeds and things are more complicated. Nevertheless, some of the traditional ideas still hold good:

A cow with a large, coarse head will seldom fatten readily, or give a large quantity of milk. A coarse head increases the proportion of weight of the least valuable parts, while it is a sure indication that the whole bony structure is too heavy. The mouth should be large and broad; the eye bright and sparkling, but of a peculiar placidness of expression, with no indication of wildness, but rather a mild and feminine look.

These points will indicate gentleness of disposition. Such cows seem to like to be milked, are fond of being caressed, and often return caresses.

Robert Jennings, *Cattle and Their Diseases* (1864)

The age of cattle can be determined by the eight incisors at the front of the lower jaw which, for the first six years, are in the shape of an arch. Beyond that age the curve reduces so that by twelve the teeth are in a more or less straight line. Another indication is that around the age of seven only the central teeth are noticeably worn, but by the age of ten all of them are worn.

SHEEP

The first step in buying sheep is to decide on a breed that both pleases you and is suitable for the local conditions. The three main classes of sheep in Britain are the Down sheep (in which the length of the wool or 'staple' is rather short), the Mountain sheep (with a medium-length staple) and the Leicester-founded breeds (with a staple that can be as long as 18in):

Milk breeds: Awassi, Chios, Fries Melkschaap, Lacaune.
Wool breeds: Bradford Count, Gotland, Karakul, Longwools, Merino, Polworth, Romney.
Primitive breeds: Hebridean, Jacob, Manx Loghtan, Soay.
Hill breeds: Cheviot, Derbyshire Gritstone, Exmoor Horn, Herdwick, Scottish Blackface, Shetland, Swaledale, Welsh Mountain, Whitefaced Woodland.
General purpose breeds: Clun Forest, Corriedale, Devon Closewool, Dorset Horn, Portland.
Meat breeds: Oxford Down, Suffolk, Texel, Wiltshire Horn.

Before buying, ask to see any performance records. Once again, teeth are a guide and should be broad and in good condition. 'Gummies' – sheep without teeth – are best avoided, as are any animals that are lame or that look unhealthy.

Wool nowadays is usually sold *in-the-dirt*, but hand-spinners prefer *washed* which simply means the sheep are thrown into a pond or stream a day or so before shearing. This is the origin of English village names such as Sheepwash.

GOATS

Strictly speaking, there is no such thing as a 'British goat' because goats evolved in arid regions of the tropics. But if it's a 'British' goat you want then the Anglo-Nubian, derived from four males imported at the end of the 19th and beginning of the 20th centuries, comes close. Anglo-Nubians have a range of colours but are often dappled and are otherwise identified by their large size (males are up to 140kg), small heads and pendulous ears. On the other hand, if you want a goat that really looks like a goat then the Saanen, which is white with pricked ears and originally from Switzerland, may be for you. For hair, choose the Angora, from which you can derive mohair as well as cashmere (using the soft undercoat only). For an immediate return, buy 'milkers'. Otherwise buy kids between one and two years or, if you're willing to wait a while for production, at as little as a week. The signs of good condition are an alert appearance, bright eyes, glossy coat, pink mucous membranes and pellets that are round and separate. Clumps of droppings may indicate worms, while pale ones can be a sign of a disease called coccidiosis.

Angora goats
© *Juniors Bildarchiv / Alamy*

PIGS

The first pigs that people ate were what we now call wild boar. It was only in the 18th century that British farmers began selective breeding, including crossing local pigs with Chinese. Pig farming was transformed again in the late 1940s following the importation of the Swedish Landrace which, together with the Large White, now dominates. As *Pratt's Practical Pointers* observed in 1919, 'As a rule, it is best to select that breed which is most popular locally, because such popularity indicates that the breed in question thrives under local conditions'. Ask to see performance records before buying and favour pedigree animals.

CHICKENS

You'll first have to choose between having pure breeds, first crosses or hybrids. Pure breeds, which include the famous Rhode Island Red, have generally fallen out of favour for being insufficiently productive. However, a first cross between a Rhode Island Red and a Light Sussex is a popular choice for smallholders, particularly because the day-old chicks can be sorted by sex very easily – the males are silvery while the females are orangey. The disadvantage of first crosses is that their offspring will not have the same characteristics. For maximum egg production hybrids are best.

Commercially, hens are considered productive for only one year. If you'd like to 'rescue' some year-old hens (which will still lay eggs) see www.bhwt.org.uk.

Sharpening Knives

KNIFE SHARPENING

In the kitchen, we often either tolerate blunt knives, or use a specially manufactured sharpening stone to give a knife back its edge, which can then be maintained with a sharpening steel. In the great outdoors you are unlikely to have such equipment with you, but with a little knowledge it is still possible to sharpen your blade (using due care and consideration for its cutting properties of course).

GETTING STROPPY

A flat rock is the most basic of sharpening tools for a flat-bladed knife. You should look for one that has been flattened (perhaps through the action of water if it has been in a stream) and is fine-grained, giving it abrasive properties (sandstone is a good choice, as is granite). The sharpening stone should be wetted with water, and the blade should be pushed away from you, across the surface of the stone. Turn the blade over and then draw it carefully towards you. Alternate from one side to the other, wetting the stone as necessary, until both are sharp – don't be tempted to test this by running your finger along the blade; use something inanimate. If possible, the blade should then be finished by stropping (in fact, unless a blade is very blunt, stropping on its own is often enough). A strop is a strip of leather, and blades are kept in good order by being swept up and down against it. A leather belt can be used as a strop if necessary, or even a piece of wood or the side of a boot.

KNIFELORE

All sorts of superstitions have been attached to knives over the centuries. One which relates directly to sharpening knives is that it is unlucky to do so after sunset (or sometimes after supper). In some instances it was thought that to sharpen a knife after sunset would lead to your house being burgled or visited by enemies, although the connection between this and evening knife sharpening has never been explained. Deliberately spinning a knife on a table was sometimes used as a method of divination – if the knife stopped spinning with its blade pointing towards you, your future husband would be a dark-haired man, whereas if it stopped with the handle pointing towards you, the husband would be fair-haired. Unfortunately, if a knife was set spinning accidentally, and it came to rest with the blade pointing towards you, it did not indicate your future husband's hair colour, but was instead an omen of death, or at least very bad luck. Death, or a nasty argument, was also presaged by knives (or sometimes a knife and fork) laid across each other on a table:

It is unlucky to lay one's knife and fork cross-wise: crosses and misfortunes are likely to follow.

Francis Grose, *A Provincial Glossary* (1787)